T0299270

Graph Learning and Network Science for Natural Language Processing

Advances in graph-based natural language processing (NLP) and information retrieval tasks have shown the importance of processing using the Graph of Words method. This book covers recent concrete information, from the basics to advanced level, about graph-based learning, such as neural network-based approaches, computational intelligence for learning parameters and feature reduction, and network science for graph-based NLP. It also contains information about language generation based on graphical theories and language models.

Features:

- Presents a comprehensive study of the interdisciplinary graphical approach to NLP
- Covers recent computational intelligence techniques for graph-based neural network models
- Discusses advances in random walk-based techniques, semantic webs, and lexical networks
- Explores recent research into NLP for graph-based streaming data
- Reviews advances in knowledge graph embedding and ontologies for NLP approaches

This book is aimed at researchers and graduate students in computer science, natural language processing, and deep and machine learning.

Computational Intelligence Techniques

Series Editor: Vishal Jain

The objective of this series is to provide researchers a platform to present state of the art innovations, research, and design and implement methodological and algorithmic solutions to data processing problems, designing and analyzing evolving trends in health informatics and computer-aided diagnosis. This series provides support and aid to researchers involved in designing decision support systems that will permit societal acceptance of ambient intelligence. The overall goal of this series is to present the latest snapshot of ongoing research as well as to shed further light on future directions in this space. The series presents novel technical studies as well as position and vision papers comprising hypothetical/speculative scenarios. The book series seeks to compile all aspects of computational intelligence techniques from fundamental principles to current advanced concepts. For this series, we invite researchers, academicians and professionals to contribute, expressing their ideas and research in the application of intelligent techniques to the field of engineering in handbook, reference, or monograph volumes.

Computational Intelligence Techniques and Their Applications to Software Engineering Problems
Ankita Bansal, Abha Jain, Sarika Jain, Vishal Jain, and Ankur Choudhary

Smart Computational Intelligence in Biomedical and Health Informatics
Amit Kumar Manocha, Mandeep Singh, Shruti Jain, and Vishal Jain

Data Driven Decision Making Using Analytics
Parul Gandhi, Surbhi Bhatia, and Kapal Dev

Smart Computing and Self-Adaptive Systems
Simar Preet Singh, Arun Solanki, Anju Sharma, Zdzislaw Polkowski, and Rajesh Kumar

Advancing Computational Intelligence Techniques for Security Systems Design
Uzzal Sharma, Parmanand Astya, Anupam Baliyan, Salah-ddine Krit, Vishal Jain, and Mohammad Zubair Kha

Graph Learning and Network Science for Natural Language Processing
Edited by Muskan Garg, Amit Kumar Gupta, and Rajesh Prasad

For more information about this series, please visit: www.routledge.com/Computational-Intelligence-Techniques/book-series/CIT

Graph Learning and Network Science for Natural Language Processing

Edited by
Muskan Garg,
Amit Kumar Gupta,
and Rajesh Prasad

CRC Press is an imprint of the
Taylor & Francis Group, an informa business

First edition published 2023
by CRC Press
6000 Broken Sound Parkway NW, Suite 300, Boca Raton, FL 33487-2742

and by CRC Press
4 Park Square, Milton Park, Abingdon, Oxon, OX14 4RN

CRC Press is an imprint of Taylor & Francis Group, LLC

ISBN: 9781032224565 (hbk)
ISBN: 9781032224572 (pbk)
ISBN: 9781003272649 (ebk)

DOI: 10.1201/9781003272649

Typeset in Times
by Deanta Global Publishing Services, Chennai, India

Contents

Editors

Muskan Garg is a postdoctoral research associate at the University of Florida, USA whose research focuses on the problems of natural language processing (NLP), information retrieval, and social media analysis. She received her Masters and Ph.D. from Panjab University, India. Her current focus is on research and development of cutting-edge NLP approaches to solving problems of national and international importance and on initiation and broadening of a new program in NLP (including a new NLP course series). Her current research interests are causal inference, mental health on social media, event detection, and sentiment analysis.

Amit Kumar Gupta is an Assistant Professor at Manipal University Jaipur, India, and has more than 15 years of teaching as well as research experience. He has published more than 50 international research papers in the reputable journal of indexing *Scopus*. He has also been guest editor of nine *Scopus* indexed journals. He has edited one book for IGI Global and organized three international conferences sponsored by the All India Council for Technical Education and the third phase of the Technical Education Quality Improvement Programme. His research areas are information security, machine learning, NLP and operating system CPU scheduling.

Rajesh Prasad is a Professor of Computer Science and Engineering at MIT Art, Design and Technology University, Pune, India. He has more than 25 years of academic and research experience, during which he has been instrumental in developing course curriculums and content. He is associated with several universities in different roles. He has a Ph.D. in Computer Engineering, and 7 research scholars have been awarded Ph.D.s under his guidance. He has published more than 90 papers in international and national journals, and has 3 patents and 6 copyrights. His areas of interest include text and data analysis, and speech processing. He has been associated with various industries for research collaboration. He is an active member of various professional societies.

Contributors

Shaikh Ashfaq Amir
Information Technology Department
M. H. Saboo Siddik College of Engineering
Mumbai, India

Prakash Andugula
Independent Researcher

Mangesh Bedekar
Department of Computer Engineering
MIT World Peace University
Pune, India

A. A. Bhange
MIT School of Engineering
MIT Art, Design and Technology University
Pune, India

H. R. Bhapkar
Department of Mathematics
MIT School of Engineering
MIT Art, Design and Technology University
Pune, India

Ujwala Bharambe
Department of Computer Science
Thadomal Shahani Engineering College
Mumbai, India

Surbhi Bhatia
Department of Information Systems
College of Computer Science and Information Technology
King Faisal University
Hofuf, Saudi Arabia

Vijaykumar S. Bidve
Information Technology Department
Marathwada Mitra Mandal's College of Engineering
Pune, India

S. V. Gayetri Devi
Department of Computer Science and Engineering
Bharath Institute of Higher Education and Research
Chennai, India

Manish Dubey
Department of Computer Engineering
Poornima College of Engineering
Jaipur, India

Jyoti Gavhane
Department of Computer Science and Engineering
MIT Art, Design and Technology University
Pune, India

Archit Gupta
Computer Science and Engineering
Software Development
Ekfrazo Technologies
Bengaluru, India

Sunita Gupta
Department of Computer Science and Engineering
Swami Keshvanand Institute of Technology
Jaipur, India

Vanita D. Jadhav
Department of Computer Science and Engineering
SVERI's College of Engineering
Pandharpur, India
and
Ph.D. Research Scholar
Smt. Kashibai Navale College of Engineering
Pune, India

Nikita Jain
Department of Computer Science and Engineering
Poornima College of Engineering
Jaipur, India

Rekha Jain
Department of Computer Science and Engineering
Manipal University Jaipur
Jaipur, India

Siddharth Jain
Cyber Security Team
Paytm
Noida, India

Vishal Jain
Department of Allied Health Sciences
Jaipur Engineering College and Research Centre University
Jaipur, India

Neha Janu
Department of Computer Science and Engineering
Swami Keshvanand Institute of Technology
Jaipur, India

Mahesh Kumar Joshi
Department of Computer Science and Engineering
Sangam University
Bhilwara, India

Vinod V. Kimbahune
Department of Computer Engineering
Nutan Maharashtra Institute of Engineering and Technology
Pune, India

B. Suresh Kumar
Department of Computer Science and Engineering
Sanjay Ghodawat University
Kolhapur, India

Tapesh Kumar
Department of Computer Science and Engineering
Swami Keshvanand Institute of Technology
Jaipur, India

Rajeev Kumar
Computer Engineering, Senior Project Manager, PMP, CSM Agilist
Johannesburg, South Africa

Manisha Sharma
Department of Computer Science
Banasthali Vidyapith
Radha Kishnpura, India

Pratistha Mathur
Department of Information Technology
Manipal University
Jaipur, India

Sharayu Mirasdar
Department of Computer Engineering
MKSSS's Cummins College of Engineering for Women
Pune, India

Rahesha Mulla
Department of Computer Science and Engineering
MIT Art, Design and Technology University
Pune, India

Namrata Naikwade
Department of Computer Science and Engineering
MIT Art, Design and Technology University
Pune, India

C. Nalini
Department of Computer Science and Engineering
Dr. M. G. R. Educational and Research Institute
Chennai, India

Chhaya Narvekar
Department of Information Technology
Xavier Institute of Engineering
Mumbai, India

Meenakshi Nawal
Department of Computer Science and Engineering
Swami Keshvanand Institute of Technology
Jaipur, India

Lalit V. Patil
Department of Information Technology
Smt. Kashibai Navale College Engineering
Pune, India

Jayashree Prasad
Department of Computer Science and Engineering
MIT Art, Design and Technology University
Pune, India

Rajesh Prasad
Department of Computer Science and Engineering
MIT Art, Design and Technology University
Pune, India

Pathan Mohd. Shafi
Department of Computer Science and Engineering
MIT School of Engineering
MIT Art, Design and Technology University
Pune, India

Suresh Shanmugasundaram
Department of Computer Engineering
Botho University
Gaborone, Botswana

Anjali Singh
Department of Computer Science and Engineering
Swami Keshvanand Institute of Technology
Jaipur, India

Vijendra Singh
Norwegian University of Science and Technology
Ålesund, Norway

Sheetal Sonawane
Department of Computer Engineering
Pune Institute of Computer Technology
Pune, India

Devansh Srivastava
Software Development
Dell

Carlos M. Travieso-Gonzalez
Signals and Communication Department
Institute for Technological Development and Innovation in Communications
University of Las Palmas de Gran Canaria
Las Palmas de Gran Canaria, Spain

K. G. S. Venkatesan
Department of Computer Science and Engineering
Megha Institute of Engineering and Technology for Women
Telangana, India

Narendra Singh Yadav
Department of Information Technology
Manipal University
Jaipur, India

Preface

Graph learning is an emerging interdisciplinary field of graph analytics and deep learning. In the recent COVID-19 pandemic era, development of secure and ethical learning-based algorithms is of the utmost importance. Recent research and developments in deep neural networks and areas of artificial intelligence such as interpretable and explainable machines have shown significant progress in creating ethical models for natural language processing (NLP).

Advances in graph-based NLP and information retrieval tasks have shown the importance of the Graph of Words approach to processing. The structure and semantics of word co-occurrence networks (WCNs) have been studied in existing literature, however, the study of the dynamics of WCNs is still in its initial phase. Study of the dynamics of linguistic networks may help in determining patterns among words and extracting useful insights in areas such as concept drift, topic detection, and event detection, to name a few. Thus, complex networks of words evolved from streaming data may contain latent patterns.

This book contains recent and concrete information, from the basics to advanced level, about graph-based learning approaches such as neural networks, computational intelligence for learning parameters and feature reduction, and network science for graph-based NLP. It also contains information about language generation based on graphical theories and language models.

OBJECTIVES

The chapters by the contributors to this book seek to propose concrete and feasible solutions in the domain of graph-based NLP and information retrieval:

1. To form a bridge between industry and academic institutions to develop their knowledge about graph analytics
2. To establish the need for graph-based NLP and information retrieval in the worldwide research community and software industry
3. To make significant progress in developing ethical models for NLP
4. To describe innovative applications such as neural network-based approaches and computational intelligence to establish learning parameters, feature selection, and dimensionality reduction
5. To impart a basic understanding of recent designs and models of graphical NLP
6. To build industry-capable talent, start-up communities, and an entrepreneurial ecosystem for handling text data

7. To energize the research mind-set and reduce costs in research and development by providing neutral and interoperable multi-technology stack laboratory facilities
8. To provide an environment to promote product creation and testing, and also validation and incubation

SCOPE OF THE BOOK

The book describes recent research, from the basics to advanced level, about graph-based learning, such as neural network-based approaches, computational intelligence for deriving learning parameters and feature reduction, and network science for graph-based NLP. It also covers language generation based on graphical theories and language models. Graph-based theories in WCNs may help in identifying useful patterns from streaming data. It aims:

a. To highlight viewpoints, surveys, and reviews of graph-based NLP
b. To explore existing and possible future research directions in graph analytics with explainable deep learning for NLP
c. To incorporate recent advances in the areas of graph learning and network science for NLP

The topics covered include:

1. Advances in graph-based NLP and information retrieval
2. Self-supervised learning of language representations
3. Graph-based learning, such as neural network-based approaches
4. Computational intelligence for establishing learning parameters and feature reduction
5. Network science for graph-based NLP
6. Graph-based theories in word co-occurrence networks
7. Explainable deep neural networks for NLP
8. Knowledge graph embedding
9. Learning and data mining ontologies
10. Random walk methods
11. Semantic webs
12. Information networks
13. Approximation algorithms for the Graph of Words approach
14. Graph-based data stream mining
15. The structure and dynamics of Graphs of Word models
16. Language dynamics
17. Lexical networks
18. Dynamic graph representation

MATLAB ® is a registered trademark of The MathWorks, Inc. For product information, please contact:

The MathWorks, Inc.
3 Apple Hill Drive
Natick, MA 01760-2098 USA
Tel: 508 647 7000
Fax: 508-647-7001
E-mail: info@mathworks.com
Web: www.mathworks.com

1 Graph of Words Model for Natural Language Processing

Sharayu Mirasdar and Mangesh Bedekar

CONTENTS

DOI: 10.1201/9781003272649-1

1.1 INTRODUCTION

Computers are machines, and cannot understand the free-flowing language used by humans for communication. They understand the language of 0s and 1s, which is a machine language called binary language. Without processing natural language, it's difficult for humans to talk to computers. For this reason, an artificial intelligence-based solution called natural language processing (NLP) has been developed. NLP techniques help computers to interpret, understand and manipulate human language (Daniel and James 2009).

Input text passes through five main NLP steps:

1. Lexical and morphological analysis
2. Syntactic analysis (parsing phase)
3. Semantic analysis
4. Discourse integration
5. Pragmatic analysis

1.1.1 Lexical and Morphological Analysis

In *lexical and morphological analysis*, the input text of natural language is scanned and converted into meaningful lexemes. In this phase, the input is divided into paragraphs, sentences and then into words. Morphological analysis determines the original words of a language from which a given word is constructed. While identifying the base word, the system also needs to look for the correct place for prefixes and suffixes in the word. For example, for the word "globalization," the base word is *globe* and *-al* is the suffix. *Global* would be the base for the suffix *-ize*. *Globalize* is the base for the *-ation* suffix, and the word "globalization" would be the final derivative.

1.1.2 Syntactic Analysis

Syntactic analysis focuses on whether the input statement is grammatically correct. The syntax of the input is verified against the grammar of the respective language. Syntactic analyzers are the modules which carry out these checks on input statements, checking the logical meaning and correctness of sentences.

For example, the sentence "School go a boy" does not convey any logical meaning, nor does it follow grammatical rules of the English language. So in this level of parsing or syntax analysis, the sentence is checked for grammar and logical meaning.

1.1.3 Semantic Analysis

During semantic analysis, input sentences' meaning representation is examined. The main focus of this phase is determining the basic meaning of words, various sentences and phrases in the input. With semantic analysis, computers are able to interpret documents, paragraphs and sentences. This is achieved by analysis of the grammatical structure of the language and finding associations between individual words occurring in the sentence with respect to a particular context. Hence, during semantic analysis, the input is processed to find the dictionary or exact meaning of the text. The basic task of a semantic analyzer is to check for meaningfulness in the text.

The following example will make semantic analysis clearer. Let's consider a sentence: "Your customer service is a joke! I've been on hold for 30 minutes!"

When a human reads this sentence, it is understood that the sentence is uttered by a customer who is very frustrated because the customer service agent is taking very long time to respond.

However, machines first need to be taught/trained to interpret and make sense of human language and identify the context in which particular words are used, otherwise, for example, the word "joke" might be misinterpreted by the machine as positive. With the use of algorithms in machine learning (ML) and NLP, semantic analysis systems can understand the context of natural (human) language, can differentiate between human emotions and words expressing sarcasm, can extract information from semi-structured or unstructured data, and can achieve human-level accuracy. Lexical analysis systems use smaller chunks of text, while semantic analysis uses larger ones.

1.1.4 Discourse Integration

Discourse integration usually depends upon the sentences that precede a particular sentence, and also identifies the meaning of the sentences that follow a particular sentence. Conducting discourse analysis not only examines how a language functions, but also interprets the meaning of sentences in different social contexts. It can be applied to languages which are in written or oral form, and can also be applied to non-verbal aspects of communication, such as tones and gestures.

The discourse analysis process focuses on:

- The purposes and effects of different types of languages
- Communication conventions and cultural rules
- The ways in which values, beliefs and assumptions are communicated
- How use of language relates to social, political and historical perspectives

1.1.5 Pragmatic Analysis

The pragmatic analysis phase helps to discover the intended effect by applying a set of rules that characterize mutual dialogues. This analysis is primarily used for extracting information from input text. It primarily deals with taking a structured set of text and identifying the actual meaning of the input text. It operates primarily in the domain of linguistics, where text is analysed to identify its context.

For example, "Open the door" is interpreted as a request rather than an order.

1.2 MACHINE LEARNING AND TEXT MODELLING

Machine learning algorithms are used for NLP and text analysis to establish the meaning of text documents. The documents which serve as input to ML modules can be anything that contains text, like comments on social media platforms, online product/service reviews, responses to survey questionnaires, financial statements, medical records, or legal or regulatory documents. The role of ML and artificial intelligence in NLP and text analytics is to improve, accelerate and automate the underlying text analytics functions and NLP features that turn this unstructured text into usable data and insights.

As the natural language text will be messy and in free format, we need ML techniques to pre-process it and convert it into well-defined, fixed-length inputs. As a part of the pre-processing of raw language, the text is broken down into numerical format, which is easier for computers to interpret. This method is called "feature extraction" or "feature encoding," and is the process of text modelling. As document data is not suitable for computation, it must be transformed into numerical data such as vector space models. Feature extraction techniques are used to transform document data into numerical data. Using these techniques, input text is converted into a matrix of features. Popular feature extraction methods include the Bag of Words (BoW) model and the Term Frequency-Inverse Document Frequency (TF-IDF) score.

1.3 BOW MODEL

1.3.1 INTRODUCTION

Bag of Words is a representation which is very simple to understand and easy to implement. This approach can be used in multiple ways to extract various features from documents. The model is also flexible and can be applied to variety of inputs. It is called *Bag* of Words, because it only considers whether the known words are present in the input document and ignores their position in it, just like a bag can carry multiple items, their location in it is insignificant. The model does not consider the order or structure of words in the document.

The following example explains the step-by-step process for construction of the Bag of Words.

1.3.1.1 Step 1: Collect the Data

In this example, a few lines from Charles Dickens' famous book *A Tale of Two Cities* are considered:

> It was the epoch of belief,
> It was the epoch of incredulity,
> It was the season of light,
> It was the season of darkness.

In this four-line example, it can be assumed that every line is a separate "document" and these four lines together form the complete input collection (document corpus).

1.3.1.2 Step 2: Vocabulary Design

A list of all the words from the vocabulary can be gathered to form a model. This is a list of the distinct words present in these documents (ignoring case, punctuation, but retaining their order of occurrence):

- it
- was
- the
- epoch
- of
- belief
- incredulity
- season
- light
- darkness

The vocabulary consists of ten words, and the corpus consists of 24 words.

1.3.1.3 Step 3: Document Vectors Creation

In this step, scores for the words present in each document are generated. The main purpose of this step is to create a vector for each free-text input document which can be used as an input and output to an ML model. As the vocabulary in the example contains a total of ten words, a document representation with fixed length can be used.

We will create a vector of length 10, where each location in the vector will be used to score every single word. Boolean values can be used to show the word score. 0 (zero) can be used to show a word is *not* present, and 1 (one) indicates the presence of the word. We can randomly order the words listed in the vocabulary and convert Document 1, “it was the epoch of belief” into a binary vector.

The score of this document can be represented as follows:

“it” = 1 (present in Document 1)
“was” = 1 (present in Document 1)
“the” = 1 (present in Document 1)
“epoch” = 1 (present in Document 1)
“of” = 1 (present in Document 1)
“belief” = 1 (present in Document 1)
“incredulity” = 0 (not present in Document 1)
“season” = 0 (not present in Document 1)
“light” = 0 (not present in Document 1)
“darkness” = 0 (not present in Document 1)

The binary vector representation of this document will appear as: [1, 1, 1, 1, 1, 1, 0, 0, 0, 0].

The vectors for the other three documents would be:

"It was the epoch of incredulity" = [1, 1, 1, 1, 1, 0, 1, 0, 0, 0]
"It was the season of light"= [1, 1, 1, 0, 1, 0, 0, 1, 1, 0]
""It was the season of darkness" = [1, 1, 1, 0, 1, 0, 0, 1, 0, 1]

We can see clearly see that in this approach, the order of the words is not considered, and it offers a consistent way to extract the document features in the corpus. A document which has an overlapping vocabulary of known words can still be coded with this approach. Here, the known word's occurrence score will be counted, and other words will be ignored. Large documents and vocabularies also can be handled using this method. In this example, it can be observed that the document vector length is the same as the total number of known words. In cases where the corpus is very large, perhaps thousands of lines in books, then the vector length will extend up to thousands or millions. Furthermore, the documents' vocabulary may contain far fewer known words. The document vector for these types of documents will then have more zeros, which results ina sparse vector. More memory and computational resources are required to model sparse vectors as they have a large number of dimensions/positions. Obviously, this makes the modelling process really challenging if traditional algorithms are used.

In using the BoW model, a decrease in the size of the vocabulary will be an advantage.

As the first step in BoW construction, the following text cleaning methods can be used:

- Ignore cases.
- Ignore punctuation marks.
- Ignore words which occur frequently but do not hold much information (such as "a," "of," etc.).
- Fix words which are not spelled properly.
- Reduce inflected (or derived) words to their stem form (root word) – for example, the root word "play" will be obtained from "playing" (stemming algorithms are used for this).

Creation of a grouped words vocabulary can be a sophisticated approach. As this method changes the scope of vocabulary, it allows BoW to extract more meaning from the input document. This approach focuses on the *gram*, which refers to each word (token) present in the input document. If a sequence of two words is considered, it is referred to as a *bigram*. The bigrams which appear in the corpus will be modelled, and all possible bigrams will not be considered.

An *N-gram* means a sequence of Ntokens of input words: a bigram means a sequence of two words, such as "please complete," "complete your or "your assignment," and a *trigram* is a sequence of three words, such as "please complete your" or "complete your assignment" (Daniel and James 2009).

For the last line in the example shown in Step 1, "it was the season of darkness," the bigrams are:

- "it was"
- "was the"
- "the season"
- "season of"
- "of darkness"

The N-gram model is a general approach to track N words, where N is the number of words present in the same group. In documentation classification, the bigram approach has proven to be better than a single-gram model. A Bag of Bigrams representation is considered more powerful than the BoW approach, and has proven hard to beat in many cases (Yoav 2017).

1.3.1.4 Scoring Words

After finalizing the vocabulary of the documents, the word occurrences in them are scored. In the example discussed earlier, a straightforward approach of scoring would be used: binary scoring (indicating whether a word is present or absent).

Other methods used for scoring are:

- *Counts* – this method calculates how many times every word appears in the input document
- *Frequencies* – this method calculates the frequency of each word in the document in comparison to the other words

The vocabulary can also contain a *hash* representation of known words. This will address the problem of having a large vocabulary for a very large text corpus because we can select the appropriate size of the hash space, which in turn hasan impact on the size of the document vector representation.

An issue with the word frequency scoring approach is that the words which occur frequently in the input will dominate in the document (as they will have a larger score) even though they may not have any informative content in the model. The words may be domain-specific: for instance, a financial document will contain multiple words related to financc, but these words might not contain complete document information. This issue can be solved by rescaling the word frequency. We can count how often these words are present in all input documents so that the scores for recurrent words like "the," which appears commonly in all the documents, are penalized.

1.3.2 Limitations of the BoW Model

The BoW model takes two factors into account to establish the occurrences of words in the input document. The first is *the vocabulary of known words*, and the second is *the measure of presence of these words*. The model focuses on occurrences of the words, and ignores their structure in the document. However, in a language, the position of words is equally important.

The BoW model does not respect the semantics of the words, so it often fails to extract the exact meaning of sentences in specific contexts. It ignores the order of words and distances between words.

The BoW model's shortcomings can be summarized as follows:

1. Vocabulary – The vocabulary is set of all words present in the document. It has to be designed very carefully because as new words are added, the vocabulary size and consequent size of the vector grow. It also has an effect on the sparsity of the document representations.
2. Sparsity – If the document contains far fewer known words, then the resultant vector will be sparse. Sparse vector representation is harder to model in terms of time and space complexity. It may also include insignificant information in this large representation space.
3. Meaning – Neglecting the order of words ignores the context present in the input document, which may change the meaning of words. This means the semantic aspect is completely ignored. Context and meaning can add much to the model, and if included in it may enable distinction between words which are the same but are arranged differently ("meaning is important" versus "is meaning important"), synonyms ("old car" versus "used car") and many more aspects.

There are millions of N-gram features when dealing with thousands of news articles, but only a few hundred are actually present in every article, and only tens of class labels.

The N-gram model fails to capture word inversion and subset matching (e.g., "article about news" versus "news article").

The accuracy of the BoW model depends on the range of vocabulary. If the words are not known, then the model simply ignores them. Because of these limitations, the BoW model is often inefficient. Therefore, the alternative approach would be to consider semantics and pay attention to the context of words.

1.4 GRAPH OF WORDS (GOW) MODEL

Graph of Words is a technique focused on graphical representation of documents. Graphs are very flexible mathematical models, and can represent any system in terms of objects and the relationship between them. Many different aspects of natural language can be represented in the form of graphs. Syntactic analysis of sentences can be depicted as parse trees, showing how the words are structurally related to each other. GoW is a text mining approach which considers the order of words and the distance between them. This model is superior for tasks of text categorization, keyword extraction, sub-event detection from text streams and many other information retrieval tasks.

1.4.1 Basic Terminology of Graphs

Graphs are flexible mathematical models used for frequent and diverse problems. Any system which can be considered as combination of objects and relationships/interactions between them can be represented in the form of a graph. Graphs are represented as ordered pairs of vertices and edges, G = (V, E).

Leonhard Euler is said to have used graphs and networks first in solving mathematical problems, such as is famous solution of "The Seven Bridges of Königsberg" using graph representation. Many real-life problems can be represented as graphs called networks. Networks are visible everywhere – for example, road, railway and airline networks. A network of cables is formed between telephones or computers which transmits voice calls or emails. The widely used World Wide Web is a network of Web pages which are linked with each other by hyperlinks. We ourselves are part of networks of people connected with each other, like a network of friends or professional associations. The human body also contains numerous networks, including the network of bio-chemical reactions between cell molecules. The brain is also a complex network, consisting of neurons and synaptic connections between them. Human languages can also be treated as networks of words, sentences or concepts which are connected with each other meaningfully. Different types of graphs are used to present different real-life situations. Line and curved graphs are used in health applications. Sales and marketing application data are represented using bar charts and column charts. Histograms are used to summarize continuous or discrete data.

1.4.1.1 Real-world Graphs

Graphs are used in many fields, including biology, sociology, computer science, engineering, and many other diverse complex systems like markets and ecosystems. Graphs also play a significant role in linguistics. They are widely used to represent semantic information (Fellbaum 1998). Furthermore, representation of human language as a graph of interacting words (Dorogovtsev and Mendes 2001; Ferrer-i-Cancho 2001) has thrown light on the very nature of language, especially on how words are structured in the brain and how language evolves from them. The neural network of the *human brain connectome* can be modelled using brain graphs (Edward and Danielle 2010), which define the nervous system as a set of nodes (recording electrodes or anatomical regions) and edges (functional or structural connections).

1.4.1.2 Graphs in Linguistics

The use of graphs has become ubiquitous in language processing. Multiple perspectives of a language can be represented as graphs. In dealing with words in lexical resources or words connected in sentences, the use of graphs is an obvious solution. Parse trees are used by language researchers, where syntactic analysis of sentences shows how the words appearing in a sentence are related with each other and the structure of their relationships. The links of a parse tree represent semantic relationships. By correctly choosing criteria to draw nodes, edges and weights, graphs can be extremely powerful in determining and representing data patterns, regularities, language identification, word sensing and parts of speech induction.

1.4.2 Semantic Similarity and Ambiguity

When an identical word form is used to refer to multiple different concepts, semantic ambiguity occurs. The phrases "rock music" and "rock stone" have similar written forms, but are totally different from each other in meaning. Natural language is full of such ambiguities, so machine translation systems have to be able to choose possible translations of an ambiguous word based on its context. This is the main bottleneck in lexical analysis. One way to overcome this is by learning the inventory of sense labels directly from the text to be disambiguated. One method is to represent the text in graph format. The network representation of the nouns in a text provides a very effective way of predicting the multiple meanings of a word automatically from the web of connections among its neighbouring words.

Many different aspects of language can be depicted as graphs. Linguists generate parse trees after syntactic analysis to depict structural relationships between the words appearing in sentences. The links in a parse tree are used to show syntactic and semantic relationships. The graph structure can also be used to describe how words are semantically related.

The ambiguity of the word "rock" can be overcome if it is represented as a graph (as shown in Figure 1.1).

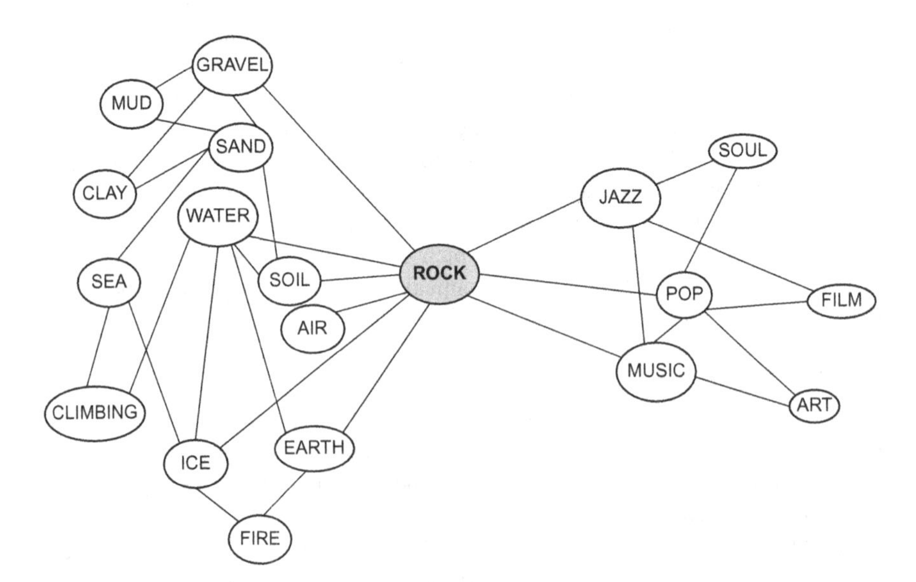

FIGURE 1.1 Different meanings of the word "rock" represented as a graph

1.4.3 How to Build a GoW

Let's consider text categorization as a graph classification problem. Here, a text document is represented as a GoW rather than showing it using the traditional N-gram BoW model, to identify more discriminative features which correspond to long-distance N-grams using frequent sub-graph mining. The sequence is as follows:

1. Construct GoW for each document in the set.
2. For each graph from Step 1, extract its main core for cost-effective.
3. Find all frequent sub-graph sizes *n* in the obtained set of graphs from Step 2.
4. Remove the isomorphic sub-graph to reduce the total number of features.
5. Finally, extract N-gram features from the remaining text.

1.4.3.1 Preliminary Concepts

1.4.3.1.1 GoW Model

An undirected graph G is expressed as G = (V, E), where V is the set of vertices, which represents unique terms of document, and E is the set of edges, which represents co-occurrences between the terms within a fixed-size sliding window.

1.4.3.1.2 Sub-graph Isomorphism

Given two graphs G and H, an isomorphism of G and H is a bijection between the vertex sets of G and H such that any two vertices *u* and *v* of G are adjacent in G if and only if *f(u)* and *f(v)* are adjacent in H:*f*:V(G) → V(H) (Figure 1.2).

1.4.3.1.3 K-core and Main Core

A sub-graph H = (V', E') induced by the subset of vertices V' ⊆ V and the subset of edges E' ϵ E of graph G = (V, E) is called a k-core, where *k* is an integer if and only if H is the maximal sub-graph that holds the property ∀ v ϵ V', deg(v) >= k.

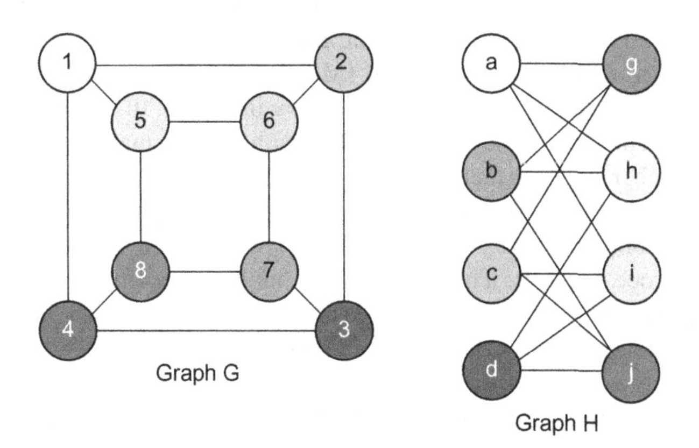

FIGURE 1.2 Sub-graph isomorphism

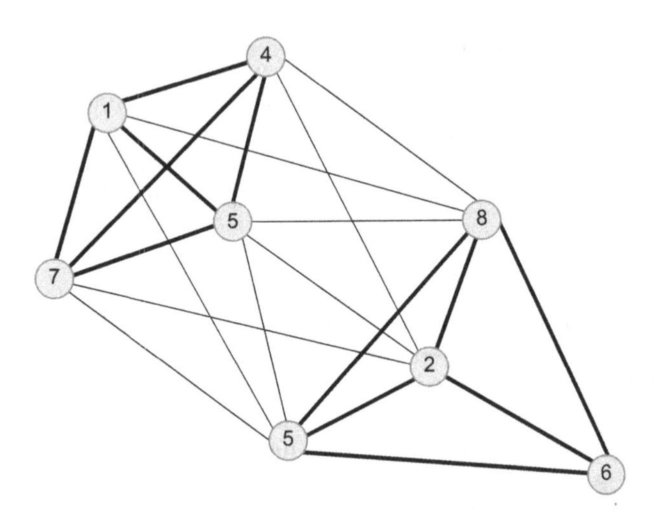

FIGURE 1.3 Two 3-cores of the graph example

A k-core is a maximal connected sub-graph whose vertices are at least of degree k within that sub-graph.

The main core is the k-core with the largest *k* (Figure 1.3).

1.4.4 Construction of a GoW

Nodes of a GoW model are the words which are unique and used during the pre-processing steps. By adding edges between these *n* nodes, the GoW is constructed. The complexity of this is written as *O(nW)*, *W* being window size. The following are some of the parameters used while constructing the GoW:

Window size – This is an integer with a value between 2 and 12, with the default value set to 3. This parameter specifies the size of the window that is slid over the input document. It has been observed that a window size of around 3 or 4 works well (Mihalcea and Tarau 2004;Malliaros and Skianis 2015). As the size of window increases, the graph becomes denser. This is because the number of graph nodes remains constant, but the number of edges increases.

Build on processed text (a Boolean process with a default value of TRUE) – The point of interest can be the window sliding over the processed or unprocessed text. This can produce multiple results, depending on the pre-processing steps. Two words which are initially very faraway in the original, non-processed text and whose co-occurrence would consequently not be captured may end up close to one another in the processed text if multiple words appearing between them (e.g., commonly used words – stop-words) are removed as the result of pre-processing. Subsequent construction of a graph from the processed text tends to relate more words which are faraway in the unprocessed text and produce denser graphs from it.

Overspan sentences (this parameter takes a Boolean value with a default value of TRUE) – For the FALSE value, an edge between two co-accompanying words is created (and only edge weight is incremented if it is already present) if and only if the two words are from the same sentence. Punctuation marks like inverted commas, exclamation marks, question marks and 'ellipses are treated as sentence boundaries.

Colour (the data type of this parameter is List, and the default value is heat) – This consists of a set of five built-in R palettes. The palettes are used to colour the graph vertices, including colour-blind-friendly gray colours. Each node of the graph is coloured such that it matches with its core (truss) number (shown in a legend) and takes darker shade as the *k* value increases.

Figure 1.4 shows the GoW representation of a textual document. The weight of the edges corresponds to the number of co-occurrences, and the node colour corresponds to the node core number (a gray scale, as mentioned above). Table 1.1 shows the ranked lists of scored keywords extracted by weighted k-core (WK-Core), PageRank and HITs (Hyperlink Induced Topic search). Words shown in bold indicate the golden keywords, and dashed lines indicate the cut-off for each method.

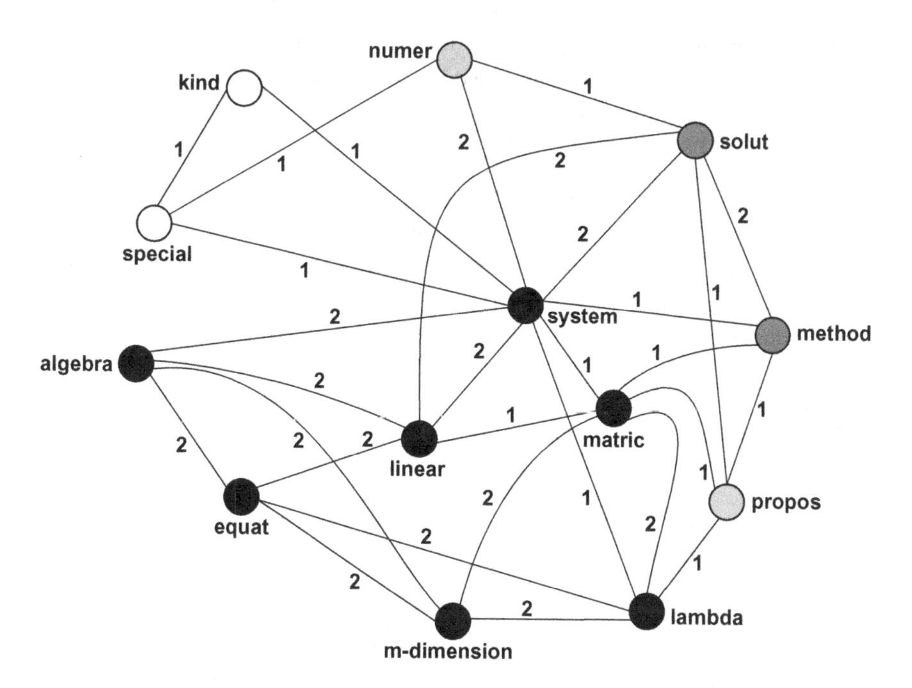

FIGURE 1.4 GoW representation of a textual document

TABLE 1.1
Ranked List of Scored Keywords

WK-Core		PageRank		HITs	
system	6	**system**	1.93	**system**	0.45
matric	6	**matric**	1.27	**matric**	0.38
lambda	6	solut	1.10	**linear**	0.31
linear	6	**lambda**	1.08	**lambda**	0.32
equat	6	**Linear**	1.08	solut	0.30
		-----------------	----------	-----------------	-------
algebra	6	**equat**	0.90	method	0.28
m-dimension	6	**algebra**	0.90	propos	0.25
-----------------	----				
method	5	**m-dimension**	0.90	**algebra**	0.25
solut	5	propos	0.89	**m-dimension**	0.23
propos	4	method	0.88	**equat**	0.22
numer	3	special	0.78	**numer**	0.18
special	2	numer	0.74	special	0.15
kind	2	kind	0.55	kind	0.12

The GoW representation in Figure 1.5 (Mihalcea and Tarau 2004) encodes a text part as an undirected graph, where nodes are distinct nouns and adjectives from the input document and there is an edge between two nodes if the terms they signify co-occur inside a window of already determined size *W* which is slid over a whole document from the starting position to the end over spanning sentences. The weights written on the edges represent co-occurrence counts. This is a completely statistical approach, and it is based on the Distributional Hypothesis, on the premise that the association between words can be determined based on the frequency with which they share local contexts of word occurrence.

Consider the sentence "Information retrieval is the activity of obtaining information resources relevant to an information need from a collection of information resources."

This statement can be represented in two ways.

The BoW presentation of this information would be:

((activity,1), (collection,1) (information,4), (relevant,1), (resources, 2), (retrieval, 1)... etc for remaining words)

Here, the word "activity" has appeared once, the word "information" has occurred four times, and so on. The BoW approach only considers how many times the word has been used in the input, and simply ignores the relationship between two words.

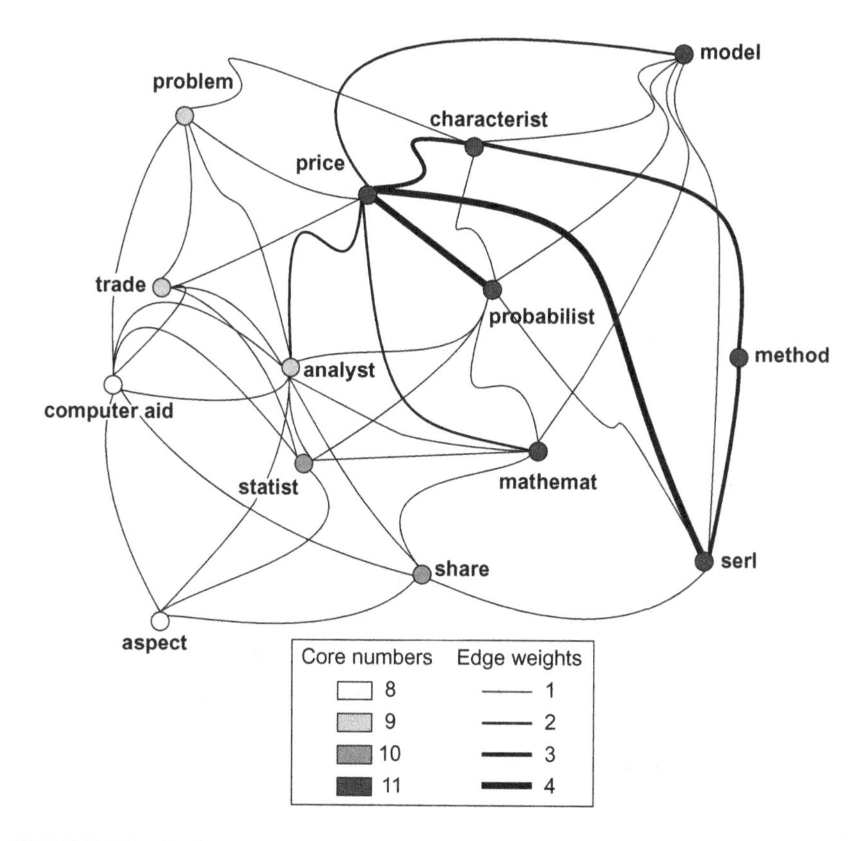

FIGURE 1.5 Undirected graph representation of computer-aided share trading

The same sentence can be represented using GoW as shown in Figure 1.6.

This approach of text mining considers word dependence, word order and distance, employing a graph-based document representation which captures the characteristics of words. Graphs are used effectively in information retrieval which includes relations and proposes meaningful weights (e.g., PageRank).

Actually, in some works, some nodes corresponded to words and others to sentences, forming a bipartite graph (Wan and Yang 2007).

An edge corresponds to a relationship between two vertices, which can be:

Statistical – e.g., simple co-occurrences or collocations in a window, a sentence, the full document or in the definition of one of the two words from a dictionary

Syntactic – e.g., an adjective pointing to the noun it modifies, and more generally grammatical relationships between pairs of words (Widdows and Dorow 2002; Ferrer-i-Cancho, Solé, and Köhler 2004), or semantic ones, e.g., based on synonymy.

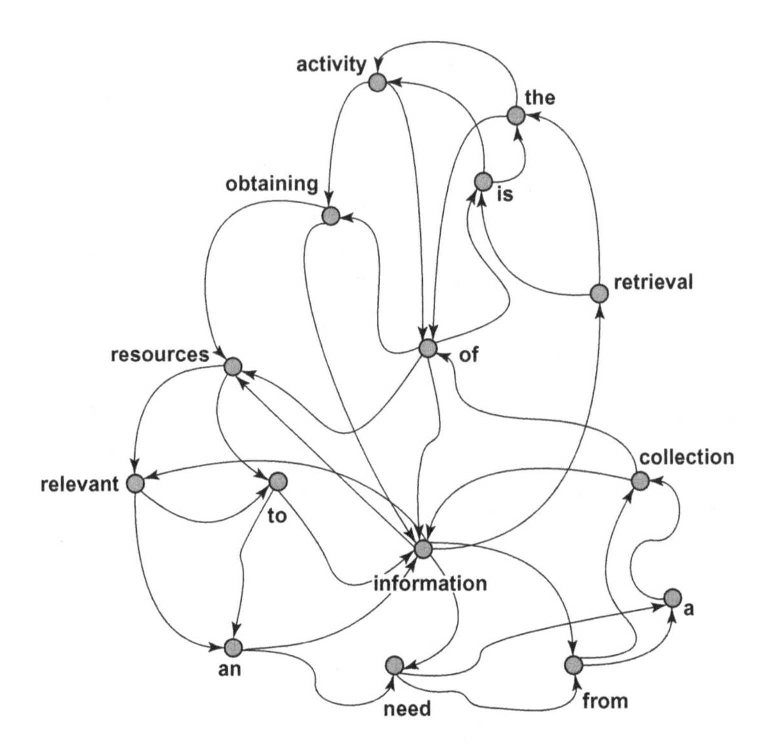

FIGURE 1.6 GoW representation of a sentence

Moreover, the graph can represent:

1. A sentence such as a dependency tree commonly used in NLP
2. A single document like in most related works
3. Multiple documents, or even
4. The entire collection of documents, depending on the application and the granularity we wish to achieve

Additionally, there exist some representations usually referred to as association graphs that mix linguistic units and linguistic labels for nodes and edges – to some extent, they are closer to the syntactic parse trees from NLP because of the use of Part of Speech (POS) tags as node labels.

1.4.5 Use of GoW in Text Mining

Text mining is used to identify facts, relationships and assertions that are otherwise ignored in the mass of textual big data. After extraction, the information is transformed into a structural format which can be further analyzed or represented directly using mind maps, charts, clustered HTML tables etc. The process of text mining employs a variety of methodologies over the input text, one of the most essential of them being NLP. The structured data generated by text mining can be integrated into databases, data warehouses or in business intelligence dashboards. The data also can be used for descriptive, predictive or prescriptive analytics.

The process of text mining can be used in various real-life applications, such as:

1. Web search engines
   - To understand user queries
   - To find matching documents
   - To group similar results together
2. Product recommendation
   - To understand product descriptions
   - To understand product reviews

Text mining involves:

1. Information retrieval
2. Single-document keyword extraction
   - Election of representative words for a document that best describe it
   - Sub-event detection in textual streams
   - Keyword extraction
   - Text categorization
     - Graph classification problem
   - Sentence-based kernels for short text categorization
   - Data mining and machine learning

The text mining technique is applied to a collection of documents. Here, the collection forms the data set, while the documents form the data points. As the input text is unstructured, it is first converted into some common representation and then processed. Input text can be represented in BoWor GoW format.

1.4.6 GoW Mining

After text pre-processing and building the GoW, the next step is analysis of the drawn graph.

1.4.6.1 Graph Degeneracy

A core of order k (or k-core) of a graph G is defined as a maximal connected sub-graph derived from G where minimum degree of each vertex v is k. This is a relaxation of a clique. (a clique is a sub-graph with $k + 1$ members where every two nodes of the sub-graph are adjacent to each other) (Seidman 1983). In a classical unweighted graph, edges do not carry any weight, so the degree of node v is the total number of its neighbours. In a weighted (or generalized) graph, the degree of a vertex v is equal to summation of the weights of edges incident on that vertex.

1.4.6.2 K-core Decomposition

The k-core decomposition of a graph G is the list of all its cores from 0 (G itself) to *k-max* (main core). It constructs a hierarchy of sub-graphs which are recursively included in each other, and their size and cohesiveness increases or decreases as per *k* value (Seidman 1983). The linear time algorithm for k-core decomposition can be observed in for the unweighted case. These algorithms perform a pruning process in which the lowest degree nodes are removed at every step. The highest order of the core in which node *v* is present will be the core number of *v*. The nodes which carry large core numbers have the property of being at the centre. These nodes are also elements of a cohesive sub-graph with other central nodes (members having high cores). This is the reason why these nodes make influential spreaders (the important nodes) and good keywords.

The central core of a graph results in a quick approximation of its densest sub-graph. For some cases, it might contain larger portion of graph nodes. As mentioned (Seidman 1983), k-cores should be regarded as seedbeds inside which one can find some more cohesive sub-graph.

1.4.6.3 K-truss

This is an extension of k-core which results in the densest sub-graph.

The k-truss of a graph G is defined as its largest sub-graph where every edge belongs to minimum $k - 2$ cycle and forms a triangle with that specific edge (the sub-graph having length 3). In short, every edge in the k-truss joins two vertices which have minimum of $k - 2$ common vertices adjacent to it.

1.4.6.3.1 K-truss Decomposition

The k-truss decomposition of a graph G is a set of all its k-trusses from $k - 2$ to *k-max*. The k-trusses are densely connected subsets of the k-cores which are their essential parts. The maximal k-truss results in a small but dense sub-graph of G which properly approximates its densest sub-graph. To obtain finer resolution of k-truss decomposition, one has to bear thecost of major complexity, polynomial in number of edges.

Similar to k-core, the truss number of an edge is the highest order of the truss in which the edge is present. The truss number of a given node is defined as the maximum truss number of its incident edges (Malliaros and Vazirgiannis 2016).

This GoW is plotted in parallel with text summarization. This helps to plot a dynamic and interactive browser-based representation of the GoW with the help of igraph and the Vis Network R packages (Almende and Thieurmel 2016).

1.5 DISCUSSION AND FUTURE SCOPE

Knowledge representation using a graph-based approach is not new, but has nowadays become a trend, especially when it comes to understanding text, information storage and knowledge transfer. Throughout this chapter, we have tried to focus on the need for GoW representation of text, how it can be plotted and the use of it in text mining work. The GoW method can perform far better than the BoW model in multiple tasks such as text categorization, sub-event detection in textual streams, single-document keyword extraction and ad-hoc information retrieval. Ongoing research will focus on in-depth analysis for the processing of natural language using the GoW approach.

REFERENCES

Almende, B. V., Thieurmel, B. (2016). visNetwork: Network Visualization using 'vis.js' Library. R package version 0.2.1.

Daniel, J., James H. M. (2008). *Speech and Language Processing*. Second Publisher, Prentice Hall.

Dorogovtsev, S. N., Mendes, J. F. (2001). Anomalous Behaviour of the Contact Process with Aging. *Physical Review. E, Statistical, Nonlinear, and Soft Matter Physics* 63(4), 046107. https://doi.org/10.1103/PhysRevE.63.046107

Edward, B., Daniel, B. (2010). Brain Graphs: Graphical Models of the Human Brain connectome. DOI: 10.1146/annurev-clinpsy-040510-143934.

Fellbaum, C. (1998). A Semantic Network of English: The Mother of All WordNets. *Computers and the Humanities* 32, 209–220. https://doi.org/10.1023/A:1001181927857

Ferrer-i-Cancho, R. (2001). The small world of human language. *Proceedings of the Royal Society B: Biological Sciences* 268(1482), 2261–2265.

Ferrer-i-Cancho, R. Sole., Kohler, (2004). Patterns in syntactic dependency networks. DOI: 10.1103/PhysRevE.69.051915.

Fragkiskos, D., Malliaros, A., Papadopoulos, M., Vazirgiannis, (2016). Core decomposition in graphs: concepts, algorithms and applications. *Proceedings of the 19th International Conference on Extending Database Technology*. Pp. 720–721. EDBT.

Malliaros, F. D., Skianis, K. (2015). Graph-Based Term Weighting for Text Categorization. In *The 2015 IEEE/ACM International Conference*. https://doi.org/10.1145/2808797.2808872

Mihalcea, R., Tarau, P. (2004). *TextRank: Bringing Order into Texts*. Department of Computer Science University of North Texas. https://aclanthology.org/W04-3252

Seidman, S. B. (1983). Network Structure and Minimum Degree. *Social Networks* 5, 269–287. https://doi.org/10.1016/0378-8733(83)90028-X

Wan, X., Yang, J., Xiao, J. (2007). Towards an Iterative Reinforcement Approach for Simultaneous Document Summarization and Keyword Extraction. In *Proceedings of the 45th Annual Meeting on Association for Computational Linguistics*, ACL2007, 552–559. https://aclanthology.org/P07-1070.

Widdows, D. (2002). *A Graph Model for Unsupervised Lexical Acquisition*. https://doi.org/10.3115/1072228.1072342

Yoav, G. (2017). *Neural Network Methods in Natural Language Processing*. https://doi.org/10.2200/S00762ED1V01Y201703HLT037.

2 Application of NLP Using Graph Approaches

Narendra Singh Yadav, Siddharth Jain, Archit Gupta, and Devansh Srivastava

CONTENTS

DOI: 10.1201/9781003272649-2

2.1 INTRODUCTION

The paradigm of Natural Language Processing (NLP) is vast and dynamic. NLP, as the name suggests, directly deals with automation and machine intelligence with high precision, which can be sub-classified as data processing for machines. Any input provided is just data without meaning for systems such as computers, analysis engines, etc. Using NLP, we can create an understanding of the data which is being processed and analyzed. This data can be in many forms, such as visual, sound, digital, etc. NLP mostly deals with the analysis of human linguistics, but is not limited to this use case.

In human linguistics, there are many applications where NLP is integrated to assist processing. NLP can be applied in the contexts of handwriting, speech, hand signs (not to be confused with computer vision, a method in which the object is detected and using this, NLP is being achieved in physical context), signature fraud detection, etc. NLP can help to ensure that human interaction with complex systems is rendered effortless and swift through applications such as such as chatbots, and can be useful in fraud detection, spam filtering, language translation, automatic form filling, text summarization, sentiment analysis, deep-fake detection, abuse detection, threat detection, and many more areas.

2.1.1 What Is a Graph?

A graph is a type of data structure or visualization of connected data which is non-linear, comprising finite sets of nodes and edges. This type of data structure is essential in computer science as it is used to model real-world connections or complex networks between various data points (nodes), providing more insights into complex structures by defining relationships (edges). Graphs have many applications in the real world:

- Graphs are used to design and implement computer networks. They help in understanding the relations inside the network (intranet) and outside the network (Internet). They can help network administrators to answer many questions about how to implement a network, such as: what is the relation between different networks, and what connections can be made to enable successful communication between different entities? As illustrated in Figure 2.1, each node can be considered as a machine (server, laptop, endpoint), and each edge as a connection between them. In the real world, the Internet is a network of servers connected by cables which span oceans and continents, thus connecting each country to the net. This was made possible with the help of graphs, which enable companies to plan the optimum ways to connect and spread the network to improve speed, convenience, and profitability.

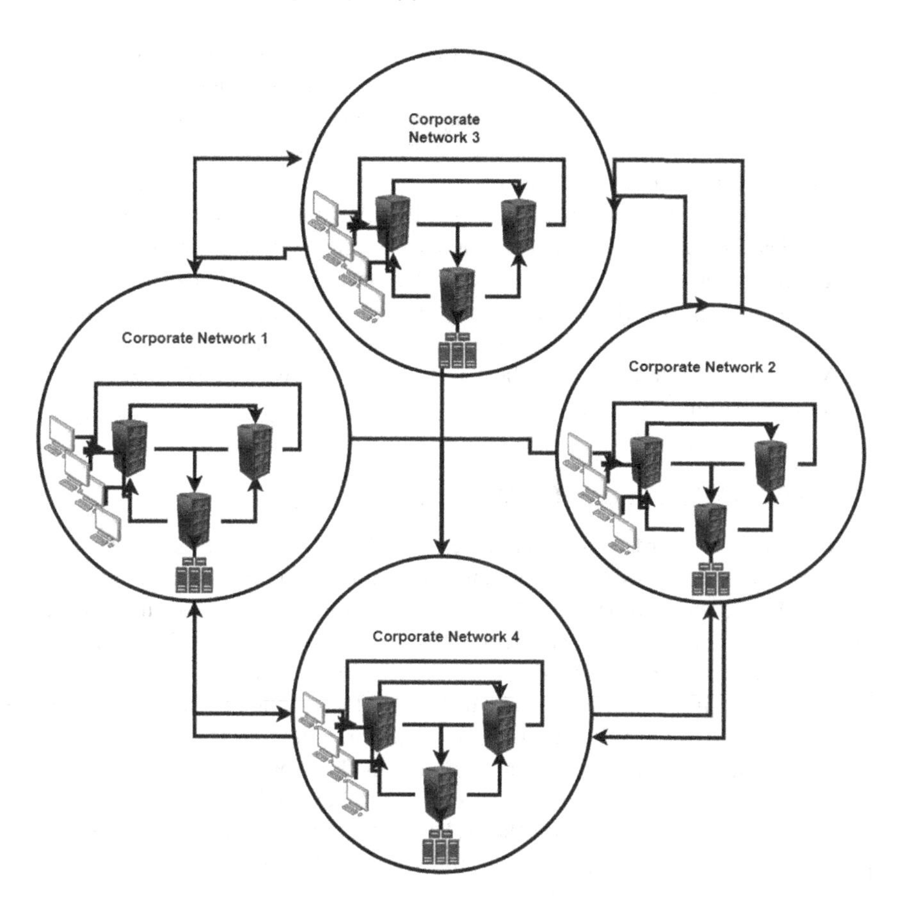

FIGURE 2.1 How graphs are implemented in networks

- Graphs play a huge role in social network platforms, such as mapping user connections on Facebook, LinkedIn, and other social media platforms, where each user and their information are represented by a vertex (node), and these nodes are connected to each other via multiple edges.
- Road networks, postal services, and many algorithmic metrics implement NLP, such as the traveling salesman problem.

We will now discuss some applications which are essential to understanding the graphical approach to NLP.

2.2 GRAPH EMBEDDINGS

Interest in incorporating graphs into artificial intelligence is booming. Graphs can display information about a specific value in an efficient way, showing connections and their respective relationships, which has proven to be useful in training machine learning (ML) models with high precision. Applying graphs as a data input to different ML algorithms is problematic. A large amount of data is required for training highly accurate models with large numbers of connections, which can become memory-extensive. Since each node will have connections to multiple different nodes, this increases the complexity, thus increasing training time.

This has led to the introduction of graph embeddings – the transformations of graphical information into a vector or a set of vectors. Embeddings attempt to capture the graph topology, node-to-node relationships, and other relevant information about graphs and sub-graphs and vertices. This transformation of graphs into a set of vectors drastically reduces the memory load and time spent in training ML models while increasing their accuracy. In this way, graphs can be used in many algorithms.

2.3 DYNAMIC GRAPH OF WORDS

In NLP, graph of words is an alternative to the bag of words approach. The bag of words method has been used for many years for information retrieval and text mining. While this approach has been used for a long time, it disregards words' order and the distance between them within a document. Graph of words techniques challenge word independence and take into account the words' order in the document. Graph of words can be used in various applications, such as information retrieval, keyword extraction, text categorization, and sentiment analysis. A dynamic graph of words stores not only the keywords and their respective frequencies, but also the distances between each keyword in a document. Due to this, the algorithm also establishes relationships between those words, which provides more accurate results after training with an ML model compared to the bag of words approach.

2.4 CROSS-LINGUAL AND MULTILINGUAL GRAPHICAL APPROACHES

In these approaches, we convert one form of language to another while keeping the grammar and the context the same. Mapping of words is one approach, which can be achieved using a graphical approach where the similarity of the words and their usage is maintained; thus, using the correct nomenclature, we can amplify in the following manner.

There are many kinds of multilingual knowledge graphs, such as DBpedia and YAGO, which contain structured knowledge of distinct entities in many languages. The cross-lingual knowledge group alignment approach matches the entities with different language counterparts, thus creating different types of one-to-many relationships.

The major use cases include Google Translate, which tries to convert words and sentences from one language to another while retaining the context (this task is very difficult to achieve with high precision, as taking the grammar of each language into consideration is a very CPU-extensive and not all rules apply similarly in different languages, so that the meaning of language A can become something else in language B).

The second major use case is customer support systems, which need to cater to the needs of users from all over the globe. These systems improve efficiency and help to avoid incorrect communication with customers, which can solve many problems in the initial stages of a customer query (faster resolution), thus increasing customer satisfaction. There are many solutions present in the market, and many more will surely be developed.

2.5 TOPOLOGICAL ANALYSIS OF GRAPHS

Topology is the study of the geometry of an object that remains preserved under stress and deformation, which includes twisting, bending, etc. It defines the object and its exact properties in terms of shape. This is an integral part of mathematics.

Topological analysis is data analysis which provides a greater understanding of data at a more granular level.

Topological analysis is required to understand information about datasets that are high-dimensional, incomplete, and noisy, which helps to create stronger models by accounting for the data points, bringing them out into the open where they can be observed. This prevents false predictions by training models resulting from anomalies in datasets.

A graphical model containing a complex network of graphs may include noisy values or "zombie nodes," which may taint the output because of false values (bad sources). This needs to be taken into account to understand a graph's boundary conditions or weaknesses.

2.6 ADVERSARIAL NETWORKS FOR NATURAL LANGUAGE PROCESSING

Adversarial networks are neural networks that compete against each other to generate synthetic data derived from the logic of the training sets provided.

Adversarial networks are used in situations where there are few training datasets, in situations where new kinds of data are required for a model, or to teach a model all the cases required for it to run seamlessly (for instance, when sending rockets to outer space, agencies may have little data, but can predict the parameters required for a successful mission).

Before exploring adversarial networks in more depth, it will be useful to summarize supervised versus unsupervised learning. In *supervised learning*, the dataset contains the labeled output of each row, which is derived from many experiments conducted by the source of the dataset. This helps in training the model according to the task (for example, to train a model to distinguish a malicious packet from a non-malicious packet). Here, the dataset will be divided into a ratio of testing versus training (which is variable and depends upon the data; the highest ratio is usually 30% testing and 70% training). The creation of labeled data is very costly and time-consuming, but the resulting model accuracy is much higher. In *unsupervised learning*, the data is not labeled, so some patterns are observed, and a generic trend for the model is then created using their input. Generative adversarial networks (GANs) are a type of unsupervised learning.

GANs rely on two primary models: the generator and the discriminator. The *generator* is the model which will create the data based on the patterns derived from the problem. The *discriminator* is based on supervised learning, and checks whether the data created by the generative algorithm is real or fake. Basically, it is a type of classifier. Together, they form the GAN algorithm. The data from the generator, which is synthetic, is provided to the discriminator; meanwhile, the real data from the dataset is also provided to it, and the discriminator then tries to identify which data is real and which is fake. If the discriminator does not detect any fake values from the generator, then the generator has great accuracy and has achieved its aim. GANs are very difficult to set up in an NLP-based model because it needs continuous data, and different combinations of data should make some sense. Many researchers are trying to implement GANs using an NLP approach. Some researchers are using GANs with a zero-shot algorithm to provide the classification of data in real time [1]. Many researchers use GANs to create different texts, and then use these as inputs to an auto-encoder to create a flow of sentences [2]. Graphical approaches are used to correlate different outputs so that the integrity of a sentence's meaning is maintained. This helps in creating applications with abundant knowledge so that the models can provide appropriate responses (Readers can refer to various published research papers on this aspect, some of which are listed in the references section.) [3].

2.7 HETEROGENEOUS INFORMATION NETWORKS FOR TEXTUAL INFORMATION

An heterogeneous information network (HIN) can be thought of as a graphical model for extrapolating real-world information into some kind of network model. The main problem in the paradigm of text analysis is to understand the meaning of sentences containing data from different sources.

The ways different words are represented and how they are chosen can cause massive differences in the output. Use cases include politicians, journalists, writers, lyricists, scientists, and many more, and the way they present their thoughts can provide many opportunities for research. Some developers use HINs to create artificial intelligence chatbots. The flows of such bots are designed using HINs so that the bot can answer customer queries from the data which is modeled in the back end, where mapping between different words and the formulation of sentences based on context is established. The words and sentences formed as an output to the user are semantically and grammatically precise. In a similar way, some bots use HINs to extract new information from different sources by mapping the text to a common context or by mapping a path that leads to new information. In threat detection, they can also be used to directly map posts on the Internet that express extreme views using strong words, thoughts of violence, or harmful or negative thoughts to a particular person and their network. But this does not mean that every person (node) who is in the identified threat's network presents a threat. HINs for those are created separately or unionized with the real threat. By randomly walking these paths or brute-forcing each path (which is CPU-intensive), one can correlate the semantics and the purpose of the sentence.

2.8 SUMMARY OF ONTOLOGY AND KNOWLEDGE GRAPHS

A knowledge graph depicts the relationships between real-world entities as a network. It has three essential parts: nodes, edges, and labels. Schemas, identities, and context all work together to give the data structure. When a knowledge graph is full, search engines can give comprehensive responses to specific queries.

A formal representation of the entities in a graph is called an ontology. An ontology is based on a taxonomy, but may also contain many taxonomies. If we look at a specific venue, such as Eden Gardens in Kolkata, India, we can see an example of an ontology. Finally, the technological infrastructure, such as databases and algorithms, assists this knowledge organization.

2.9 TOPIC IDENTIFICATION

Topic identification is an NLP technique for detecting topics in a group of text documents. Assume we have a set of reviews for a product. We can discover the features of the product that have most impressed reviewers by extracting a few topics the positive reviews have in common. Assume we have several newspapers, each reporting on a subset of the news. Detecting common topics will help to identify a publication's leanings and current trends.

2.10 MAJOR PROCESSES OF NLP USING GRAPHICAL APPROACHES AND THEIR APPLICATIONS IN THE REAL WORLD

Having discussed the different uses of graphs in NLP and how they can be used in research, we will now discuss real-world applications in more detail so that readers can relate them to practical contexts.

There are many use cases for applications of graphs in NLP. This is an extremely wide field whose limits in terms of the combinations of applications are bounded only by the capabilities of the human mind, so this section will only cover some of the major applications:

1. Summarization
2. Semi-supervised passage retrieval
3. Keyword extraction

4. Information extraction
5. Question answering
6. Cross-language information retrieval
7. Term weighting
8. Topic segmentation
9. Machine translation
10. Discourse analysis

2.10.1 Summarization

In this fast-paced world where a quintillion bytes or more of data are created every day, there is a demand for solutions where data can be provided in a much cleaner and more concise format so that human readers can understand the context quickly while maintaining the integrity or the semantics of the data (see Figure 2.2).

In earlier times, this task of summarization was performed by humans. Nowadays, advancements in machine learning and neural networks have provided systems with the capability to understand the context of the given information, which has helped in advances in solving summarization problems. This means that summarization is a use case of NLP which is simply an automation task.

How did humans solve summarization problems in earlier times? It was done in steps. First, the input was provided to the human end-user, then the end-user took rough notes. These notes would emphasize the topic and key features.

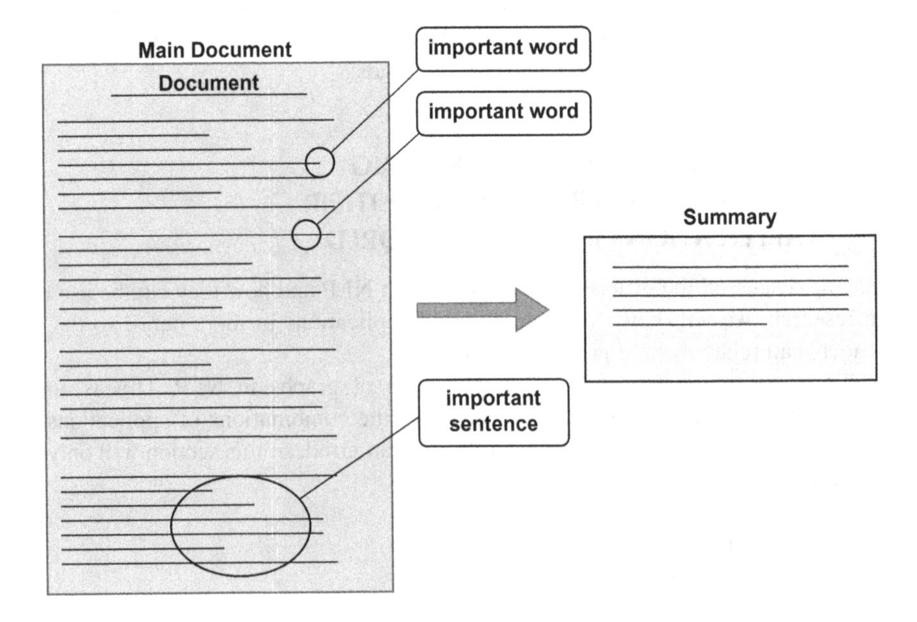

FIGURE 2.2 Example of summarization

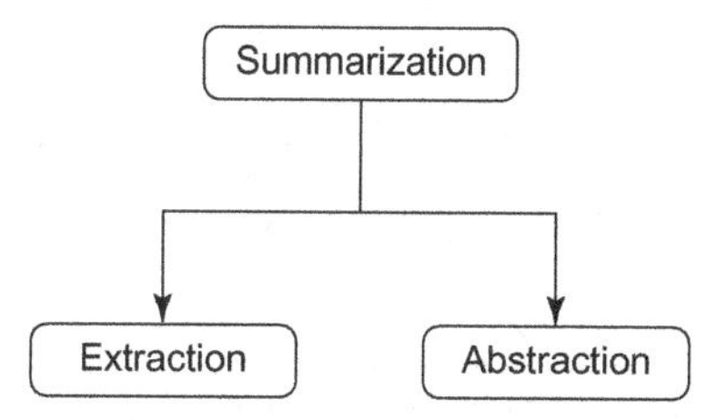

FIGURE 2.3 Types of summarization

The note taker then researched and took into account each note so that the premises and aims of the input could be presented in a suitable format so that there was no ambiguity. In this process, more notes would be created, so the content would incorporate all the data required to present it. These notes would then be polished by the note taker into a presentable form using their expertise in language, thus completing the process of summarization.

Summarization can be achieved using two approaches: extraction and abstraction (see Figure 2.3).

1. *Extraction* involves identifying the important parts, like words, sentences, phrases, names, and other information, which are combined to form the sense of the original sequence. Here is an example depicting the process of extraction:
   Original sentence: "The *UN doesn't appreciate* the *actions of many countries***.** As from the *intelligence gathered* by agencies and allies, many countries have *state-sponsored hacking groups* like *North Korea, Russia* etc. These countries are targeting other countries and companies by *spreading propaganda and also gaining ransom*, thus removing the direct competitions by cyber-terrorism."
   The italic text in this passage shows the focuses of the extraction-based algorithm, and its resulting output would be as follows: "UN doesn't appreciate the actions of many countries. Intelligence gathered, shows that state-sponsored hacking groups by North Korea, Russia, etc, are spreading propaganda and also gaining ransom"
2. *Abstraction* is a more advanced approach, where the whole input topic is shortened using deep learning algorithms to create sentences and phrases that take into account grammar and semantics. This provides an optimized version of the original text. Let's take into consideration the same example taken above in the extraction method, assuming the extraction keywords are the same. The optimized solution presented by the abstraction method would be: "The UN condemns countries like North Korea, etc., for having state-sponsored hacking groups, and for targeting countries and companies for propaganda and ransom."

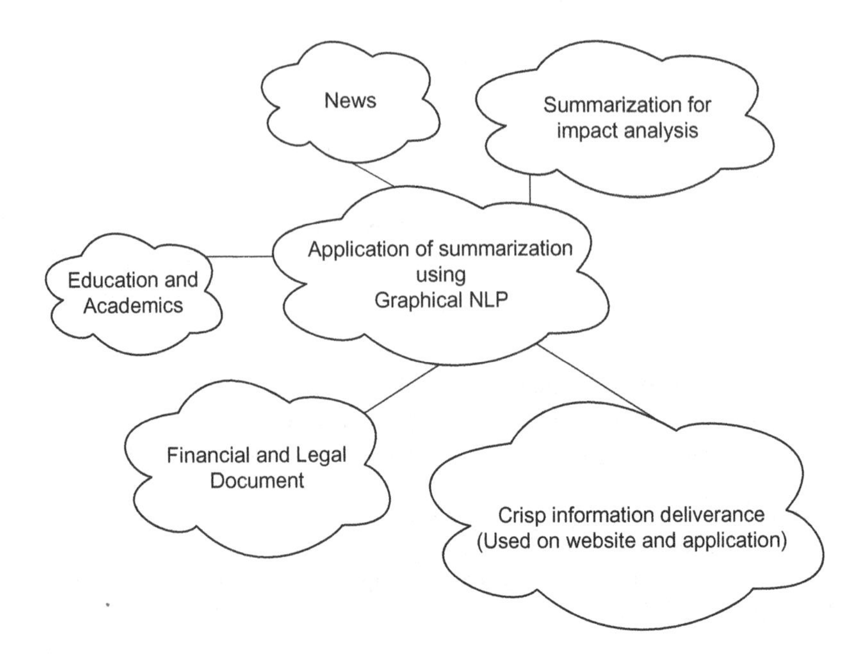

FIGURE 2.4 Applications of summarization

This process used to be a very arduous task, taking up much human time, along with the risk of introducing inaccuracies, which can cause catastrophic results in fields such as media, journalism, politics, business operations, and even defense [4].

Readers can assume that all the negative aspects illustrated in the above passage are kept in mind when creating an NLP-based solution using graphs, which is well suited to summarization problems (see Figure 2.4).

Summarization of text can be achieved using many graphical approaches. One approach is by visualizing each sentence or word as a node. The meaning of the passage is represented by the interconnection of different nodes. The distance between each node will provide a comparison of the meaning of the sentence or word [5]. The closer the nodes, the more similar the words or sentences are. Similarly, the further the nodes are from each other, the greater the contrast in meaning of words or sentences. Sentences and words with similar meanings will be removed. After segregating the passage into a granular and sanitized graph with a myriad of nodes, the model will calculate the number of times a node was accessed, providing the priority of the word. This provides the keywords and the context of the passage or sentence.

Another approach is to divide passages into sentences, then determining the structure of the sentences by representing them in a tree format where each node will be some kind of identifier of the sentences' features. For example, a word's function as a verb, noun, or determiner, etc. is to be understood as a feature of the sentence that maintains the core idea of the sentence and is represented as a sub-child, where the sentence is at the top, and the words and their nature are sub-children of the node. By dividing the sentences into graph-based semantic, lexical, and syntactical elements, one can assume that any problems can be solved.

Different dictionaries rely on different databases. For example, the WordNet multilingual lexical semantic database contains words and their meanings, which can be represented in the format of graphs. In the WordNet lexical database for English, nouns, adjectives, verbs, and adverbs are grouped based on synonyms (synsets). Each word may have a different concept or meaning when used differently (see Figure 2.5; see also http://wordnetweb.princeton.edu/perl/webwn), which is then integrated into the graph's format, which provides better interpretation, as shown by the following sentence example:

India is a great country to live in. All citizens live in harmony and peace [6].

The model will start parsing the sentence, the first word, "*India*," will be searched, and a map will be created as a graph where all the meanings of the word are mapped to each sub-word. This process will continue until the full stop at the end of the sentence. The word "*live*" occurs twice in the sentence. As a result, the model will prioritize it and assume something revolving around the word "live." Each word has a different meaning, but obeys the basic rules of semantics and grammar, and the model will delineate the sentence elements: "'India' is a noun,"

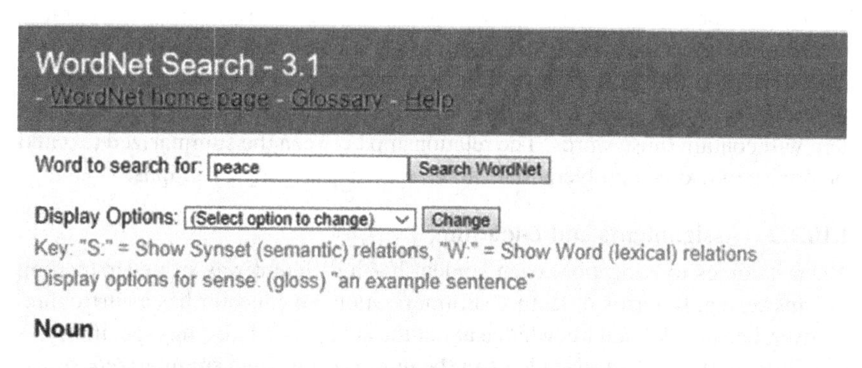

FIGURE 2.5 WordNet screenshot for the word "peace"

"'great' is an adjective," and so on. From that, the model will parse the sentence multiple times and remove the noise words, providing us small sentences like:

> "India is a great country where all live in harmony and tranquility" ("tranquility" because peace and harmony have common synonyms, so the model will choose the node convergence or distance – Euclidean distance or Levenshtein, etc.). Please remember the model can choose different words based on the dictionary used and how well the model was constructed.

We will now discuss the different applications of summarization (Figure 2.4). The inner workings of some applications may be intellectual property, but we will try our best to work around this to provide some ideas for readers.

2.10.1.1 News

One major approach to summarization can be found in the news industry. On the Internet, there are many sources and many people providing information, so it is not humanly possible to read all the information available, and not all the information may be relevant to a particular end-user. This is where NLP is useful. The NLP model will try to extract information from articles and convert it into smaller sentences/simpler words, after which some content may be curated by humans to provide a service to readers. This human intervention is necessary because full trust in such models has not been achieved and not all news sources can be said to be 100% reliable. One major example is the Inshorts news app from India, which provides news to its users as 60-word summaries. These are curated according to a person's interests, and provide a condensed version of the main article, which is linked at the end of the summary. Let's take a use case where the preference of words by the end-user is noted, and as a result the summarized news item will contain those words. The relationship between the summarized text and the preferred text is a problem that can be solved efficiently by graphs.

2.10.1.2 Assignments and E-learning

When it comes to education, each student has a different way of understanding and answering. In terms of lecture summarization, an educator has a curriculum to cover, has pre-defined knowledge about the subject, and also has specific ways of delivering the subject to students in the most coherent and summarized format possible within the time limits. NLP and graphs can be useful here. Graphs can define specific relationships between the topic and sub-topics, and how each sub-topic is important within the whole context. This can be approached by calculating the number of times the same node is accessed, to establish a priority. Each node will have a child node which may be defined content of the sub-topics, after which the context is organized into a form which should be semantically and lexically easy for the student to understand. After this, the flow can be decided based on the original database provided to the model, either using exaction positioning of sub-topics or priority-based positioning of content. It is a good practice to retain the flow of the original content, as this will ensure all the required knowledge is provided to the students, rather than just covering the higher-priority subjects.

The database can consist of multiple books and research papers from which content has been extracted. Here is an example of a possible process for a book:

Input a book's content.
Summarization occurs, and texts are extracted from the dataset.
Priority is decided for the nodes.
Sub-content is organized.
Output is humanly checked for coherence.

In terms of assessment, there can be two scenarios, depending on whether the assessment is for language (a proficiency test for English or any other language) or content-based (a science test or any test of content proficiency). In language proficiency, lexical, grammatical, and semantic coherence are essential. How well the student has answered a question must be judged on the content provided and how the content was represented.

In *language proficiency assessmen*t, the order of the sentence elements, how the sentence is planned, rating of vocabulary, and coherence regarding meaning should meet the standards set, which provide the boilerplate for the model. For example, the words which need to appear in the answers should be provided to the model. The graph which will be generated for this may be expansive, as the answers provided may contain words from eclectic sources, but the marking can be carried out based on Euclidean distance or other practices regarding synonyms of the boilerplate words provided. When it comes to summarization of the answers, either the answers can be summarized and then re-parsed for marking, or they can then be checked by human intervention.

In *content proficiency assessment*, the answers must be coherent and correct, with higher weighting allocated to their meaning. Grammatical errors can be given lesser weights, but the model needs to be able to judge the answers against the training inputs or marking limits. In this case, the graph may not be expansive, as the nouns used and their properties should be in the dictionary provided while training the model. Diagrams and extensive formulas need to be processed using machine vision to decipher handwriting. If digital input is provided, then character recognition can be carried out so that the input correlates with the logic. In testing content proficiency, deviation from the boilerplate will be easily noticed and marking will be much easier than in a language proficiency assessment. Therefore, summarization may be much easier, as the relationships in the context will be established, so the correctness of the summarized answer can be determined easily by a machine or human eyes.

It is important to understand that these are not fully autonomous systems: one cannot trust the system to judge the correctness of answers by itself, but it can summarize the answers and play a role in judging their coherence.

2.10.1.3 Summarization of Financial or Legal Documents

These documents are usually very wordy and lengthy. Even professionals like lawyers and accountants can take weeks to review such documents, so newcomers can be overwhelmed by them. The methods discussed earlier in this section will give a basic approach, and graphs can be used to define relationships between all the technical terms and their synonyms, which should be decided based on the usage trends of the words. Capturing the main words and deciding their impact on a passage will provide the basis for the summarization of that passage. The utmost accuracy is essential in these fields, as errors in summarization can change the meaning of the text, and may result in large damages.

2.10.2 Semi-supervised Passage Retrieval

In supervised learning, the ML model is provided with labeled data during use or while training; in unsupervised learning, the data which is provided is not labeled, so the ML model has to understand the data by itself. Semi-supervised learning is a combination of these two types of learning, where labeled and unlabeled data are used to train the model. Unlabeled data is more common, and when coming to applicability of topic this is most ideal situation the readers may face, as the data labeling is a very costly activity, one will neither ingest non known data in the model. It is important not to confuse these processes with summarization or information extraction. Summarization will render a passage in a shorter form using the same or different words to describe the context. In information extraction, the main context is extracted and derived from the whole input. Passage retrieval, on the other hand, delivers a precise passage which properly describes the context or answers questions from large amounts of data or passages. In this approach, the data is not changed, but the machine has to choose the appropriate paragraphs, delivering the relevant data and removing the irrelevant (see Figure 2.6).

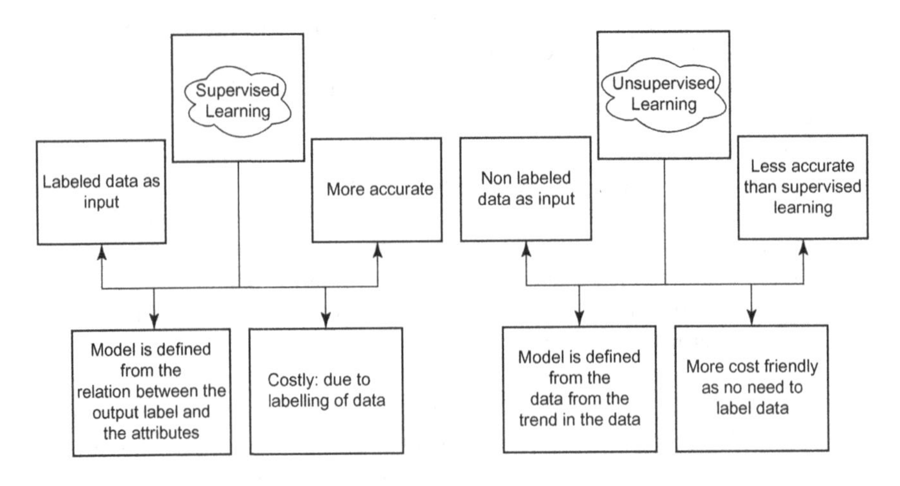

FIGURE 2.6 Supervised versus unsupervised learning

Real-life processing of data or texts about any subject requires detailed understanding of the subject, so it takes lots of human time to go through these materials. Students, doctors, teachers, researchers, and especially lawyers, doctors, engineers, or any profession where correct information is essential, all need easy and rapid access to precise data from books or documents. Summarization may partially answer these needs, but at the end of the day, the user may still need to go through the source text. Summarization can be used to address some retrieval problems, but information extraction will focus on the key points which users may need to search for in a vast document to bolster their arguments.

How is semi-supervised passage retrieval approached? Suppose there is a book titled *Computer Networks*. This is a topic where there are a large number of definitions, protocols, architectures, nomenclatures, and case studies. A fledgling student will need lots of time to read the whole book, starting from page one and going on till the end, highlighting important passages that will be useful in future for understanding the concepts. These passages will be the core of the topic, and will present the main ideas for quick reference. This is called passage identification and extraction. Similarly, a machine seeking to understand a topic for which it does not know any context can use lexical analysis (which is a great way to approach semi-supervised retrieval) to try to understand some context about the topic. A very useful algorithm known as LexRank offers a graph-based approach to unsupervised and semi-supervised passage retrieval [7].

Where is semi-supervised passage retrieval used? One of the major applications is question answering systems, where the system tries to answer an input question using the limited data which was used to train the model, then using knowledge about the specific product or topic. This can be achieved by finding the relationships between the data and creating some kind of trend. This can be achieved using a feature extraction question-type classifier, named-entity recognizer (NER), etc., [8] and applying some custom algorithm in the model, after which the model will provide an answer.

Other practical uses of semi-supervised passage retrieval are as follows:

1. For diagnosis, where doctors have to refer to books and databases, which takes a lot of time
2. For lawyers, who have to refer to large bodies of caselaw to carry out their work
3. For bots, which can use it to understand ranking and website data
4. For researchers, who can use it to speed up the review of published data, and can also use it for assessment and providing faster teaching methods
5. This can create crisp content in media houses, which can sway more users.
6. For cost and storage optimization in storage facilities where the data can be derived using an optimized retrieval process (using concepts of efficient meta-tagging), keeping the main content intact
7. For threat profiling of digital data, where data from the speech or published text of a threat actor can be used for profiling and can serve as evidence

2.10.3 Keyword Extraction

Highlighting words from which the topic can be deduced or deducing the words which act as buttresses/classifiers for a sentence is called keyword extraction. The keyword extraction process is carried out by the human brain when one tries to read a passage, so why the need for automated keyword extraction? This process helps to save time by extracting words so that context of the text can be deduced, and decreasing the complexity of the passage by dividing it into a granular format with or without better words chosen from the dictionary based on synonyms and usage trends. Many of the NLP applications which this section has covered involve keyword extraction in one way or another (see Figure 2.7).

There are many approaches to keyword extraction – statistical (TF-IDF, YAKE, etc.), graphical (RAKE etc.), neural networks, etc. – but this the section will only focus on how it is achieved using graphs [9].

In a graph-based approach, the relationships between words are defined in terms of where the word was used, node convergence, link importance, and weighting of the link. The process runs as follows:

1. A page with multiple paragraphs of text is provided as input to the algorithm.
2. Noise is removed, or normalization is carried out.
3. Data segregation is carried out on words on the basis of their traits.
4. An interconnected graph is be created (nodes and edges).
5. Ranking of the graph elements is carried out to establish the most optimal ones.
6. The highest-weighted words are chosen, which will be ranked on the basis of their weights to establish the best keywords.
7. The scores are calculated, then all the weights of the words which are chosen are added.

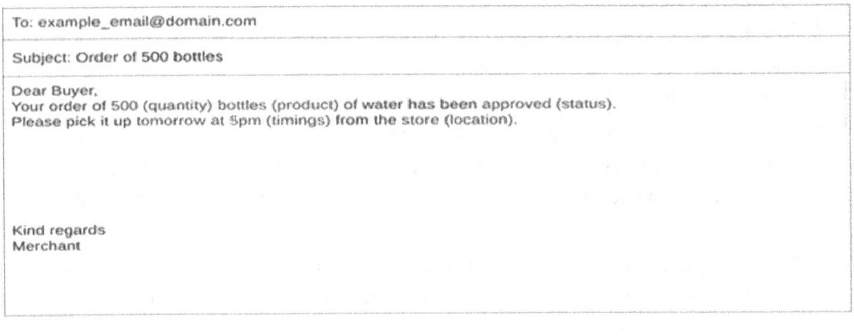

To: example_email@domain.com

Subject: Order of 500 bottles

Dear Buyer,
Your order of 500 (quantity) bottles (product) of water has been approved (status).
Please pick it up tomorrow at 5pm (timings) from the store (location).

Kind regards
Merchant

FIGURE 2.7 Extraction of entities from an email body: an example of information extraction

2.10.3.1 The Steps of the TextRank Algorithm

1. Tokenization is carried out using labeling, called part of speech tagging (POS-T), which in simple terms defines the effect or purpose of the words in the sentence.
2. Graph creation: using POS-T, the selected words like nouns, adjectives, verbs, adverbs etc. are created as nodes or vertices, after which the connections are created on the basis of the distance of the words from each other or using the KNN algorithm, where *K* would be the number of words from word of comparison. This graph will be undirected in nature.
3. A graph ranking algorithm is applied to each node. It will be necessary to apply the algorithm multiple times as this is an undirected graph. Node convergence will be observed as a result of refining the graph.
4. The nodes are then sorted from the highest scores to the lowest, choosing the words in accordance with the required limits.
5. Now the words are combined, extraction is completed, and the scoring is carried out, with summation of the scores of the words [10,11].

There are many approaches with which these problems can tackled. The authors advise readers to study the article "An overview of graph-based keyword extraction methods and approaches", which provides more conceptual knowledge [12].

One of the major keyword extraction algorithms in use is Rapid Automatic Keyword Extraction (RAKE).

To quote the algorithm's creators: "RAKE is based on our observation that keywords frequently contain multiple words but rarely contain standard punctuation or stop words, such as the function words and, the, and of, or other words with minimal lexical meaning" [13].

Let's simplify a sentence:

1. Candidate keywords: let's call this stage possible keyword combination identification. In this process, the model tries to extract the possible keywords on the basis of the delimiter. Words which are between two delimiters may be good candidates to become keywords or may be classed as possible keywords, maintaining the order of occurrence. Stopwords (common words like "a," "our," "the," "is," "and," etc.) are removed, which helps save memory, as in the following example:
   a. Input: "India is a great country, with great people with great minds."
   b. Output:
      - India-great country
      - Great people-great minds
2. Graph construction: similarly to TextRank, the words serve as nodes. Maintaining the indexing of the matrix, the links between the nodes are decided on the basis of whether a specific node has come after or before other possible keywords.

3. Keyword scores: graph scoring is carried out using the following attributes:
   a. word frequency (*freq(w)*)
   b. word degree (*deg(w)*)
   c. ratio of degree to frequency (*deg(w)/freq(w)*)
4. Adjoining keywords: sometimes these are stopwords, so the algorithm will deduce pairs of keywords concatenated with a stopword in a text and update the stopwords dictionary. (They must appear at least twice in the text to be added.) The score of the new keyword is the sum of its member keywords.
5. Keyword extraction: after which the ⅓ of the words are extracted.

For the differences between RAKE and TextRank, see Table 2.1.

In practical terms, keyword extraction is the backbone of NLP, and one of its major applications is search engine optimization. Search engines are built by content mapping their input. The content only maps to a keyword if the content is present in the site, more relevant keywords, good code quality of the site, and more number of clicks results in a higher ranking/score. Keywords are mapped/indexed to a site, and when a user enters a query in a search engine, the results will only include sites where the content contains the specific words searched for in the context the user is looking for, which is achieved using lexical-semantic and other techniques. In terms of site ranking, to achieve the maximum number of user clicks on a particular site's URL, the site must appear in the earlier pages of the search engine results. To achieve this, site administrators need to maximize the keyword count in their sites' content, which will be scored using the search engine's algorithms. Graphically this can be achieved using the relationships between words and their context. If a node is parsed a high number of times (heavily weighted), then it can be assumed that the word is the keyword for the context. There is more probability that the user will also search for the same in the same combinations, this set of keywords will be extracted from larger text/content so that the whole scope is covered.

Creating tags for documents so that they can be filtered to remove incorrect domains and purposes is another major application of keyword extraction. If a paper on NLP is published, keyword extraction will automatically create nodes,

TABLE 2.1
Where Is Keyword Extraction Used?

RAKE	TEXTRON
Considers the co-occurrences inside candidate keywords	Fixed windows approach
Simpler scoring procedure (statistical)	Complex scoring procedure
Can work with single document	Needs many document for extraction

and on the basis of the training provided, it will index all the sub-keywords it contains. Sub-topics like dataset names, keyword-related topics, unique methods, and algorithm names will be extracted, and the publisher will add these as tags so that any researcher who is searching for a paper in specific domain can find it.

In behavior analysis, threat detection, and anomaly detection, specific keywords which may indicate threats can be extracted from the context. For example, if someone posts on social media proposing an extremist act, then that person can be profiled on the basis of the keywords they use, and risk calculation can be carried out to prevent them taking any steps which may cause harm. This can be achieved using a graph of where these extreme words are mapped lexically and semantically within the post. Also, inn digital forensics, it may be possible to identify the perpetrator of a forgery or fraud from the keywords they use or their distinctive word usage.

2.10.4 Information Extraction

There is a huge explosion of information as the number of Internet users is increasing rapidly every day, leading to a substantial rise in the amount of data on various digital platforms. Due to this vast increase in information generation, the demands for processing and analyzing large volumes of data have increased. This makes it difficult to navigate through the large amounts of data to find reliable information, so there is a need to extract specific information from online documents, which is termed information extraction.

Information extraction is a type of text processing which extracts fact-based information present in a document. Such a system performs its tasks based on the user's information requirements. For example, a user may be interested in extracting all the references to a specific author from a variety of research papers, including papers which the user was not aware of previously [14]. An information extraction system can accurately extract and present all the occurrences of the author's references contained in a text document. This therefore reduces human effort and expense, and makes the process less error-prone and more efficient. It is an important process that extracts sub-sequences from a given sequence of instances that represent insightful information for further use, and has a wide range of practical applications, such as in business intelligence to enable analysts to gather structured information from multiple sources, in financial investigation for analysis and discovery of hidden relationships, in scientific research for automated reference discovery or to find relevant papers, etc.

One of the applications of information extraction is automating the identification of certain information in the body text of emails, as depicted in Figure 2.7. In this case, the buyer is able to extract certain data, such as the quantity of the product, the status of the order, the timings, and the location where the order is to be picked up.

This automation of the task of extracting certain features from given information is less error-prone and more efficient compared to human involvement. Looking at the example in Figure 2.7 from a different perspective, the user of this system may need to search through the large number of emails received to find those where orders have been approved, and this workload can be reduced by automating the task. The user can simply extract the data and then formulate further queries to gather any more specific information required.

Another application of information extraction is spam email detection, where the information extraction system can be used to fetch various sub-sequences from a given sequence present in the body of an email. After extracting those sub-sequences, they are fed to a machine learning algorithm (a classification algorithm, such as logistic regression, decision trees, etc.) that classifies whether the email is spam. Here, information extraction plays a crucial role for extracting the required keywords from the email body, so it is a vital first step in any natural language processing task.

We will now look at how graph-based approaches can be applied to these techniques and the benefits of using them compared to traditional ones. We will also look at different applications that can leverage these relatively new techniques and benefit from them.

When we turn to any new technique, the first questions that come to mind are: why this technique, or how is this better than the previous one? The rest of this section will shed some light on how we leverage graphs in our traditional information extraction techniques, what their applications are, and how these approaches are better than earlier ones.

Graphs are being used with neural networks to improve the processing of information and training better deep learning models. In NLP, graph convolutional networks (GCNs) can be applied to structured documents such invoices and bills to automate the process of extracting insightful information by learning the relationships between various text entities. We will discuss different approaches along with various methodologies to convert text documents to graphs as the first step before using GCNs, but first, let us briefly describe what a GCN is.

A GCN is a neural network architecture for applying machine learning algorithms to graphs. These neural networks are powerful enough to produce useful feature representations of nodes in networks with a minimum of a two-layer GCN which is randomly initialized. GCNs are quite similar to convolutional neural networks (CNNs), with one difference. CNNs perform operations where the model learns features by inspecting neighboring nodes. GCNs learn to insert feature vectors of a node by a vector of real numbers that represents the input node as a set of vectors in N-dimensional space. These features will then be mapped to those which are closely neighboring in order to help the training model to classify these nodes.

The major difference between the two is that CNNs are developed to operate on structured data, whereas GCNs are generalized and can work on unstructured data where the number of nodes can be different and the order of these nodes does not matter. The field of GCNs is an active area of research, and many different techniques are being proposed to compute convolutions on graphs, so let us move to discussion of how they can be utilized in information extraction.

There are different ways in which a graph can be constructed from a text document. Most of these processes develop by using text sequences as nodes, and the edges connect each node with a number of its closest neighboring nodes. As explained in detail in the article "GraphIE: A graph-based framework for information extraction," [15] the approach utilizes the graph component within an encoder-decoder framework. The core of this algorithm is a recurrent neural network that encodes the text sequences, which are then fed to the GCN, and the nodes are processed. The output from the graph then advances back into the recurrent neural network decoder to perform word-level tagging. This application with use of graphs has shown an increase of around 1–2% in accuracy, as discussed in article cited.

Having seen how the addition of graph methodologies is working wonders in the area of natural language processing, in the next section we will explore a related topic – question answering by incorporating graphical methods.

2.10.5 Question Answering

Question answering is a branch of artificial intelligence within the fields of natural language processing and information retrieval which primarily focuses on building systems that can answer questions posed by humans in a natural language. These question answering systems are able to formulate answers by querying a knowledge base – a structured database of knowledge – or an unstructured collection of documents in a natural language. Question answering systems are divided into two types – closed domain and open domain.

In closed domain systems, the answers are fetched from a specific source such as a database, whereas open domain systems fetch data from different sources and then form the answer to a given question. After a brief explanation of how the process works in both domains, we will explore the applications of each of them.

To begin with closed domains, the sentence structure is either a database query or a simple query that can be translated easily into a database query which then fetches the results and presents them to the user. This can deal with simple answers that are stored in a database, such as what is the capital of India. The system fetches the required entities from the sentence with the help of some simple rules that translate the natural language into a database query like "Select capital from country where country = 'India.'" This will then return the output to the user as "Delhi."

On the other hand, in open domain answering systems, natural language questions are transformed into a structured query, keyword extraction is used to determine the type of question, and entity extraction, parts of speech tagging, and syntactic parsing are used to define the nature of the answer the user requires. An information retrieval system is used to find relevant answers from different sources, then parsing is carried out to translate the answer into meaningful text.

One example of this domain is IBM's Watson question answering system, which uses NLP, information retrieval, knowledge representation and reasoning, and ML technologies.

We will now discuss how graphs are playing a role in question answering systems.

Figure 2.8 shows a knowledge graph that represents the information present in a given text document as graphical and more structured information, which makes it easier to infer insights or extract answers for the questions posed by users. The technique basically extracts the subjects, objects, and the relationships between them to form a graph. In Figure 2.8, we can easily make out that we have two entities that are connected not only in a one-to-one relationship, but a many-to-many relationship. This makes it easier for the algorithm to find the answer based on the missing link in a given question. For example, for a question posed by a user such as "Who painted the Nikumb portrait?", the algorithm transforms the text sequence into a structured query, extracts the given entities, and looks for the missing part in the question – either the subject, the object, or the relationship. In this way, the algorithm returns the answer "Awasthi." We can expect the question to be posed in a different way as well, such as if the user asks "How are Awasthi and Nikumb related?" This will lead the algorithm to extract the relationship from the knowledge graph and provide the user with the answer, "Awasthi painted the Nikumb" [16].

There are some publicly available knowledge graphs that readers can study to explore this topic in more depth, such as Wikidata and DBpedia. These knowledge graphs can be queried using a standard querying language like SPARQL.

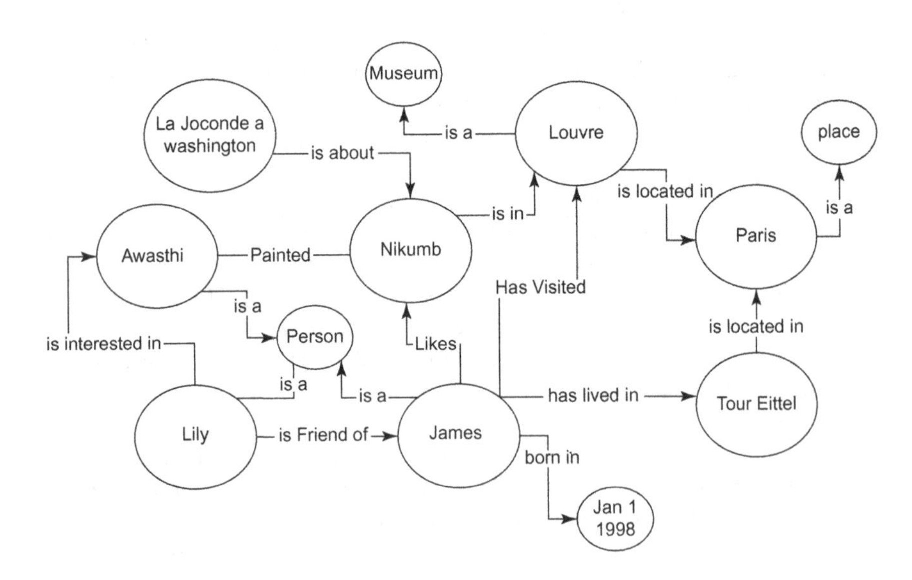

FIGURE 2.8 The graph method of question answering

2.10.6 Cross-language Information Retrieval

Cross-language information retrieval (CLIR) is an information retrieval technique which is utilized when the language of the document cannot be processed without first being converted into a processable language. For example, if an Englishman visits China and is handed a map to visit different places in the country, his first step is to deal with the difficulty of understanding the language in order to find the directions to his desired destinations. In the same way, CLIR comes into play when the language that needs to be queried has to be understandable by the algorithm. There are many situations where CLIR is essential because the information is not in the user's native language.

Therefore, we need to have a machine translation before the user can query a document. Machine translation is a core part of CLIR, or we can say that CLIR is the combination of machine translation and information retrieval. So machine translation is an essential block whose applications will be discussed later.

CLIR uses two approaches to retrieve information from a text document in a non-native language.

The first approach is known as *document translation* (see Figure 2.9). In this approach, we take the text document and feed it to the machine translation algorithm, which translates the given information into the English language so that the user can read through the document or query anything in it.

The language of the document is now processable, and structured queries can be used to extract the required information from it [17].

The second approach is *query translation* (see Figure 2.10). In this approach, only the query posed by the user is translated into the specified language and used to fetch the information from the given document. This approach is often considered more suitable, as the translations are rapid due to the shortness of the query sentences. However, query translation can suffer from translation ambiguity due to multiple possible translations when translating the query and then translating the information fetched into the English language. This problem is difficult, as the query sentences are short and may provide an incorrect context or lose context in the course of the translation processes.

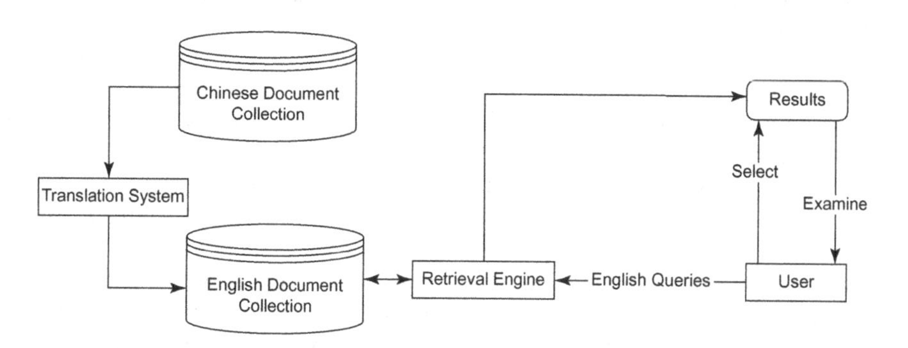

FIGURE 2.9 The CLIR document translation approach

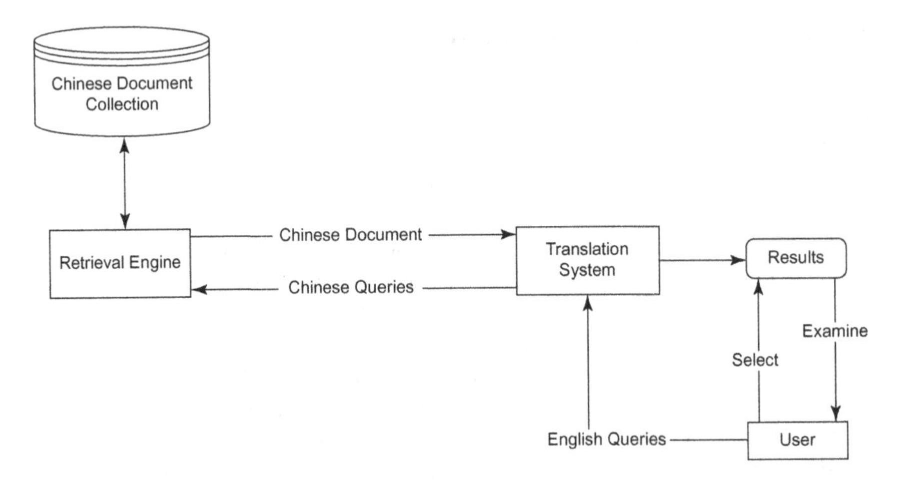

FIGURE 2.10 The CLIR query translation approach

2.10.7 Term Weighting

Term weighting is the process of assigning numerical values to each term in a document so that when it is used in the information retrieval process, it is easier for an algorithm to extract information based on the importance assigned to the term to improve retrieval effectiveness. It takes into account the relative importance of the terms in the document, as not all the terms are equally important [18].

Term weighting has two approaches: the first is to find items which are relevant to the user's needs, while the second is to ignore or reject peripheral items that add noise to the information required by the user. The two measures which can be used to assess the performance of the term weighting system are recall and precision [19]. *Recall* provides the ratio of the number of relevant items retrieved to the total number of relevant items in the collection, whereas *precision* gives the ratio of the number of relevant items to the total number of items in the collection. We will provide a brief description of these two approaches to term weighting and assess their performance, then move on to how graphs can be used to enhance the processes.

In the term weighting technique, a graph of each document is created where each node represents a word or word sequence and the edges represent the relationships between the nodes. Once the graph creation process is completed, we can proceed with the process of term weighting.

Let's consider a document which is represented as a bag of words model, where the term frequency criterion forms the foundation for weighting the terms within it. To proceed with this scenario in a graphical manner, we utilize the technique of node centrality criteria of graphs. Node centrality is a technique which is used to measure the importance of the different nodes that are present in the graph, and their importance in the document is inferred by how many connections a node has – the greater the number of edges or connections the node has, the more importance is assigned to it. This is the basic idea of how node centrality can be used to define importance in the text sequence. However, each node could be important from a different angle depending on how the measure of importance is defined. Several different centrality criteria have been explored in the field of graph theory and network analysis, and some of them have already been used in graph-based information retrieval and keyword extraction systems. Among the centralities that are being utilized are degree centrality, in-degree/out-degree centrality in directed graphs, and weighted degree in weighted graphs. To find the importance of a node based on the properties of the node globally in the graph, PageRank centrality, eigenvector centrality, betweenness centrality, closeness centrality, etc. are utilized. However, the use of these centrality processes depends on the type of graph, because some centrality criteria can be applied only to directed or undirected graphs.

2.10.8 Topic Segmentation

Today, there are various significant applications of natural language processing, like sentiment analysis, market intelligence, and survey analysis. All these applications require the data to be segmented and labeled. This is where topic segmentation comes in.

Topic segmentation is the automatic breaking up of large transcripts into smaller, contextually cohesive segments (see Figure 2.11). It deals with identifying where the shift from one topic to another occurs within a document [20–22].

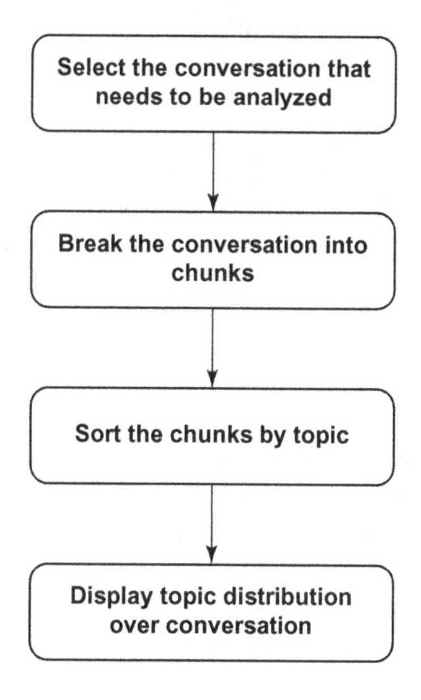

FIGURE 2.11 Sequence of steps in topic segmentation

Why would we want to do this? It makes browsing and searching for results much easier for users. In some natural language processing tasks, segmenting the text into topics may be useful as it can improve information retrieval significantly by indexing documents more precisely or by returning the specific part of a document that corresponds to a query as a result. Hence, topic segmentation serves as a vital precursor for various applications of NLP [23], as we will now explore.

Information retrieval is a process that controls the organization, storage, retrieval, and assessment of data from document repositories, particularly textual data. The system helps users discover the information they need, but it does not provide direct results for queries. Instead, it notifies users of the presence and locations of papers that may contain the information needed. Relevant documents are those that meet the requirements of the user. A flawless information retrieval system will retrieve only relevant articles.

The performance of an information retrieval model may be improved if documents, particularly long ones, are first broken up into smaller parts and then indexed as independent documents [24]. Many publications cover a whole host of topics or varied aspects of a single topic, therefore the vocabulary will shift as the topic changes. Word frequency statistics gathered from complete papers are used to drive most information retrieval algorithms. In this case, they may not indicate any specific topic section in a document. The statistics will be more informative if they are derived from individual topic segments.

Hence, an information retrieval model can use topic segmentation to improve its efficiency significantly, as it allows further classification of documents and can be used to return more specific parts of a document in response to a search query. At the same time, it expands document indexing, allowing for more precise identification of relevant documents.

Information extraction is the method of obtaining specific (pre-specified) information from various sources. One of the most basic examples is when software extracts an email message's data for the user to enter into their calendar.

The following vital sub-tasks are typically involved in extracting structured information from unstructured texts: pre-processing, identifying and classifying concepts, connecting the concepts, unifying, and getting rid of noise.

Topic segmentation is helpful in two scenarios for information extraction. First, it can be applied during the pre-processing of text to increase the efficiency of the process. However, the amount of data being worked on will determine whether the resources consumed increase or decrease. Second, topic segmentation can be applied after unifying the document to make it easier to remove noise from the data [25].

Text summarization is an essential application of natural language processing. It is a technique in which computer software shortens lengthy texts and provides summaries to convey the desired information. This is a common problem in machine learning and NLP. Text summarization presents several issues, including text identification, interpretation, summary generation, and analysis of the resulting summary.

Text structuring is a crucial component of solving summarization problems. Meaningful sentences can only be taken from a document once it has been structured. The summary is then generated from these sentences. Identifying the relevant sentences in a lengthy document is a difficult task. Topic segmentation comes in very handy in this situation. Segmenting the document before attempting to find the relevant sentences makes the process much smoother and more efficient [26].

Language modeling (LM) is the use of various probabilistic and statistical methods to determine the likelihood of a specified sequence of words appearing in a sentence. Language models examine large amounts of text data to establish a foundation for word predictions. Many NLP systems commonly employ these models, particularly those that create text as output.

Language models analyze text data to calculate word probability. They use an algorithm to interpret the data, which establishes rules for context in natural language. The model then uses these principles to accurately predict or construct new sentences in language tasks. The model learns the basic properties and qualities of language, then applies them to new phrases.

Language modeling is used to create speech recognition models. Some of these models employ previously recognized sentences to find documents closely linked to the contents of those sentences. The words from these documents are then used to train the speech recognition model by increasing the probability of these words. However, as with information retrieval, the documents may cover a wide range of topics, and using words from the entire document may introduce many unrelated words into the model. This may cause the model's accuracy to suffer and the model's processing demands to increase. Using topic segmentation allows the speech recognition model to only use words from relevant parts of a document.

Topic segmentation is also used to create language models based on topics. However, because these models are created by clustering pre-segmented documents, they are usually static [27].

2.10.8.1 Graph-based Topic Segmentation

To implement topic segmentation using a graph-based approach, one method is to create two sets: *s* for all the sentences in the given text, and *w* for all the unique words that are nouns or verbs.

This approach works by visualizing each sentence as a node. The relationships between words in different sentences are considered to be the edges in the graph.

The frequency of occurrence of the different words in the text gives a preliminary idea of broad topics. These frequently occurring words are chosen as target words. A graph is then individually created for each target word, leading to the creation of multiple graphs, each containing nodes of sentences in which that target word appears. Every unique graph created represents a single topic.

The graphs may further be weighted based on the distance between the appearance of target words on the two sides of the edge. Topic segmentation is often carried out as a pre-process for other NLP techniques. The weighting of the graphs makes the ensuing applications more accessible and efficient.

This approach has been implemented based on the research paper "A new graph-based text segmentation using Wikipedia for automatic text summarization" by Mohsen Pourvali and Mohammad Saniee Abadeh.

2.10.9 Machine Translation

Machine translation is a process in which text is translated from one language to another using computer software without the intervention of a human translator. At its most basic level, machine translation is the simple replacement of whole words in one individual language with words in another. Aggregation methods, including improved treatment of phonetic typology contrasts, expressing acknowledgment, idiom translations, and the seclusion of outliers, can carry out more intricate translations. Such systems are currently unable to perform as well as human translators, but this will be attainable in the future [28].

There are four types of machine translation (see Figure 2.12):

- *Statistical machine translation (SMT)* – This operates by referring to statistical models that rely on the analysis of massive amounts of bilingual information. It predicts the relationship between a source language word and a destination language word. Some examples of this are Google Translate and DeepL Translator (see Figure 2.13) [28].

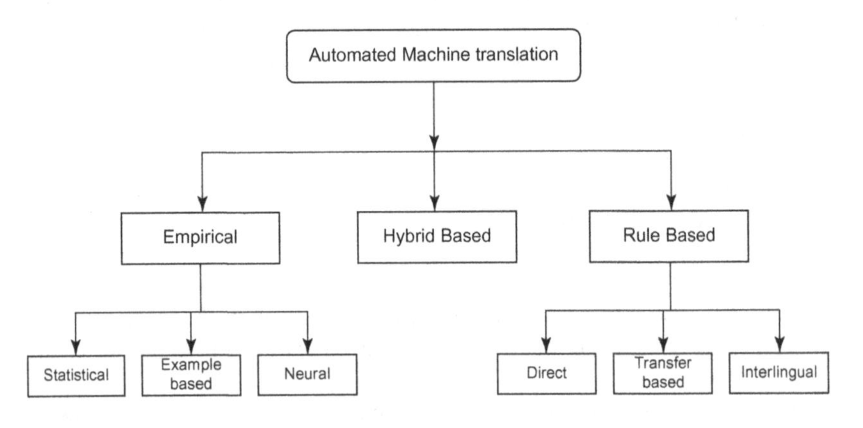

FIGURE 2.12 Different types of machine translation

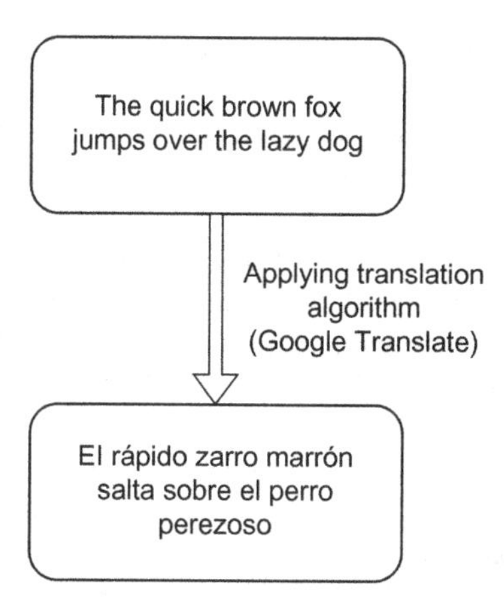

FIGURE 2.13 The process of SMT

- *Rule-based machine translation (RBMT)* – This uses millions of bilingual dictionaries and thousands of established grammatical rules for all language pairs.
- *Hybrid machine translation (HMT)* – This machine translation model incorporates several approaches into a single machine translation system. The various types of HMT are:
  - Multi-engine
  - Statistical rule generation
  - Multi-pass
  - Confidence-based
- *Neural machine translation (NMT)* – This uses a neural network architecture to develop a statistical model for machine translation.

One of the essential advantages of machine translation is speed. Computer systems can quickly translate large amounts of text. While human translators can produce more accurate translations than computers, they cannot match their speed.

Machine translation provides a useful blend of quick and cost-effective translation. It is significantly cheaper than employing a human translator. A properly trained machine can detect the tone and context of complete sentences before translating them. This results in an excellent, human-like output [29].

The following are applications of machine translation:

Text translation – Text translation is widely used in a variety of sentence-level and text-level translators. Translations of query and recovery inputs are components of sentence-level translators. The translation of a wide range of unfiltered reports and the translation of archives containing organized data are included in text translation. Organized data includes customization of aspects of the presentation of text material, such as text styles, hyperlinks, colors, and tables. A sentence may completely convey a subject, which often defines an articulation unit. The importance of each word in a sentence can be resolved to a large extent based on the sentence's environment.

Speech translation – Speech translation is the process of instantly translating spoken phrases into a second language, which may be presented as subtitles or computer-generated speech in the second language. This is in contrast to phrase translation, in which the algorithm only translates a handful of manually entered phrases.

Other applications – Machine translation changes a set of phrases from a source language to a target language based on various identified patterns and rules. However, on a basic level, it changes one succession of objects into another following some logic, as shown by the algorithms used. Thus, when the idea of these objects solely being some spoken language is let go, machine translation can be applied to many other comparable change scenarios.

2.10.9.1 Graph-based Machine Translation

Graph-based machine learning algorithms use a similarity graph with nodes representing data samples and weighted edges reflecting pair-wise similarities between samples.

A weight matrix, whose elements represent the similarity values for edges between neighboring vertices, and a label vector, which defines labels for the points up to that vertex, constitute the graph. The weight matrix will be empty if there is no edge connecting two nodes.

Data samples are represented as fixed-length feature vectors in most graph-based machine learning applications, with edge weights depending on cosine similarity or Euclidean distance. The weights can be chosen with a great deal of flexibility. The graph structure is determined by the similarity measure used to compute the edge weights, and it is the most significant factor in properly using graph-based machine learning.

The nodes in the machine translation algorithm represent the sentences of the text. The edge weights represent similarity by comparing the source and target sides with a pair of nodes.

This approach can be studied in further detail in the research paper "Graph-based Learning for Statistical Machine Translation" by Andrei Alexandrescu and Katrin Kirchhoff [30].

2.10.10 Discourse Analysis

Discourse comprises a sequence of sentences that must be interpreted regarding the context. A set of sentences only makes sense when they are related to each other.

Discourse processing is a set of NLP tasks that extract linguistic elements from texts at several levels, allowing for various downstream applications. For conversational discourse, this entails determining the topic structure, coherence structure, conversation structure, and coreference structure. These structures can help with text summarization, question answering, sentiment analysis, machine translation, and information extraction [31,32].

A language comprises organized and coherent collections of sentences, rather than unrelated and isolated sentences. Discourse refers to these coherent collections of sentences.

Discourse analysis, which involves developing algorithms and models for how statements combine to produce coherent discourse, is one of the most challenging problems in NLP.

Coherence and discourse structure are linked. The output quality of a natural language generation system is evaluated using coherence. For example, collecting ten sentences from ten consecutive pages of a book will not form a discourse because these sentences will not display coherence.

For example, let us consider the following sentences:

> Mr. Sourav Ganguly was unanimously elected as the President of the Board of Control for Cricket in India (BCCI). The decision was taken at the General Body Meeting in Mumbai on Wednesday after the former India Captain had filed his nomination for the post last week at the BCCI headquarters in Mumbai. Mr. Ganguly was the only candidate who filed his nomination for the President's post.

The above text can be summarized as:

> Sourav Ganguly was unanimously elected as the President of the Board of Control for Cricket in India (BCCI). The decision was taken at the General Body Meeting in Mumbai on Wednesday.

It is essential to know that the first part of the text is more important than the second to build the above summary. This can be inferred because a relation exists between the different sentences in the text passage – the sentences are coherent. This relationship between different sentences in a discourse is called *coherence relation*. Determining the coherence structure between the sentences based on coherence relations is a crucial task in discourse analysis.

Let's take another example:

> Rohit went to New Delhi to meet a potential investor and present his business proposal. After he presented it, the entrepreneur waited for the capitalist's response.

A few inferences that can be drawn from these sentences:

- "He" refers to Rohit, not the potential investor.
- "It" refers to the business proposal, not New Delhi.
- "Entrepreneur" refers to Rohit, and "capitalist" refers to the potential investor he was meeting.

These inferences are reasonably easy to make for humans. However, using pronouns such as "he" and "it" and other references like "entrepreneur" for Rahul may lead to ambiguities at the machine level. Resolving the ambiguities surrounding such references is one of the most critical aspects of discourse analysis. This is called *coreference resolution.*

These two analyses comprise discourse analysis, and help us to find coherence among the different sentences of the text, and to determine the meaning behind different references – i.e., the pronouns and adjectives used for the entities in the text.

The following are applications of discourse analysis:

Pre-processing text – Discourse analysis is one of the preliminary steps for pre-processing data in several NLP techniques. Coreference resolution and coherence relations are both of utmost importance in pre-processing data to prepare it for information retrieval, information extraction, and text summarization, as well as working in parallel with topic segmentation for language modeling.

Detecting misrepresentation – Often, words can be slightly changed to convey something in a subtly more positive or negative light. The publicists of celebrities and print and electronic news media employ often these tactics to achieve their goals. Applying discourse analysis to such broadcasts and articles can give new insights on the discourse and help us dissect the document and see through these patterns to recognize what subtle changes are being made to change our impression about the content. This helps avoid being led astray.

2.11 CONCLUSION AND FUTURE SCOPE OF NLP

This chapter has illustrated that NLP helps in automation and provides the ability for computer systems to interact with users in more human-friendly ways (see Figure 2.14).

The main goal for now will be to optimize current technology. We have the technology for chatbots, but their output is still robotic in nature, so if customers or users have a query regarding a service or product, they will select a human operator if given a choice, as they want the most accurate output to their query with the least input from them in the shortest possible time. This statement also applies to e-commerce or banking bots which large organizations have deployed – at the end of the day, customers will want the human touch.

One solution to this is simply to improve the way chatbots reply. One approach is to use data based on demographics and the pre-existing linguistics at the particular location so that the bot is prepared to respond in the same format as well as able to anticipate what questions may come next. This will also help the bot to understand any new situations. The other is to deploy data-based learning, where users may have queried or interacted with the system earlier, so we can teach the bot based on the past data. Similarly, the bot can be taught based on the user's profile in the company's database. If a user works in a media-based company and another user from the same company has posed a similar question, the bot can automatically recall that earlier query's answer, which can help to save much time.

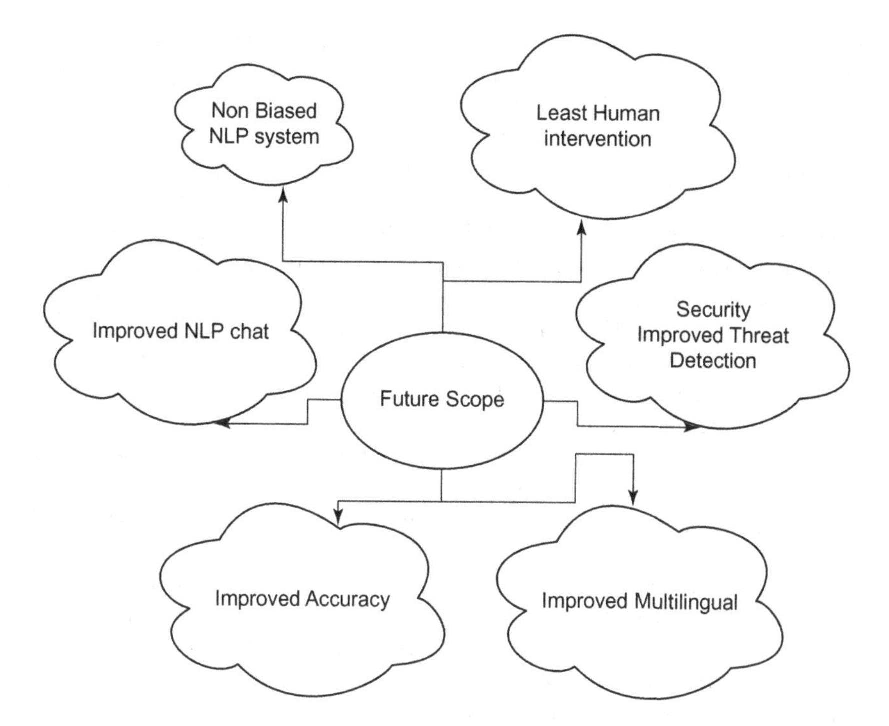

FIGURE 2.14 Future scope

In cyber security, there is major scope for NLP. Intelligence is essential in enabling organizations to prepare for cyber threats. As the Internet contains so much data, it is very arduous for humans to identify information on threats before an attack takes place, so crawlers have been invented to sift through websites for intelligence. With so much data to go through, even automated methods of gathering such intelligence can be time-consuming, potentially making it worthless if the parsing time is too high. NLP can be used to identify true positive and discard false positive intelligence, using sentiment analysis or fact correlation-based analysis.

Another application is log parsing and alerting, where a log created by any system can be fed into an NLP application for analysis, be it behavioral-based or a normal system log, allowing the automation of some decisions or provision of a much simpler view to analysts.

Other applications for NLP include:

1. Scanning computer code for vulnerabilities
2. Scanning network data using .pcap, metadata, headers, etc. to detect intrusions with malicious intent
3. Data leak prevention

The majority of the information presently available to us is still unstructured. As discussed earlier, NLP systems can extract structured data from a variety of sources, including texts, films, and audio. They are able to gather data by analyzing the voice, word choice, and positive or negative tones in the manner of speech. They can also collect information from legal documents, medical records, and other sources, thus increasing the amount of structured data available to us.

So far, NLP applications have primarily focused on the English language. But now companies such as Facebook and Google are teaming up with NLP solution providers to introduce pre-trained multilingual NLP models. Successful large-scale implementation of these models will greatly increase the usability and reach of NLP applications. Multilingual support will increase applications that can assist users to find any required information using voice commands in their preferred language rather than by typing them, thus increasing convenience for users and making systems more accessible to members of the population who have special needs.

There will be improvements in the ability of virtual assistants to comprehend and respond to sophisticated, real-time conversations. Over time, these assistants will speak more naturally with people and be able to carry out tasks such as suggesting improvements to business agreements, interpreting complex requests, and taking dictation.

One major application of NLP is creating unbiased moderator systems. As there is a human tendency to be opinionated about any topic, it is literally impossible for humans to be unbiased in all scenarios. Because of this tendency, many users of sites like Twitter get banned by moderators just because the users expressed ideas which are opposed to a moderator's beliefs. As a solution to this, NLP can be used to decide whether the users are complying with the rules.

2.12 DATASETS FOR NLP APPLICATIONS

Table 2.2 lists some datasets which are used in natural language applications.

TABLE 2.2
Datasets for NLP Applications

Dataset Name	Link	Purpose
Stanford Sentiment Treebank	http://nlp.stanford.edu/sentiment/code.html	Sentiment analysis
Free Spoken Digit Dataset	https://github.com/Jakobovski/free-spoken-digit-dataset	Speech recognition
WordNet	https://wordnet.princeton.edu	Lexical database of English
SMS Spam Collection Data Set	https://archive.ics.uci.edu/ml/datasets/sms+spam+collection	Spam detection
University of California Irvine Paper Reviews Data Set	https://archive.ics.uci.edu/ml/datasets/Paper+Reviews	Scientific paper reviews from an international conference on computing and informatics
Deepmind Question Answering Corpus	https://github.com/deepmind/rc-data	Question answering using articles from the broadcaster CNN and the newspaper *Daily Mail*

REFERENCES

1. Vyas M.R., Venkateswara H., Panchanathan S. (2020). Leveraging seen and unseen semantic relationships for generative zero-shot learning. In Vedaldi A., Bischof H., Brox T., Frahm J.M. (eds) Computer Vision – ECCV 2020. ECCV 2020. *Lecture Notes in Computer Science*, vol 12375. Springer, Cham. Retrieved from https://doi.org/10.1007/978-3-030-58577-8_5.
2. Haidar M.A., Rezagholizadeh M. (2019). TextKD-GAN: Text generation using knowledge distillation and generative adversarial networks. In Meurs M.J., Rudzicz F. (eds) Advances in Artificial Intelligence. Canadian AI 2019. *Lecture Notes in Computer Science*, vol 11489. Springer, Cham. Retrieved from https://doi.org/10.1007/978-3-030-18305-9_9.
3. Li C., Su Y., Liu W. (2018). Text-to-text generative adversarial networks. In *2018 International Joint Conference on Neural Networks (IJCNN)*. Retrieved from https://doi.org/10.1109/ijcnn.2018.8489624.
4. Garbade D.M.J. (2018, September 19). A quick introduction to text summarization in machine learning. *Medium*. Retrieved September 24, 2021, from https://towardsdatascience.com/a-quick-introduction-to-text-summarization-in-machine-learning-3d27ccf18a9f.
5. Vashisht A. (2019, November 29). Graph based approach for text summarization (reduction). *OpenGenus IQ: Computing Expertise & Legacy*. Retrieved September 24, 2021, from https://iq.opengenus.org/graph-based-approach-for-text-summarization/.
6. Ekmekci B., Howald B. (2020). WAFFLE: A graph for WordNet applied to free-form linguistic exploration. Retrieved from https://aclanthology.org/2020.nlposs-1.21.pdf/.
7. Otterbacher J., Erkan G., Radev D.R. (2008, 5 August). Biased LexRank: Passage retrieval using random walks with question-based priors. Retrieved from https://doi.org/10.1016/j.ipm.2008.06.004.
8. Celikyilmaz A., Thint M, Huang Z. (2009). *A Graph-Based Semi-Supervised Learning for Question-Answering.* Suntec, Singapore, Association for Computational Linguistics.
9. Mihalcea R., Tarau P. (2004). TextRank: Bringing order into texts. In *Proceedings of EMNLP*. Association for Computational Linguistics, Barcelona, Spain.
10. Ying Y., Qingping T., Qinzheng X., Ping Z., Panpan L. (2017). A graph-based approach of automatic keyphrase extraction. Retrieved from https://doi.org/10.1016/j.procs.2017.03.087.
11. Godec P. (2021, September 19). Keyword extraction methods-the overview. *Medium*. Retrieved September 24, 2021, from https://towardsdatascience.com/keyword-extraction-methods-the-overview-35557350f8bb.
12. Slobodan B., Meštrović A., Martincic-Ipsic S. (2015). An overview of graph-based keyword extraction methods and approaches. *Journal of Information and Organizational Sciences* 39, 1–20. Retrieved from https://www.researchgate.net/publication/280092953_An_Overview_of_Graph-Based_Keyword_Extraction_Methods_and_Approaches.
13. Berry M.W., Kogan J. (2010). Automatic keyword extraction from individual documents. Retrieved from https://onlinelibrary.wiley.com/doi/10.1002/9780470689646.ch1.
14. Okurowski M.E. (n.d.). Information extraction overview. Retrieved from https://aclanthology.org/X93-1012.pdf.
15. Qian Y., Santus E., Jin Z., Guo J., Barzilay R. (n.d.). GraphIE: A graph-based framework for information extraction. Retrieved from https://arxiv.org/pdf/1810.13083.pdf.

16. Seth Y. (2019, October 8). Introduction to question answering over knowledge graphs. *Let the Machines Learn*. Retrieved September 24, 2021, from https://yashuseth.blog/2019/10/08/introduction-question-answering-knowledge-graphs-kgqa/.
17. Zhang R. (2019, March 7). A brief introduction to cross-lingual information retrieval. *Medium*. Retrieved September 24, 2021, from https://medium.com/lily-lab/a-brief-introduction-to-cross-lingual-information-retrieval-eba767fa9af6.
18. El-Khair I.A. (2009). Term weighting. In Liu L., Özsu MT (eds) *Encyclopedia of Database Systems*. Springer, Boston, MA. Retrieved from https://doi.org/10.1007/978-0-387-39940-9_943.
19. Salton G., Buckley C. (1988). Term weighing approaches in automatic text retrieval. Retrieved from http://www.ict.nsc.ru/jspui/bitstream/ICT/1231/1/solton-1-29-03.pdf.
20. Adarve F., Kwong H., Speriosu M. (2007, Spring). Topic segmentation of meetings using lexical chains. Retrieved from https://nlp.stanford.edu/courses/cs224n/2007/fp/adarve-kwong-speriosu.pdf.
21. Joty S., Carenini G., Ng R.T. (2013, July). Topic segmentation and labeling in asynchronous conversations. Retrieved from https://arxiv.org/ftp/arxiv/papers/1402/1402.0586.pdf.
22. Chang T.-H., Lee C.-H. (n.d.). *Topic Segmentation for Short Texts*. Retrieved from https://aclanthology.org/Y03-1018.pdf.
23. Purver M. (2011, March). *Systems for Extracting Semantic Information from Speech*. John Wiley & Sons, Ltd., Hoboken, NJ.
24. Reynar J. (1998, August). *Topic Segmentation: Algorithms and Applications*. University of Pennsylvania, The Institute for Research in Cognitive Science.
25. Nikolova I. (2016, October). What is information extraction? *Ontotext*. Retrieved September 24, 2021, from https://www.ontotext.com/knowledgehub/fundamentals/information-extraction/.
26. Impelsys Marketing Team (2021, April 27). An overview of text summarization in natural language processing. *Impelsys*. Retrieved September 24, 2021, from https://www.impelsys.com/an-overview-of-text-summarization-in-natural-language-processing/.
27. Lutkevich B. (2020, March 2). What is language modeling? *SearchEnterpriseAI*. Retrieved September 24, 2021, from https://searchenterpriseai.techtarget.com/definition/language-modeling.
28. Kumari R. (n.d.). 4 types of machine translation in NLP. *Analytics Steps*. Retrieved from https://www.analyticssteps.com/blogs/4-types-machine-translation-nlp.
29. Vadapalli P. (January 21, 2021). Machine translation in NLP: Examples, flow & models. *upGrad blog*. Retrieved from https://www.upgrad.com/blog/machine-translation-in-nlp/#Machine_Translation.
30. Pourvali M., Abadeh M.S. (2012). A new graph based text segmentation using Wikipedia for automatic text summarization *International Journal of Advanced Computer Science and Applications*, Vol. 3, No. 1, pp. 36–37.
31. Shafiq J., Carenini G., Ng R., Murray G. (2019). *Discourse Analysis and Its Applications*. Association for Computational Linguistics, Florence, Italy. Retrieved from https://aclanthology.org/P19-4003/.
32. Cheng A.Y.N. (2009). Analyzing complex policy change in Hong Kong: What role for critical discourse analysis? *International Journal of Education Management*, Vol. 23, No. 4, pp. 360–366.

3 Graph-based Extractive Approach for English and Hindi Text Summarization

Rekha Jain, Manisha Sharma, Pratistha Mathur, and Surbhi Bhatia

CONTENTS

DOI: 10.1201/9781003272649-3

3.1 INTRODUCTION

Today, the Internet is flooded with data, including information in the form of text data in digital documents. Most of these documents are large, unstructured, and unorganized, and processing them is an onerous task. We may not have time to completely read and understand all of them, but we often have to make important decisions based on what we absorb from the information they contain. Text summaries can help to extract the important information. Berry, Dumais, and O'Brien (1995) defined text summarization as: "The process of distilling the most important information from a source (or sources) to produce an abridged version for a particular user (or users) and task (or tasks)."

Automatic text summarization can be beneficial in a variety of day-to-day tasks, such as generating news headlines, making notes for students, preparing minutes of meetings, previewing of movies, designing summary reports, digests, etc. The task of summarization involves identifying information from a given document which is the most important to its content and condensing it. Several dimensions for text summarization have been reported in the literature, including methods based on the number of input documents (single-versus multi-document), the purpose (generic, domain-specific, or query-based), and the type of output required (extractive or abstractive) (Chuang and Yang, 2000).

Extractive and abstractive summarization are the two major approaches to text summarization. *Extractive summarization*s elects relevant, meaningful sentences from the text and arranges them in a comprehensive manner, whereas *abstractive summarization* produces a para phrase by importing information from the text. Our proposed method uses the extractive summarization approach, which is a popular way of carrying text summarization.

The chapter is organized as follows. Section 3.2 describes the approaches used for text summarization. The current state of art of text summarization is explored in Section 3.3 through a literature review. Section 3.4 discusses graph-based algorithms. Section 3.5 describes the term frequency-inverse document frequency (TF-IDF) method. The methodology for the experiment on which this chapter is based is discussed in Section 3.6. The experiments we undertook to access the performance of the two algorithms, Text Rank and TF-IDF, are described in Section 3.7. Finally, Section 3.8 presents our conclusions.

3.2 TEXT SUMMARIZATION APPROACHES

Text summarization approaches can be divided into various categories based on different factors such as the number of documents, the required outputs, and the purpose, language, and content. The approaches can also be categorized as single or multi-document, extractive or abstractive, generic or query-based, supervised or unsupervised, mono-, multi- or cross-lingual, web-based, email-based, personalized, updating, sentiment-based, or survey-based. El-Kassas et al. (2021) described different approaches used for text summarization, as shown in Figure 3.1.

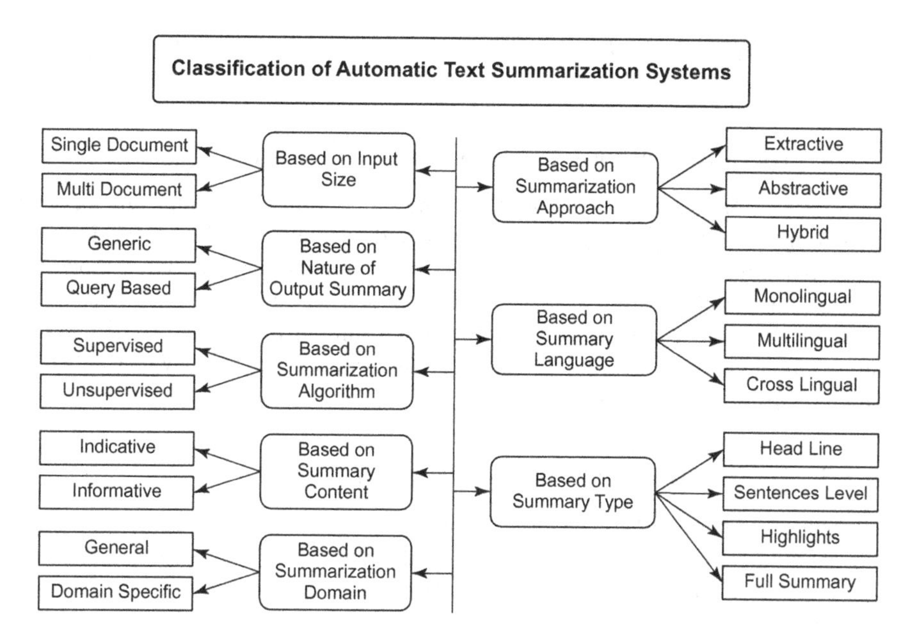

FIGURE 3.1 Approaches to text summarization

3.2.1 Text Summarization Based on Number of Documents

Automatic summaries can be generated for either a single input document or multiple documents. More challenges are posed by summaries generated using multiple documents. Redundancy reduction is a key parameter which has been subject to experiments by different researcher to get the best results when of summarizing multiple documents.

3.2.2 Text Summarization Based on the Summary's Purpose

According to the purpose, summaries can be either generic or query-focused. Query-focused summaries are also sometimes referred as topic-focused or user-focused. Generic summaries convey a general sense of the information in documents.

3.2.3 Text Summarization Techniques

Text summarization can be carried out using supervised or unsupervised learning techniques (Allahyari et al., 2017). Supervised learning requires a huge amount of annotated data to identify important content among the information. Support vector machines (SVMs)and neural networks are among the most popular techniques. Unsupervised techniques do not require any training data.

These techniques extract highly relevant content from the documents based on clustering.

3.2.4 Text Summarization Based on Level of Language

Summaries can be categorized into three types – mono-lingual, multi-lingual, or cross-lingual. In mono-lingual summarization, the language of the source document and target summary is the same. In multi-lingual summarization, documents in more than one language are used as the source, and the summary is also represented in these languages. In cross-lingual summarization, the source and target languages are different – for example, the source language may be English and target summary may be in Hindi.

3.2.5 Text Summarization Based on Output Style

Summaries generated by a system can be indicative or informative. An *indicative* summary presents an overview of the document, whereas an *informative* summary gives the information in elaborative form in keeping with the topic coverage.

3.2.6 Text Summarization Based on the Summary's Characteristics

This is the most important method of categorization in automatic text summarization. Summaries can be classified as extractive or abstractive. An *extractive* summary is the result of taking a few relevant sentences from the original document. The summary's length will depend on the compression ratio used. An *abstractive* summary does not use words and phrases from the source document (Gupta and Gupta,2019). It uses an abstract of the content to reinterpret and generate a summary which includes the meaning of important information (Gerani et al., 2014). The new sentences that result are generally called paraphrases.

Extractive summarization methods generate summaries by taking a subset of the sentences from the original source document or documents. The main idea of summarization, as given by Nenkova and McKeown (2012), is represented in the following three-step process:

Step 1: Create an intermediate representation of the source text.
Step 2: Using any scoring method, calculate the score of the sentences based on the intermediate representation
Step 3: Extract a summary using the top-scored most important sentences with the help of any optimization technique.

El-Kassas et al. (2021) described the complete architecture of the extractive text summarization process as shown in Figure 3.2.

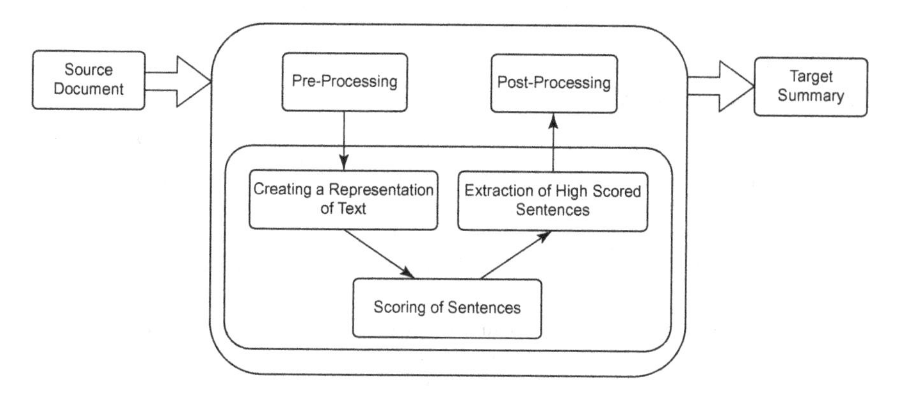

FIGURE 3.2 Extractive text summarization system

3.3 LITERATURE SURVEY

Mishra et al. (2012) designed an effective stemmer for the Hindi language: Maulik. It works purely on devanagari script, and uses a combination of the brute force and suffix removal approaches for stemming.

Kaur and Singh (2013) proposed a procedure that produces a summary by applying five unique provisions. First, loads are determined for explicit sentences, then an outline is created. Next, deadwood rules are applied to the resultant outline to eliminate words and expressions with no significance. This approach will abbreviate a text while retaining meaning.

Thaokar and Malik (2013) proposed an idea for summarizing Hindi text based on the sentence extraction method. The Hindi WordNet is used to carry out parts-of-speech tagging of words to checking the subject-object-verb structure of the sentence. Agenetic algorithm is used to optimize the generated summary to maximize the theme coverage and to minimize redundancy.

Singh and Verma (2014) proposed a system where new features are represented for Punjabi text using an extractive approach. It consists of two phases:(1) pre-processing and (2) processing. Pre-processing recognizes word and sentence boundaries as well as eliminating Punjabi stop words and identifying root words. In the processing phase, weight is assigned to each sentence so that unwanted sentences can be eliminated from the input text.

Kumar et al. (2015a) worked on automatic text summarization by using a graph-based algorithm for the Hindi language. It uses the weighted graph technique for summarization.

Kumar and Yadav (2015b) presented an improvised extractive technique for Hindi text summarization based on a thematic approach.

Gupta et al. (2016) explored text summarization using a rule-based approach to remove dead phrases and deadwood.

TABLE 3.1
Recent Research in NLP

Year	Authors	Title	Work Done
2017	John X. Qiu and Hong-Jun Yoon	"Deep Learning for Automated Extraction of Primary Sites from Cancer Pathology Reports"	Implementation of extractive summarization using convolutional neural networks to extract topographical codes
2020	Reda Elbarougy, Gamal Behery, and Akram El Khatib	"Extractive Arabic Text Summarization Using Modified PageRank Algorithm"	An approach for Arabic text summarization that focuses on retrieval of important information
2021	William Chen, Kensal Ramos, Kalyan Naidu Mullaguri, and Annie S. Wu	"Genetic Algorithms for Extractive Summarization"	Investigation of various genetic algorithms that provide more efficient solutions
2021	Mohd Khizir Siddiqui, Amreen Ahmad, Om Pal, and Tanvir Ahmad	"CoRank: A Clustering cum Graph Ranking Approach for Extractive Summarization"	Two-stage selection model for sentences that involves clustering and then ranking of sentences

Gulati et al. (2017) discussed a novel technique for Hindi text summarization for multiple documents. It is based on a fuzzy inference system, and is used for feature extraction for news articles.

Dalal et al. (2017) described a method of automatic text summarization using semantic graphs and particle swarm optimization for the Hindi language. It is based on linguistic, semantic, and syntactic feature extraction and semantic graph construction.

Yao, Pengzhou, and Chi (2019) proposed a keyword extraction technique using Text Rank and a TF-IDF algorithm to produce a summary of text.

Jain (2019) proposed an extractive approach for text summarization based on a cosine similarity approach that calculates the similarity score between sentences to generate a summary. More recent work on natural language processing (NLP) is shown in Table 3.1.

3.4 GRAPH-BASED ALGORITHMS

The Internet can be represented as a directed graph in which each node is a webpage and links are present between node *i* and node *j* if there is a link from page *i* to page *j*. Let *in(i)* be the*in* degree of webpage, meaning the number of websites linking to this page, and let *out(i)* be the websites that page *i* links to (see Figure 3.3).

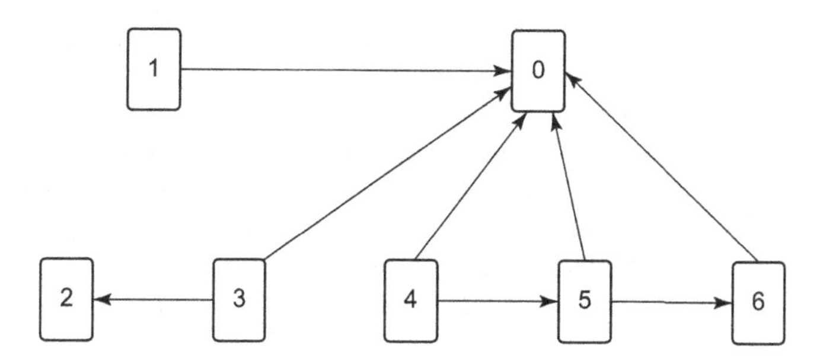

FIGURE 3.3 Graphical representation of Web Graph

In Figure 3.3, there are seven pages, numbered from 0 to 6, and their *in*degree and *out*degree can be expressed as in(0) = 1,3,4, 5,6},out(0) = {}.

A variety of graphical algorithms are used to rank Internet sites, including the PageRank algorithm and the Text Rank algorithm.

3.4.1 PageRank Algorithm

The PageRank algorithm was developed by Larry Page, one of the founders of Google. Initially, it was used to rank web pages (Brin and Page, 1998). It defines the importance of a web page by counting the number of links to it. This is based on the assumption that the number of external links to a webpage indicates its importance (Bryan and Leise, 2006). Scores are allocated to every page to signify their importance. PageRank values lie between 0 and 1.

PageRank Calculation:

$$PR(u) = \sum_{v\ in(u)} \frac{PR(v)}{|out(v)|} \quad \text{(Equation 3.1)}$$

The PageRank value of a page u is dependent on the PageRank values of each page v contained in the set *in(u)* (the set of all pages linked to page u) divided by the number $|out(v)|$ of outgoing links from page v.

PageRank is an iterative procedure. Iteration 1 initializes all ranks to be *1/(number of total pages)*, and the next iteration applies the algorithm *For each page u, update u's rank to be the sum of each incoming page v's rank from the previous iteration, divided by the number total number of links from page v.* This algorithm uses many passes or iterations.

3.4.2 Text Rank Algorithm

PageRank provides the basis for the Text Rank algorithm, which is used for the automatic summarization of text (Mallick et al., 2018). It is used in NLP applications. This is unsupervised method of extractive summarization. It is language-independent, so it can be used for any language.

Text Rank is similar to PageRank in many ways. In Text Rank, a sentence plays the same role as a web page in PageRank, and PageRank's webpage transition probability is equivalent to Text Rank's similarity between two sentences.

In Text Rank, sentences are the units, and they are ranked by finding similarities to other sentences (Mihalfcea and Tasrau,2004).

The steps for Text Rank are as follows:

1. Extract text from given documents.
2. Split the text into individual sentences.
3. Convert the sentences into vectors (word embeddings).
4. Calculate the similarity between the sentences and store it in the form of a similarity matrix.
5. Convert the similarity matrix into a graph where sentences are the vertices and similarity scores are the edges in order to calculate the sentences' rankings.
6. The top-ranked sentences are chosen to generate the summary.

3.5 TF-IDF ALGORITHM

Term frequency-inverse document frequency is a statistical measure that finds how relevant a word is to a text document (Kim and Gil,2019; Yao et al., 2019). The algorithm weighs keywords in the input text and assigns importance to each of them on the basis of the number of times they are present in the document.

This is calculated with the help of two values. The first is *term frequency*, which means, how many times a word is present in a document. This can be calculated by counting the instances of a word in a document. The second is *inverse document frequency* of the key word across a set of documents. It finds how rare or how common a word is in a set of documents (Manning et al., 2008). If the value is closer to 0, the word is very common. The TF-IDF score is calculated by the formula given in Equation 3.2, where t is the keyword, d is the document, D is the entire document set, and N is the total number of documents in the document set:

$$tf\,idf\left(t,d,D\right)=tf\left(t,d\right)*idf\left(t,D\right) \qquad \text{(Equation 3.2)}$$

where:

$$tf\left(t,d\right)=\log\left(1+freq\left(t,d\right)\right) \qquad \text{(Equation 3.3)}$$

and

$$idf\left(t,D\right)=\log\left(\frac{N}{Count\left(d\in D:t\in d\right)}\right) \qquad \text{(Equation 3.4)}$$

This algorithm has many uses, most importantly in text analysis, and is widely used for scoring key words in machine learning algorithms for NLP.

3.6 METHODOLOGY

The research for this chapter focused on the extractive summarization method, which finds the most relevant sentences in an input document. Extractive text summarization starts with text pre-processing, such as stop word removal and extraction of sentences based on features, after which the sentences are selected and combined to produce a summary. This is an unsupervised technique which does not use a labeled dataset. Figure 3.4 shows the workflow.

The most important aspect of this work was calculation of similarity values among the sentences, and TF-IDF and cosine similarity methods were used for this. Text in two different languages was used for the summary generation: English and Hindi.

Initially, the input text data was taken and split into sentences, and pre-processing took place to clean the input data.

Cosine similarity is used to determine how similar documents are irrespective of their sizes. It calculates the cosine angle between two n-dimensional vectors in an n-dimensional space. It is calculated by following formula:

$$\cos\theta = \frac{\vec{a}.\vec{b}}{\vec{ab}} = +\frac{\sum_{i}^{n} a_i b_i}{\sqrt{\sum_{i}^{n} a_i^2}\sqrt{\sum_{i}^{n} b_i^2}} \qquad \text{(Equation 3.5)}$$

where $\vec{a}.\vec{b} = \sum_{i}^{n} a_i b_i = a_1 b_1 + a_2 b_2 + \ldots + a_n b_n$ is the dot product of two vectors.

Calculation of similarity is carried out to determine the graphical structure, which is finally used to define the ranks of the sentences. In this research project, 60% compression was used, so 40% of the top-ranked sentences were used to generate the summary.

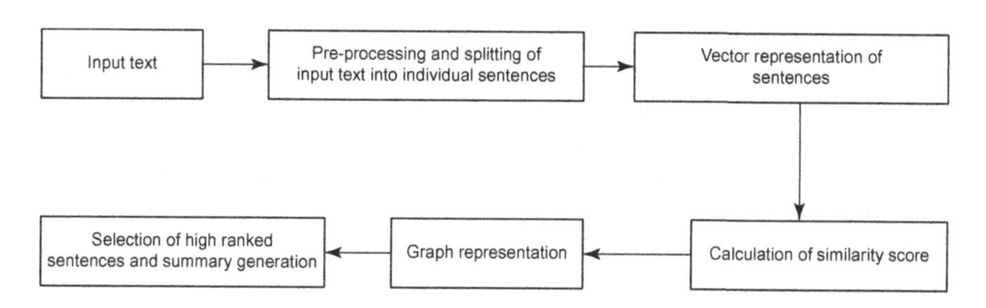

FIGURE 3.4 Workflow

3.7 EXPERIMENTAL RESULTS

For the purposes of the experiment, two datasets, one from English and another from Hindi, were considered. The Text Rank algorithm and TF-IDF algorithm were applied to each dataset. Both the algorithms were tested with a 40% summary, meaning the algorithms were tested with a 60% compression ratio. Once the same text in English was fed to both the algorithms, both were again tested for Hindi text. An ample number of datasets were available in Hindi for machine learning. They were downloaded from various sites, such as https://metatext.io/datasets-list/hindi-language; other examples of Hindi NLP datasets include HC Corpora and the Hindi English Recognition Corpus.

The Text Rank algorithm calculates the similarity between sentences on the basis of cosine similarity. Initially, vectors for each sentence are constructed, then cosine similarity is calculated among all the elements of vectors. Vectors containing higher similarity scores are included in the summarized text.

The TF-IDF algorithm computes similarity on the basis of term frequency and inverse document frequency, and sentences with higher TF-IDF scores are included in the summarized text.

3.7.1 English Original Text

There are the times when night sky glows with various colors of bands. The bands may begin with cloud like shapes and then they spread into a great arc across the entire sky. They may fall in folds like a curtain drawn across the heavens. Lights usually grow brighter, and then they suddenly get dim. During this time sky glows with pale yellow, bright pink, chloro green, violet, cyano blue, and eosino red. These lights are named as the Aurora Borealis. Some people also call them the Northern Lights. The scientists have been continuously watching them for hundreds of years. They are not so confident about what causes them. In ancient times people were very afraid of the Lights. They imagined that they saw some fiery dragons in the sky. Some even concluded that the heavens were on the fire.

The Text Rank similarity scores for this passage are shown in Table 3.2.

Figure 3.5 shows the experimental results for the English text using the Text Rank algorithm on a 60% compression ratio.

3.7.2 Summary Produced Using the Text Rank Algorithm

Some people also call them the Northern Lights. In ancient times people were very afraid of the Lights. The bands may begin with cloud like shapes and then they spread into a great arc across the entire sky. They may fall in folds like a curtain drawn across the heavens. Some even concluded that the heavens were on the fire.

The TF-IDF scores for this passage are shown in Table 3.3.

TABLE 3.2
Similarity Scores According to the Text Rank Algorithm

Sentence No.	Sentence No.	Similarity Score
1	2	0.12
1	3	0.08
1	4	0.00
1	5	0.20
1	6	0.20
1	7	0.10
1	8	0.08
1	9	0.09
1	10	0.26
1	11	0.08
1	12	0.16
2	3	0.32
2	4	0.21
..	..	..
..	..	..
10	11	0.10
10	12	0.27
11	12	0.26

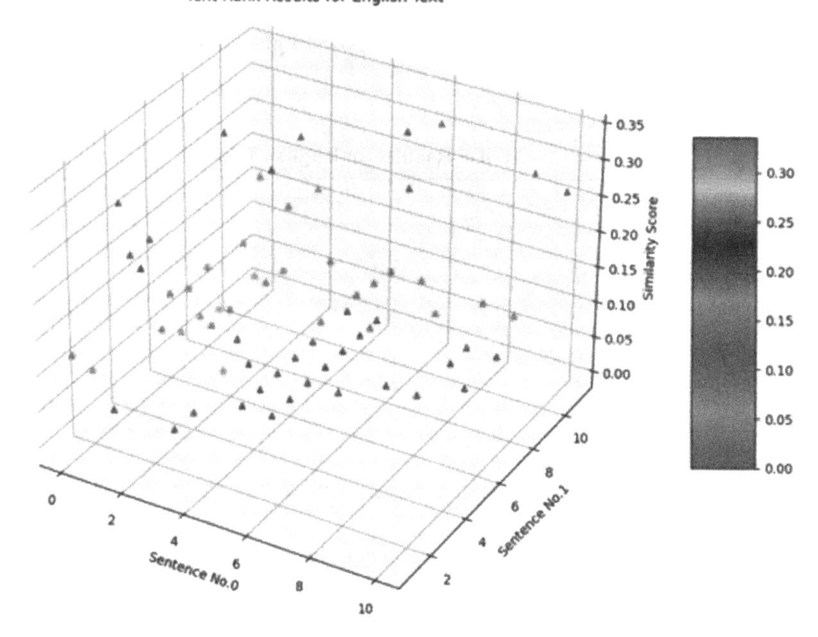

FIGURE 3.5 Text Rank results for English text

TABLE 3.3
Scores According to the TF-IDF Algorithm

Sentence No.	Score
1	0.10
2	0.07
3	0.10
4	0.11
5	0.06
6	0.19
7	0.15
8	0.18
9	0.36
10	0.12
11	0.16
12	0.20

3.7.3 Summary Produced Using the TF-IDF Algorithm

These lights are named as the Aurora Borealis. The scientists have been continuously watching them for hundreds of years. They are not so confident about what causes them. They imagined that they saw some fiery dragons in the sky. Some even concluded that the heavens were on the fire.

Figure 3.6 shows the experimental results for the English text the TF-IDF algorithm on a 60% compression ratio.

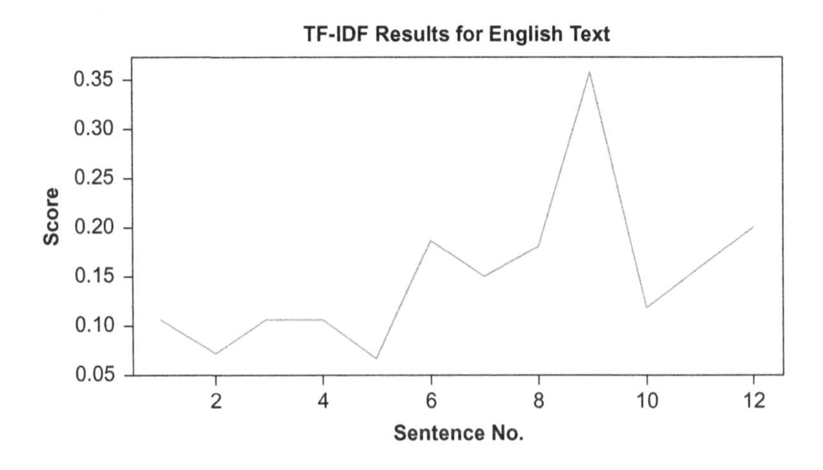

FIGURE 3.6 TF-IDF results for English text

3.7.4 Hindi Original Text

प्रदूषण की समस्या आज मानव समाज के सामने खड़ी सबसे गंभीर समस्याओं में से एक है | पिछले कुछ दशकों में प्रदूषण जिस तेजी से बढ़ा है उसने भविष्य में जीवन के अस्तित्व पर ही प्रश्नचिन्ह लगाना शुरू कर दिया है | संसार के सारे देश इससे होनेवाली हानियों को लेकर चिंतित है | संसार भर के वैज्ञानिक आए दिन प्रदूषण से संबंधित रिपोर्ट प्रकाशित करते रहते हैं और आनेवाले खतरे के प्रति हमें आगाह करते रहते हैं | आज से कुछ दशकों पहले तक कोई प्रदूषण की समस्या को गंभीरता से नहीं लेता था | प्रकृति से संसाधनों को प्राप्त करना मनुष्य के लिए सामान्य बात थी | उस समय बहुत कम लोग ही यह सोच सके थे कि संसाधनों का अंधाधुंध उपयोग हानि भी पहुँचा सकता है | हम जितना भी प्रकृति से लेते, प्रकृति उतने संसाधन दोबारा पैदा कर देती | ऐसा लगता था जैसे प्रकृति का भंडार असीमित है, कभी ख़त्म ही नहीं होगा | लेकिन जैसे-जैसे जनसंख्या बढ़ने लगी, प्राकृतिक संसाधनों का दोहन बढ़ता गया | वनों को काटा गया, अयस्कों के लिए जमीनों को खोदा गया | मशीनों ने इस काम में और तेजी ला दी | औद्योगिक क्रांति का प्रभाव लोगों को पर्यावरण पर दिखने लगा | जंगल ख़त्म होने लगे | उसके बदले बड़ी-बड़ी इमारतें, कल-कारखाने खुलने लगे | इससे प्रदूषण की समस्या हमारे सर पर आकर खड़ी हो गई | आज प्रदूषण के कारण शहरों की हवा इतनी दूषित हो गई है कि मनुष्य के लिए साँस लेना मुश्किल हो गया है | गाड़ियों और कारखानों से निकलनेवाला धुआँ हवा में जहर घोल रहा है | इससे तेजी से वायु प्रदूषण बढ़ रहा है | देश की राजधानी दिल्ली में तो प्रदूषण ने खतरे का निशान पार कर लिया है | कारखानों से निकलनेवाला कचरा नदियों और नालों में बहा दिया जाता है | इससे होनेवाले जलप्रदूषण के कारण लोगों के लिए अब पीने लायक पानी मिलना मुश्किल हो गया है | खेत में खाद के रूप में प्रयोग होनेवाले रासायनिक खादों ने खेत को बंजर बनाना शुरू कर दिया है | इससे भूमि प्रदूषण की समस्या भी गंभीर हो गयी है | इस तरह प्रदूषण तो बढ़ रहा है किंतु प्रदूषण दूर करने के लिए जिन वनों की जरुरत है वो दिन-ब-दिन कम हो रहे हैं | प्रदूषण के कारण धरती का तापमान बढ़ रहा है | ओजोन लेयर में कई छेद हो चुके हैं | नदियों और समुद्रों में जीव-जंतु मर रहे हैं | कई देशों का मौसम बदल रहा है | कभी बेमौसम बरसात हो रही है तो कभी बिलकुल वर्षा नहीं हो रही | इससे खेती को बहुत नुकसान हो रहा है | ध्रुवों की बर्फ पिघल रही है, जिससे समुद्र के किनारे जो देश और शहर हैं, उनके डूबने का खतरा बढ़ गया है | हिमालय के ग्लेशियर पिघल रहे हैं | जिससे गंगा, यमुना और ब्रह्मपुत्र जैसी नदियों के लुप्त होने की संभावना आ गई है | ऐसे गंभीर समय में यह आवश्यक हो गया है कि संसार के सारे देश मिलकर प्रदूषण की इस समस्या पर लगाम लगाए | उद्योगों के लिए प्रकृति को नष्ट नहीं किया जा सकता | जब जीवन ही खतरे में पड़ रहा है तो जीवन को आरामदायक बनानेवाले उद्योग क्या काम आएँगे | अभी हाल ही में (१२ दिसंबर २०१५) संसार के १९६ देश प्रदूषण पर नियंत्रण के लिए फ्रांस की राजधानी पेरिस में इकट्ठे हुए थे | सबने मिलकर यह निश्चय किया है कि धरती के तापमान को मौजूदा तापमान से दो डिग्री से ज्यादा बढ़ने नहीं दिया जाएगा | देर से ही सही पर यह सही दिशा में बढाया हुआ कदम है | यदि इसपर वास्तव में अमल किया गया तो पेरिस अधिवेशन मनुष्य जाति के लिए आशा की स्वर्णिम किरण साबित होगी | उम्मीद है कि हम पर्यावरण की रक्षा के लिए सही कदम उठाएँगे और आनेवाली पीढ़ी को प्रदूषण के दुष्परिणामों से बचाएँगे |

Table 3.4 shows the scores for the Text Rank algorithm.

Figure 3.7 shows the experimental results for the Hindi text using the Text Rank algorithm on a 60% compression ratio.

TABLE 3.4
Similarity scores According to the TextRank Algorithm

Sentence No.	Sentence No.	Similarity Score
1	2	0.28
1	3	0.15
1	4	0.13
1	5	0.29
1	6	0.14
1	7	0.06
1	8	0.06
1	9	0.00
1	10	0.00
1	11	0.07
..	..	..
..	..	..
39	42	0.28
40	41	0.06
40	42	0.26
41	42	0.18

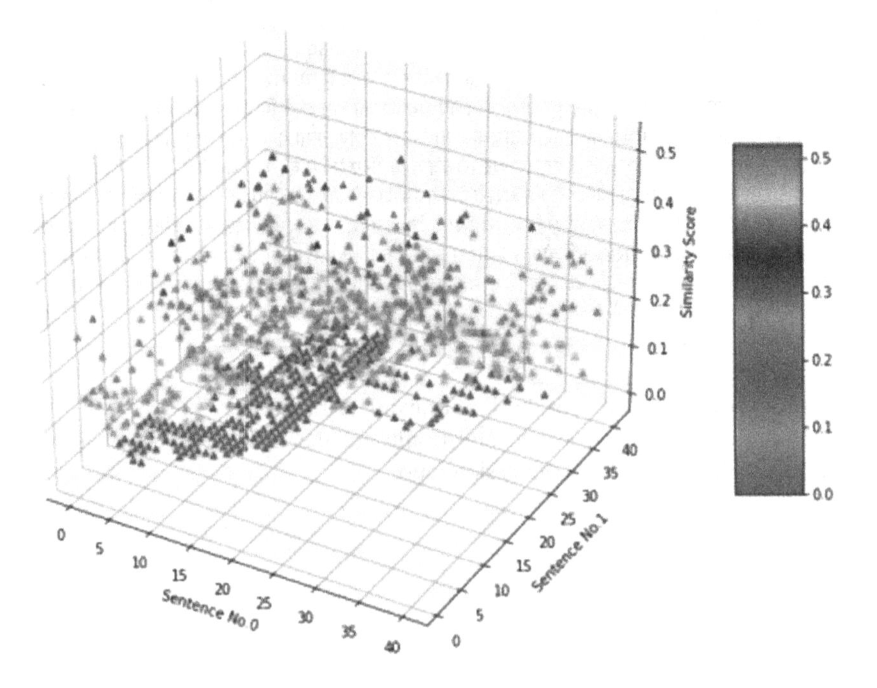

FIGURE 3.7 Text Rank results for Hindi text

3.7.5 Summary Produced Using the Text Rank Algorithm

आज प्रदूषण के कारण शहरों की हवा इतनी दूषित हो गई है कि मनुष्य के लिए साँस लेना मुश्किल हो गया है| इससे होनेवाले जलप्रदूषण के कारण लोगों के लिए अब पीने लायक पानी मिलना मुश्किल हो गया है| गाड़ियों और कारखानों से निकलनेवाला धुआँ हवा में जहर घोल रहा है| कारखानों से निकलने वाला कचरा नदियों और नालों में बहा दिया जाता है| इससे प्रदूषण की समस्या हमारे सर पर आकर खड़ी हो गई| इससे भूमि प्रदूषण की समस्या भी गंभीर हो गयी है| इससे तेजी से वायु प्रदूषण बढ़ रहा है| प्रदूषण के कारण धरती का तापमान बढ़ रहा है| इस तरह प्रदूषण तो बढ़ रहा है किंतु प्रदूषण दूर करने के लिए जिन वनों की जरुरत है वो दिन-ब-दिन कम हो रहे हैं| ऐसे गंभीर समय में यह आवश्यक हो गया है कि संसार के सारे देश मिलकर प्रदूषण की इस समस्या पर लगाम लगाए| पिछले कुछ दशकों में प्रदूषण जिस तेजी से बढ़ा है उसने भविष्य में जीवन के अस्तित्व पर ही प्रश्नचिन्ह लगाना शुरू कर दिया है| खेत में खाद के रूप में प्रयोग होनेवाले रासायनिक खादों ने खेत को बंजर बनाना शुरू कर दिया है| उम्मीद है कि हम पर्यावरण की रक्षा के लिए सही कदम उठाएँगे और आनेवाली पीढ़ी को प्रदूषण के दुष्परिणामों से बचाएँगे| कई देशों का मौसम बदल रहा है|

Table 3.5 shows the results using the TF-IDF algorithm.

Figure 3.8 shows the experimental results for the Hindi text using the TF-IDF algorithm on a 60% compression ratio.

TABLE 3.5
Scores According to the TF-IDF Algorithm

Sentence No.	TF-IDF Score
1 (प्रदूषण की समस्......)	0.15
2 (पिछले कुछ दशकों......)	0.12
3 (संसार के सारे द......)	0.21
4 (संसार भर के वैज......)	0.11
5 (आज से कुछ दशकों......)	0.19
6 (प्रकृति से संसा......)	0.23
7 (उस समय बहुत कम......)	0.20
8 (हम जितना भी प्र......)	0.20
9 (ऐसा लगता था जैस......)	0.16
10 (लेकिन जैसे-जैसे......)	0.16
11 (वनों को काटा गय......)	0.24
12 (मशीनों ने इस का......)	0.29
13 (औद्योगिक क्रांत......)	0.22

(Continued)

TABLE 3.5 CONTINUED
Scores According to the TF-IDF Algorithm

Sentence No.	TF-IDF Score
14 (जंगल ख़त्म होने......)	0.47
15 (उसके बदले बड़ी-ब......)	0.21
16 (इससे प्रदूषण की......)	0.17
17 (आज प्रदूषण के क......)	0.14
18 (गाड़ियों और कारख......)	0.21
19 (इससे तेजी से वा......)	0.20
20 (देश की राजधानी......)	0.18
21 (कारखानों से निक......)	0.24
22 (इससे होनेवाले ज......)	0.14
23 (खेत में खाद के......)	0.17
24 (इससे भूमि प्रदू......)	0.20
25 (इस तरह प्रदूषण......)	0.20
26 (प्रदूषण के कारण......)	0.21
27 (ओजोन लेयर में क......)	0.41
28 (नदियों और समुद्......)	0.38
29 (कई देशों का मौस......)	0.54
30 (कभी बेमौसम बरसा......)	0.36
31 (इससे खेती को बह......)	0.45
32 (ध्रुवों की बर्फ......)	0.13
33 (हिमालय के ग्लेश......)	0.51
34 (जिससे गंगा, यमु......)	0.16
35 (ऐसे गंभीर समय म......)	0.13
36 (उद्योगों के लिए......)	0.32
37 (जब जीवन ही खतरे......)	0.21
38 (अभी हाल ही में......)	0.09
39 (सबने मिलकर यह न......)	0.16
40 (देर से ही सही प......)	0.35
41 (यदि इसपर वास्तव......)	0.13
42 (उम्मीद है कि हम......)	0.12

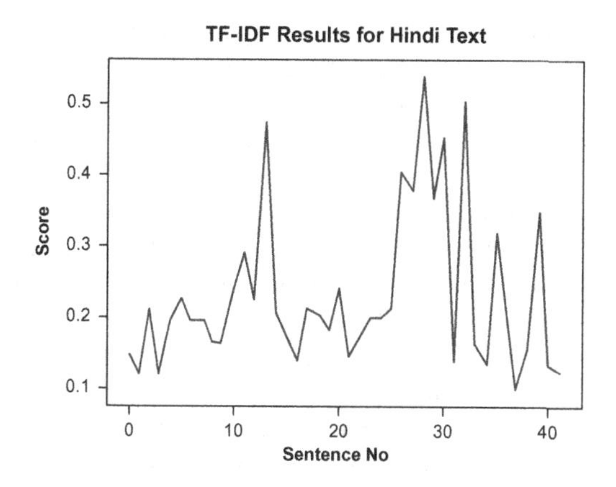

FIGURE 3.8 TF-IDF results for Hindi text

3.7.6 Summary Produced Using the TF-IDF Algorithm

वनों को काटा गया, अयस्कों के लिए जमीनों को खोदा गया | मशीनों ने इस काम में और तेजी ला दी | जंगल ख़त्म होने लगे | कारखानों से निकलनेवाला कचरा नदियों और नालों में बहा दिया जाता है | ओजोन लेयर में कई छेद हो चुके हैं | नदियों और समुद्रों में जीव-जंतु मर रहे हैं | कई देशों का मौसम बदल रहा है | कभी बेमौसम बरसात हो रही है तो कभी बिलकुल वर्षा नहीं हो रही | इससे खेती को बहुत नुकसान हो रहा है | हिमालय के ग्लेशियर पिघल रहे हैं | उद्योगों के लिए प्रकृति को नष्ट नहीं किया जा सकता | देर से ही सही पर यह सही दिशा में बढाया हुआ कदम है |

3.8 CONCLUSIONS AND FUTURE DIRECTIONS

In the experiments covered in this chapter, the Text Rank and TF-IDF algorithms were applied. Text Rank is a graph-based algorithm that summarizes text based on similarity scores. This algorithm was applied to Hindi as well as English text to show the contrasts with the TF-IDF algorithm.

The authors observed that on the given data set, the Text Rank algorithm performed better than TF-IDF. The original text in English is about some lights, bands, and the sky. These important terms were included in the summarized text by to Text Rank algorithm, but the summary produced by TF-IDF did not convey this type of relevant information.

In case of the original Hindi text, the actual context is pollution (प्रदूषण). The summary produced by the Text Rank algorithm included important sentences, as many of them contained the Hindi word for "pollution." This happened because the Text Rank algorithm compares two sentences and checks common words among them, then provides a similarity score on the basis of matching words.

But these types of important words were not present in the summary produced by TF-IDF. This is because the TF-IDF algorithm first counts the frequency of each word in a sentence (or document), then calculates the IDF by considering single occurrence of word in a sentence whether the word appears more than once.

Therefore, our conclusion is that for given datasets, Text Rank out performs the TF-IDF algorithm. In future work, more similarity measures could be used and their effect studied. Since Text Rank is language-independent, summarization of other languages could also be tested.

Judging the quality of summaries is a challenging task since it is subjective. In the future, the authors would like to compare these two algorithms in terms of various concrete parameters such as accuracy, precision, recall, etc. The summaries produced could be compared to standard summaries, and the efficiency of the algorithm would be computed accordingly. The authors would also like to develop a customized Text Rank algorithm that would give better results.

REFERENCES

Allahyari, M., Pouriyeh, S., Assefi, M., Safaei, S., Trippe, E.D., Gutierrez, J.B., & Kochut, K. (2017), Text summarization techniques: A brief survey. *International Journal of Advanced Computer Science and Applications*, 8.

Berry, M.W., Dumais, S.T., & O'Brien, G. (1995), Using linear algebra for intelligent information retrieval. *SIAM Review*, 37(4), 573–595.

Brin, S., & Page, L. (1998), The anatomy of a large-scale hypertextual web search engine. *Computer Networks and ISDN Systems*, 30(1–7): 107–117.

Bryan, K., & Leise, T. (2006), The $25,000,000,000 eigenvector: The linear algebra behind Google. *SIAM Review*, 48(3), 569.

Chen, W., Ramos, K., & Mullaguri, K. (2021), Genetic algorithms for extractive summarization. arXiv:2105.02365v1.

Chuang, W.T., & Yang, J. (2000), Extracting sentence segments for text summarization: A machine learning approach. In *Proceedings of the 23rd Annual International ACM SIGIR Conference on Research and Development in Information Retrieval* (pp. 152–159). ACM, New York. doi: 10.1145/345508.345566.

Dalal, V., & Malik, L. (2017a), Automatic summarization for Hindi text documents using BioInspired computing. *International Journal of Advanced Research in Computer and Communication Engineering*, 6(4), 682–688.

Dalal, V., & Malik, L. (2017b), Semantic graph based automatic text summarization for Hindi documents using particle swarm optimization. In International Conference on Information and Communication Technology for Intelligent Systems (pp. 284–289). Springer, Cham.

Elbarougy, R., Behery, G., & El Khatib, A. (2020), Extractive Arabic text summarization using modified PageRank algorithm. *Egyptian Informatics Journal*, 21(2), 73–81. https://doi.org/10.1016/j.eij.2019.11.001.

El-Kassas, W., Salama, C., Rafea, A., & Hoda, K.M. (2021), Automatic text summarization: A comprehensive survey. *Expert Systems with Applications*, 165.

Gerani, S., Mehdad, Y., Carenini, G., Ng, R.T., & Nejat, B. (2014), Abstractive summarization of product reviews using discourse structure. In *Proceedings of the 2014* Conference *on* Empirical Methods *in* Natural Language Processing *(EMNLP)* (pp. 1602–1613).

Gulati, A.N., & Sawarkar, S.D. (2017), A novel technique for multi document Hindi text summarization. In International Conference on Nascent Technologies in Engineering (ICNTE) (pp. 1–6). IEEE.

Gupta, M., & Garg, N.K. (2016), Text summarization of Hindi documents using rule based approach. In *2016* International Conference on Micro-Electronics and Telecommunication Engineering (ICMETE) (pp. 366–370). IEEE.

Gupta, S., & Gupta, S.K. (2019), Abstractive summarization: An overview of the state of the art. *Expert Systems with Applications*, 121.

Jain, R. (2019), Unsupervised method for text summarization using content based approach. In International Conference on Sustainable Computing in Science, Technology & Management (SUSCOM-2019).

Kaur, M., & Singh, J. (2013), Deadwood detection and elimination in text summarization for Punjabi language. *International Journal of Engineering Sciences*, 8, 51–59.

Kim, S.W., & Gil, J.M. (2019), Research paper classification systems based on TF-IDF and LDA schemes. *Human-centric Computing and Information Sciences*, 9, 30. https://doi.org/10.1186/s13673-019-0192-7

Kirmani, M., Hakak, N.M., Mohd, M., & Mohd, M. (2019), Hybrid text summarization: A survey. (pp. 63–73). Springer Nature, Singapore. K. Ray et al. (eds.), Soft Computing: Theories and Applications, Advances in Intelligent Systems and Computing 742, https://doi.org/10.1007/978-981-13-0589-4_7

Kumar, K.V., & Yadav, D. (2015a), An improvised extractive approach to hindi text summarization. (pp. 291–300). Springer, New Delhi. published in Information System Design and Intelligent Applications

Kumar, K.V., Yadav, D., & Sharma, A. (2015b), Graph based technique for hindi text summarization. In *Information Systems Design and Intelligent Applications* (pp. 301–310). Springer, New Delhi. published in Information System Design and Intelligent Applications

Kumari, N., & Singh, P. (2020), Automated Hindi text summarization using TF-IDF and TextRank algorithm. *Journal of Critical Reviews*, 7(17), 2547–2555.

Mallick, C., Das, A.K., Dutta, M., Das, A.K., & Sarkar, A. (2018), Graph-based text summarization using modified Text Rank. *Advances in Intelligent Systems and Computing*. https://doi.org/10.1007/978-981-13-0514-6_14.

Manning, C., Raghavan, P., & Schütze, H. (2008), *Introduction to Information Retrieval*. Cambridge University Press, England.

Mihalfcea, R., & Tasrau, P. (2004), Text Rank: Bringing order into texts. In *Proceedings of Empirical Methods in Natural Language Processing (EMNLP)* (pp. 404–411). Association for Computational Linguis Barcelona.

Mishra, U., et al. (2012), MAULIK: An effective stemmer for Hindi language. *International Journal on Computer Science and Engineering (IJCSE)*, 4, 711–717.

Nenkova, A., & McKeown, K. (2012), A survey of text summarization techniques. In C.C. Aggarwal and C.X. Zhai (eds.), *Mining Text Data* (pp. 43–76). Springer.

Singh, G., & Verma, K. (2014), A novel features based automated Gurmukhi text summarization system. In International Conference on Advance in Computing Communication and Information Science (pp. 424–432), Singh2014ANF.

Thaokar, C., & Malik, L. (2013), Test model for summarizing Hindi text using extraction method. In *Proceedings of 2013* (pp 1138–1143) IEEE Conference on Information and Communication Technologies.

Yao, L., Pengzhou, Z., & Chi, Z. (2019), Research on news keyword extraction technology based on TF-IDF and Text Rank. In *2019* IEEE/ACIS 18th International Conference on Computer and Information Science (ICIS) (pp. 452–455). IEEE Computer Society.

4 Graph Embeddings for Natural Language Processing

Jyoti Gavhane, Rajesh Prasad, and Rajeev Kumar

CONTENTS

4.1 INTRODUCTION

Graphs are frequently used in diverse real-world applications and presentations. Social networks are huge graphs of individuals who follow each other (e.g., Facebook, Twitter, Instagram), biologists use graphs of protein and gene relations, and data communication networks are represented with the help of graphs. Without language usage, communication is quite difficult. Are "graph" and "language" terms correlated? The answer is- Yes! A *graph* is a pictorial representation, whereas a *language* usually uses verbal concepts. Although they appear in different forms, there is a strong relationship among these terminologies. A graph

DOI: 10.1201/9781003272649-4

is nonlinear data structure. It is an influential formal tool to represent and apply multiple aspects associated to language processing. The field of natural language processing (NLP) or computational linguistics builds on techniques and insights from several different disciplines, principally theoretical linguistics and computer science, but with some input from mathematical logic and psychology.

In simple terms, natural language processing interprets the meaning of language via computational techniques. Though the term NLP may appear simple, it is quite difficult to implement and map language using computational skills and techniques, but it isn't impossible. Graphs are not only associated with NLP, but are also used to solve challenges or problems encountered by NLP. This chapter will try to provide an overview of how NLP difficulties have been treated in graphical contexts, focusing in particular on graph construction – a critical step in exhibiting data to highlight targeted phenomena.

The process of mapping some complex object, a textual document, a colored image, or a graph into something simple, a fixed-length vector – e.g., a cluster of numbers or a matrix that captures the significant key features of a complicated object while rendering it as fewer low-dimensional objects is called *embedding*.

This chapter will focus on providing an overview of graph embedding techniques for NLP and will feature a few examples of graph embeddings. This effort may help researchers to solve problems related to question answering systems, ranking for academic search, well-structured text analysis and classification, fact-checking, explanation regeneration, and many more NLP applications.

4.1.1 Natural Language and Natural Language Processing

Language is the primary means of communication that enables a human or an animal to convey messages with each other. Animals cannot talk as we do, but they are able to communicate in their own languages, and some humans are able to understand their communication. But this chapter will not focus on that domain in terms of language, but rather on language as the means by which human communicates with other human to convey his or her ideas, opinions, suggestions, or any other message. In this computational era, we need to consider not only speech (e.g., audio, video, podcasts, and webinars), but also text (e.g., news, menus, signatures, emails, text messages, blogs, web pages, articles, and bar codes). There is another form of language which we call gesture – i.e., neither speech nor text. All these aspects can be considered natural language.

Humans communicate with the help of language which consists of words, sentences, grammar, tenses, etc. "Word" is the basic unit of any language. As a child grows, he or she starts to use gestures, and after that, words. By listening to words uttered by a child, we can start to interpret the meaning he or she wants to convey. What, then, is the meaning of language? It consists of words used in a structured and conventional way and conveyed by speech, writing, or gesture. Linguistics is basically the precise study of language, which includes its syntax (grammar), meanings of words (semantics), and spoken language sounds (phonetics), and natural language processing is a branch of linguistics.

Now the next question arises: why do we process language? First, we will consider NLP as an acronym for natural language processing. In a wide sense, it covers any kind of computer manipulation of natural language. This could be as simple as calculating frequencies of words to compare different writing styles. In another sense, NLP involves "understanding and appreciating" complete human utterances or expressions to the degree of being able to give suitable responses to them [1]. We all know that computers are used to process data, like a human brain processes the linguistic data to find and understand meaning. Wherever we use the term "processing" in this chapter, we are referring to processing with the help of computational techniques and the major role played by computer systems themselves.

Natural language processing is a broad term referring to automatic computational processing of human languages. This includes both algorithms that take human-produced text as input, and algorithms that produce natural looking text as outputs [2]. Nowadays, NLP is considered a revolutionary subfield of artificial intelligence. Whereas our brain can process language data very quickly, computers cannot. Computers rely on algorithms, machine learning, deep learning, and many more strategies to do the same thing, then have to test the results to verify their accuracy. If the result is wrong, a decision may be wrong, so humans have to face consequences of that incorrect output. Therefore, it is crucial to process language in the correct manner.

4.1.2 Processing: A Module in Machine Learning

Learning is a continuous process. In this context, when we refer to a "*process*," a computer has to follow certain steps to achieve a correct result. A simple example using Amazon's popular data cloud-based voice service Alexa will demonstrate the steps:

1. A human interacts with Alexa or gives an instruction in the form of verbal communication.
2. Alexa captures the audio or human voice.
3. The system converts the audio into text.
4. The system processes the text data.
5. The system convert the processed data to audio.
6. Alexa responds to the human by playing and audio file as if it's a human speaking to a human.

There are a number of applications of NLP we use in day-to-day life, such as Google Maps voice assistance, email assistance, chatbots, spam filters, autocorrect feature in word processing software, e-commerce search engines, and home appliances (fans, lights, fridge, door locks, air conditioners, etc.).

This chapter will look at the different techniques used for NLP. Appropriate techniques are needed to help process natural language, so let's see how to achieve this.

4.2 COMPUTATIONAL TECHNIQUES

4.2.1 How NLP Works

NLP involves applying algorithms to categorize and extract natural language rules such that amorphous language data is converted into computer-understandable form. When text is provided, the computer extracts the meaning associated with sentences and words included in that text.

Terms associated with NLP include text analysis, text classification, information retrieval/extraction, and information abstraction.

Text analysis and classification use rule-based methods and machine learning-based methods.

There are some challenges posed by using these methods for text analysis. The term "graph embeddings" was coined to address some of the challenges or limitations encountered by NLP.

Graph embeddings try to address very challenging NLP issues, such as:

1) Question answering (Bordes et al., 2014)
2) Ranking for academic search (Xiong et al., 2017)
3) Text classification (Yao et al., 2019)
4) Fact checking (Zhong et al., 2020)
5) Explanation regeneration (Li et al., 2020)

4.2.2 Graph Embeddings

Graph embedding involves machine learning using graphs, and is a technique of machine learning or deep learning used to develop natural language processing. When we combine the terms "graph" and "embedding," it describes a special technique which helps in natural language processing, but first, we need to understand the basics of these two words separately.

4.2.2.1 Graph

First, we need to try to understand the simple meaning of a graph. A graph $G = (V, E)$ is a structure consisting of a set of vertices (or nodes) $V = \{v_i|i = 1, n\}$, some of which are connected through a set of edges $E = \{(v_i, v_j)|v_i, v_j \in V\}$. In a weighted graph $G_w = (V, E, W)$, the edges have associated to them a weight or cost w_{ij}: $W = \{w_{ij}|w_{ij}$ is the weight/cost associated with edge (v_i, v_j), $w_{i,j} \in R\}$. Edges can be directed or undirected. In simpler terms, a graph is considered as a collection of nodes called vertices or nodes, and collection of segments called lines or edges.

The graph $G = \{V, E\}$ is a nonlinear data structure. It is a powerful depiction formalism that can be applied to a diverse features associated with language processing. Here is an outline of how NLP problems have been projected into the graph framework, converging in particular on graph creation – a fundamental step in depicting the data to highlight the phenomena targeted.

NLP-based application development is challenging because a digital system like a computer requires structured data. A data structure is the domain with the help of which we can represent a graph by using an adjacency list or adjacency matrix. This helps us to store and organize data in a structured format so that we can access only the important data we require in an efficient way for processing. Here, embedding focuses on what is important in a generalized way. But why bother with matrices? They can be difficult to understand and manipulate because of their multidimensionality. The answer lies in the problem itself. Let's make it simpler to understand and map. Mathematics is also a language through which you can model any real-life application. Mathematics and graph theory play major roles in converting higher-dimensional data to smaller-dimensional data by employing a concept called embedding.

Let us illustrate this with pictorial representations of two different graphs. We will arbitrarily uniquely assign the numbers 1, 2,…,| V | to each vertex.

If you look at the graphs in Figure 4.1 and Figure 4.2, you can see a finite set of vertices together with a finite set of vertices (1–5) and edges.

In Figure 4.1, the vertices are connected without any direction, so this is referred to as an undirected graph. Figure 4.2 features arrows showing direction, so it is referred to as a directed graph.

$$A[i][j] = \{1 \text{ if there exists an edge } <i, j> \\ \quad 0 \text{ if an edge } <i, j> \text{ does not exist.}\}$$

$$A[i][j] = \{1 \text{ if there exists a directed edge from an edge } <i \text{ to } j> \\ \quad 0 \text{ otherwise}\}$$

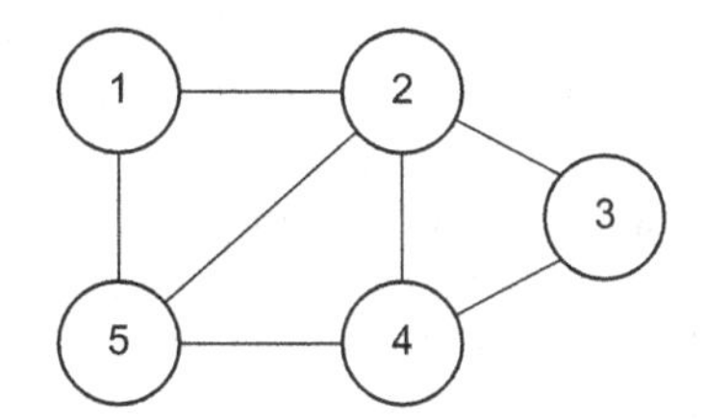

	1	2	3	4	5
1	0	1	0	0	1
2	1	0	1	1	1
3	0	1	0	1	0
4	0	1	1	0	1
5	1	1	0	1	0

FIGURE 4.1 Undirected graph and adjacency matrix to represent mathematically

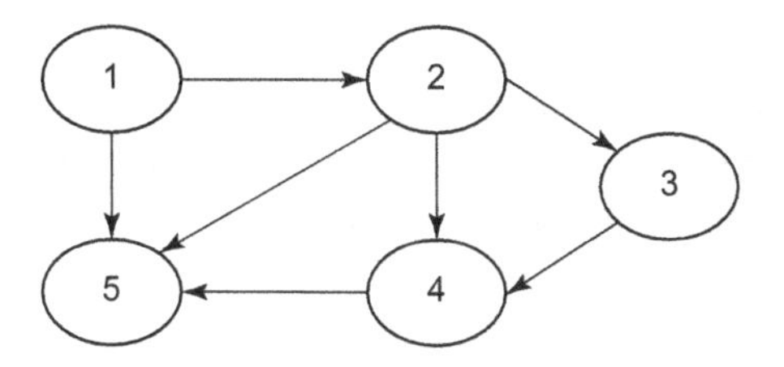

	1	2	3	4	5
1	0	1	0	0	1
2	0	0	1	1	1
3	0	0	0	1	0
4	0	0	0	0	1
5	0	0	0	0	0

FIGURE 4.2 Directed graph and adjacency matrix representation

4.2.2.2 Embedding

Embedding has been defined by different sources as follows:

1. From Wikipedia, the free encyclopedia: "In mathematics, n **embedding** (or **imbedding**) is one instance of some mathematical structure contained within another instance, such as a group that is a subgroup."
2. From dictionary.com: "*noun Mathematics* – the mapping of one set into another."
3. From Google: "An **embedding** is a relatively low-dimensional space into which you can translate high-dimensional vectors. Embeddings make it easier to do machine learning on large inputs like sparse vectors representing words. Ideally, an embedding captures some of the semantics of the input by placing semantically similar inputs close together in the embedding space. An embedding can be learned and reused across models."

Surprisingly we are neither aware nor understanding these definitions of embedding in a true sense. Because we feel 'embedding' (English meaning) means adding/implanting/inserting something in some of the form.

If we think about these definitions scientifically, we can add one more definition which is relevant to the context.

4.2.2.3 Graph Embeddings

Graph embeddings are a specific type of embedding that translates graphs and graph subparts to fixed-length vectors (tensors) [2]. A graph is represented by an adjacency matrix, which may be large and sparse. It is translated into a lower-dimensional, smaller matrix by the embedding. The translation or conversion process involves understanding, learning, and extracting significant features of a graph, then you can use that matrix for some kind of task. Embedding captures important (significant) features of objects in a compact way. Here, we should elaborate why we are considering tabular data, putting it into a graph and converting it into a vector. It is a desirable practice if you want to translate a complex entity into a simple one you want to use for a task in a convenient manner.

4.2.2.4 Word Embeddings: Classic Example

How do you represent the meaning of a word? You can use several representations to understand the meaning of word, such as a definition, an image, or a logical structure. Here is an example:

Zebra:

noun [C] [3]

UK /ˈzeb.rə/ /ˈziː.brə/ **US** /ˈziː.brə/
plural **zebras** or **zebra**

1. an African wild animal that looks like a horse, with black or brown and white lines on its body, as shown in Figure 4.3.

FIGURE 4.3 Animal "Zebra"

We can consider word embedding as a simpler way to deal with a word. We can use it mathematically. We can find similarities between two words or we can represent a word in a model. By constructing the model shown in figure 4.4, we can predict which word will come next, what are the possible words around this word, etc. We can encode all the letters of alphabet, and count how many times a particular word occurs in a document. Term frequency-inverse document frequency (TF-IDF) is one method for deriving a weighted term frequency.

Our aim is to find the relationship between an animal and its type using the following context windows:

Words exist in sentences, and the context around a word helps you to understand what it means [4].

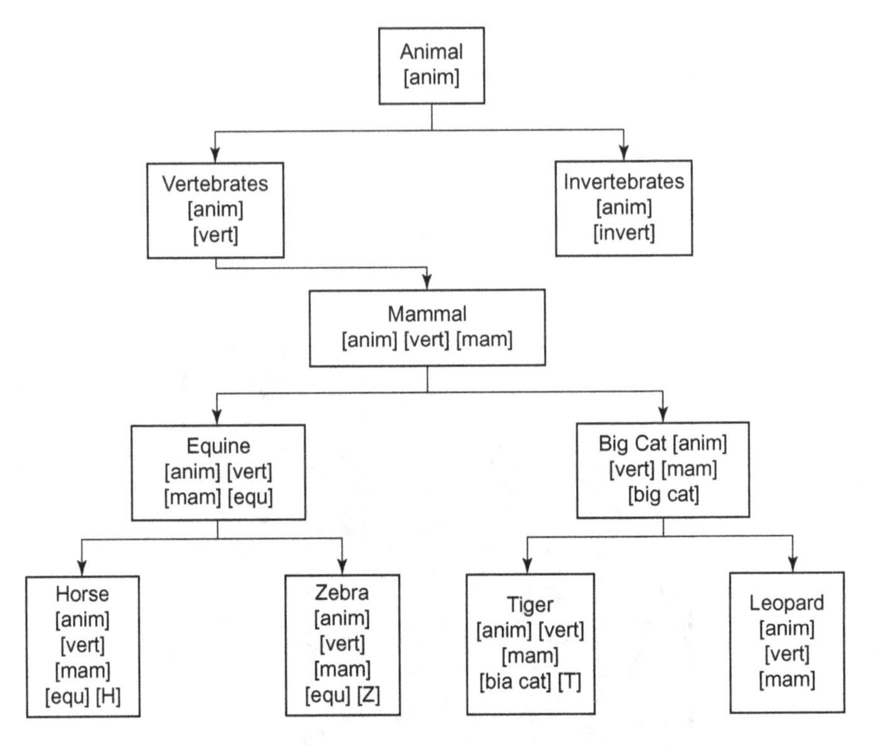

FIGURE 4.4 Animal taxonomy: "Zebra" as a word and its relationship to the animal kingdom

Tiger is a wild animal.
Lion is a wild animal.

Even if you don't know about lions, you see that the words are used in same context hence they probably share similar characteristics.

Let's look at co-occurrence – how often do two words appear in the same context window?

Context window – specific number and direction:

Animal is not invertebrate.
Animal is mammal.
Animal is warm-blooded.

We have a context window of one behind and one forward. The focal word is "is." Then what is the context for "is"? We need to know this in order to make a matrix where we can represent every word in the corpus of these three sentences – what word comes next? "Invertebrate" and "mammal" never show up together. They don't mean the same thing. And that is useful. We could do this for a lot of the words (see Table 4.1).

TABLE 4.1
Context Window

	Animal	is	not	invertebrate	mammal	warm-blooded
Animal	0	3	2	1	2	1
is	3	0	1	2	2	1
not	2	1	0	1	0	0
invertebrate	1	2	1	0	0	0
mammal	2	2	0	0	0	0
warm-blooded	1	1	0	0	0	0

The context window tells us what comes before and what comes after. The difficult part is that we need access to lots of documents to understand the context. The meaning of more documents is the larger matrix.

We end up with a huge, sparse matrix as soon as we add more documents. Large, sparse matrices are clumsy and difficult to handle, and create confusion. But this would be the input, so we you need to condense it down into something we can work with. How we do this?

The answer is with the help of linear algebra – a subfield of mathematics. In linear algebra, we need to understand singular value decomposition to apply it for condensing the matrix.

This chapter deals with a technique called *singular value decomposition* or *decay* (SVD) for dynamic graphs and graph embeddings. An illustration of a matrix embeddings can be used for dynamic graph updating and modeling. The adjacency matrix updates graph operations through which SVD (and low rank approximation) can be updated powerfully.

4.3 THE SINGULAR VALUE DECOMPOSITION FOR "GRAPH EMBEDDINGS"

Singular value decomposition is a dimension reduction technique for matrices that reduces a matrix into its component to simplify the calculation $A_{[m} \times_{n]} = U_{[m} \times_{r]} \sum {}_{[r} \times_{r]} (V_{[n} \times_{r]})^T$.

The terms used in SVD are shown in Table 4.2.

Values in the matrix: 1 represents that a word is present in the document, 0 represents that it is not. Matrix A is represented as a product of three different matrices as shown above, visualized as U, $\sum$ and V.

For example, in the matrix we can consider: rows = Student 1 and Student 2, columns = feedback for three different instructors:

$A^T . A = V$ Instructor to feedback similarity matrix
$A . A^T =$ U= Student to feedback similarity matrix
$\sum =$ Its diagonal elements: strength of each feedback

TABLE 4.2
Terms in SVD

Matrix Name	Rows	Columns
A: Input matrix	m documents	n words
U: Left singular vectors	m documents	r concepts
$\sum$: Singular values	r rank of Matrix A	r strength of each concept
V: Right singular vectors	n words	r concepts

We see strength of feedback for Instructor 1 by Student 1 and for Instructor 2 by Student 2 is highest amongst all values. Our aim is to see, when we reduce the dimension of Matrix A, whether these concepts contribute to strength accordingly. Meaning is to compute $\sum$ matrix.

When we compute the SVD, we consider the Eigen values and Eigen vectors:

$$A = \begin{bmatrix} 3 & 1 & 1 \\ -1 & 3 & 1 \end{bmatrix}_{2\times 3} \cdots \quad \text{(Matrix 4.1)}$$

$$A^T = \begin{bmatrix} 3 & -1 \\ 1 & 3 \\ 1 & 1 \end{bmatrix}_{3\times 2} \quad \text{(Matrix 4.2)}$$

$$\text{A.A}^T = \begin{bmatrix} 11 & 1 \\ 1 & 11 \end{bmatrix}_{2\times 2} \quad \text{(Matrix 4.3)}$$

$$(A - \lambda I) = 0$$

$$\begin{bmatrix} (11-\lambda) & 1 \\ 1 & (11-\lambda) \end{bmatrix} = 0 \quad \text{(Matrix 4.4)}$$

$$(11-\lambda)^2 - 1^2 = 0$$

$$(11-\lambda+1)(11-\lambda-1) = 0$$

$$(12-\lambda) = 0 \ \therefore \lambda = 12$$

$$(10-\lambda) = 0 \ \therefore \lambda = 10$$

$$\lambda_1 = 12, \lambda 2 = 10 \rightarrow \text{Eigen Values}$$

To find the Eigen vectors:

If we substitute λ_2 in first row and λ_1 in second row in Matrix 4.4, we will get:

$$\begin{bmatrix} 1 & 1 \\ 1 & -1 \end{bmatrix} \quad \text{Eigen vectors} \qquad \text{(Matrix 4.5)}$$

We can now conduct orthogonalization using the Gram-Schmidt orthogonalization process:

$$A = A.\Sigma V^T$$

We need the A and V^T matrix in orthogonal form, which is why we are following this process.

We can compute the length of Matrix 4.5:

$$\begin{bmatrix} 1 & 1 \\ 1 & -1 \end{bmatrix} = \frac{\sqrt{1^2+1^2}}{\sqrt{1^2+(-1)^2}} = \frac{\sqrt{1+-1}}{\sqrt{1+1}} = \frac{\sqrt{2}}{\sqrt{2}}$$

Putting these values into Matrix 4.5:

$$\begin{bmatrix} \frac{1}{\sqrt{2}} & \frac{1}{\sqrt{2}} \\ \frac{1}{\sqrt{2}} & \frac{-1}{\sqrt{2}} \end{bmatrix} = U \qquad \text{(Matrix 4.6)}$$

$$AT.A = V$$

$$A^T \cdot A = \begin{bmatrix} 10 & 0 & 2 \\ 0 & 10 & 4 \\ 2 & 4 & 2 \end{bmatrix}_{3\times 3} \qquad \text{(Matrix 4.7)}$$

Characteristics equation from $(A–\lambda\, I)\, X = 0 \rightarrow X$ is the column vector:

$$\begin{bmatrix} (10-\lambda) & 0 & 2 \\ 0 & (10-\lambda) & 4 \\ 2 & 4 & (2-\lambda) \end{bmatrix} \qquad \text{(Matrix 4.8)}$$

There is a simple way to solve Matrix 4.8 with the help of the polynomial equation $\lambda^3 - S_1\lambda^2 + S_2\lambda - S_3$.

Trace of $AT.A = S_{1,}$ minor of diagonals $AT.A = S_2$ determinant of $A^T.A = S_3$

$$S_1 = \text{Trace} = \text{Sum of all diagonal elements of } A^T.A \text{ i.e.}\left[10+10+2=22\right]$$

$$S_3 = \left|\left(A^T.A\right)\right| = 10(4) + 2(-20) = 40 \quad 40 = 0$$

$$S_2 = \text{minor of diagonals } A^T.A$$

$$= \begin{vmatrix} 10 & 4 \\ 4 & 2 \end{vmatrix} + \begin{vmatrix} 10 & 2 \\ 2 & 2 \end{vmatrix} + \begin{vmatrix} 10 & 0 \\ 0 & 10 \end{vmatrix}$$

$$= (20-16) + (20-4) + (100-0)$$

$$= 4 + 16 + 100$$

$$S_2 = 120$$

The final characteristic equation becomes:

$$\lambda^3 - 22\lambda^2 + 120\lambda = 0 \text{ Factorization}$$

$$\lambda\left(\lambda^2 - 22\lambda + 120\right) = 0 \text{ Put } \lambda_1 = 0$$

$$\lambda^2 - 22\lambda + 120 = 0$$

$$\lambda^2 - 12\lambda - 10\lambda + 120 = 0$$

$$\lambda(\lambda - 12) - 10(\lambda - 12) = 0$$

$$(\lambda - 12)(\lambda - 10) = 0$$

$$\lambda - 12 = 0 \qquad \lambda - 10 = 0$$

$$\lambda_2 = 12, \qquad \lambda_3 = 10$$

$$\text{Rearrange the values } \lambda_1 = 12$$

$$\lambda_2 = 10$$

$$\lambda_3 = 0$$

$$V^T = \text{column vector} \begin{bmatrix} V_1^T \\ V_2^T \\ V_3^T \end{bmatrix}$$

$$U = \text{row vector} \left[U_1.U_2.U_3\right]$$

Put $\lambda_1 = 12$ in Matrix 4.8:

$$\begin{bmatrix} -2 & 0 & 2 \\ 0 & -2 & 4 \\ 2 & 4 & -10 \end{bmatrix}\begin{bmatrix} x_1 \\ x_2 \\ x_3 \end{bmatrix} = 0 \because \text{Applying}(A - \lambda I)x = 0$$

Apply Cramer's rule to get the values of x_1, x_2, and x_3:

$$\frac{x_1}{4} = \frac{-x_2}{-8} = \frac{x3}{4}$$

After dividing throughout by 4, we define the first vector as:

= 1 2 1.

Then we take $\lambda_2 = 10$ and put it in Matrix 4.8:

$$\begin{bmatrix} 0 & 0 & 2 \\ 0 & 0 & 4 \\ 2 & 4 & -8 \end{bmatrix}$$

$$\frac{x1}{-16} = \frac{-x}{-8} = \frac{x3}{0}$$

2 –1 0 second vector

Then we take $\lambda = 0$:

$$\frac{x1}{4} = \frac{-x2}{-8} = \frac{x3}{-20}$$

1, 2, –5 third vector

$$V = \begin{bmatrix} 1 & 2 & 1 \\ 2 & -1 & 2 \\ 1 & 0 & -5 \end{bmatrix} \qquad \text{(Matrix 4.9)}$$

$$V^T = \begin{bmatrix} 1 & 2 & 1 \\ 2 & -1 & 0 \\ 1 & 2 & -5 \end{bmatrix} \qquad \text{(Matrix 4.10)}$$

$$\sqrt{1^2 + 2^2 + 1^2} = \sqrt{6}$$
$$\sqrt{2^2 + (-1)^2} = \sqrt{5}$$
$$\sqrt{1^2 + 2^2 + (-5)^2} = \sqrt{30}$$

We now apply the Gram-Schmidt process for orthogonalization:

$$\sqrt{6}, \sqrt{5}, \sqrt{30}$$

$$V^T = \begin{bmatrix} \frac{1}{\sqrt{6}} & \frac{2}{\sqrt{6}} & \frac{1}{\sqrt{6}} \\ \frac{2}{\sqrt{5}} & \frac{-1}{\sqrt{5}} & 0 \\ \frac{1}{\sqrt{30}} & \frac{2}{\sqrt{30}} & \frac{-5}{\sqrt{30}} \end{bmatrix}. \qquad \text{(Matrix 4.11)}$$

Now we will obtain Σ [diagonal matrix of singular values] $A_2 x_3 = \Sigma\, _2 x_3$

We can see the values of λ in the following two matrices:

$$\lambda_1 = 12,\ \lambda_2 = 10,\ \lambda_3 = 0 \qquad \text{(Matrix 4.12)}$$

$$\lambda_1 = 12,\ \lambda_2 = 10 \qquad \text{(Matrix 4.13)}$$

The two values are same, $\lambda_{1,}\ \lambda_2$, which equal 12 and 10 respectively:

$$\Sigma = \begin{bmatrix} \sqrt{12} & 0 & 0 \\ 0 & \sqrt{10} & 0 \end{bmatrix}_{2\times 3} \qquad \text{(Matrix 4.14)}$$

We insert the diagonal values in descending order:

$\sqrt{12} = 3.46$ is greater than $\sqrt{10} = 3.16$

$$\Sigma = \begin{bmatrix} 3.46 & 0 & 0 \\ 0 & 3.16 & 0 \end{bmatrix}_{2\times 3} \qquad \text{(Matrix 4.15)}$$

If you perceive that matrix (4.15), 3.46 and 3.16 values contribute the strength of concept which is expected out of total 6 values, we will consider these 2 values for decision making.

The advantages of SVD are that it preserves relationships and is accurate. Its disadvantage is that it requires more memory.

4.4 PREDICTIVE METHODS

We will now apply embedding to a specific task.

4.4.1 Word2vec

Word2vec is a group of related models that are used to produce word embeddings [7]. These models are shallow, two-layer neural networks that are trained to reconstruct linguistic contexts of words. Word2vec takes as its input a large corpus of text and produces a vector space, typically of several hundred dimensions, with each unique word in the corpus being assigned a corresponding vector in the space. Word vectors are positioned in the vector space such that words that share common contexts [8] in the corpus are located close to one another in the space.

The word2vec model has two different architectures to create the word embeddings:

1. Continuous bag of words (CBOW)
2. Skip-gram model

4.4.1.1 CBOW: Continuous Bag of Words [5]

CBOW uses embeddings to train neural networks where the context is characterized by numerous words for a given target word [9].

For example, we could use "bird" and "wings" as context words for "flying" as the target word.

This calls for an adjustment to the neural network architecture.

The adjustment, shown below in Figure 4.5, CBOW consists of replicating the input to hidden layer SUM connections times the number of context words and adding a divide by operation in the hidden layer neurons which gives W_0 output.

4.4.1.2 Skip-gram Model

The skip-gram model learns a vector representation for each word that maximizes the probability of that word occurring given the previous word. Input vector is one hot encoded vector for that word, in hidden layer weights have been assigned, then it is possible to find the probability for every word in the corpus. We don't care about the output layer, but we are concerned about the hidden layer because the hidden layer is a weight matrix, and after taking the values from the input vector,

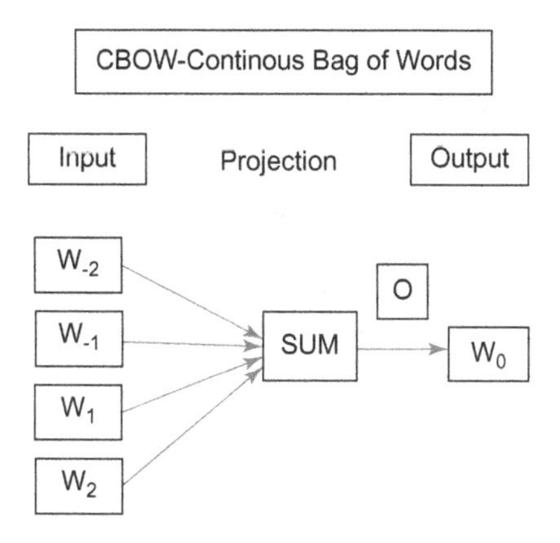

FIGURE 4.5 Simple CBOW framework

we assign a value to calculate the output layer. Here we use forward and back propagation and gradient descent to learn what the accurate weights are. You train the skip-gram model to learn a given word to find what the context is. The hidden layer is word embedding (see Figure 4.6).

What has this got to do with graphs?

As we can see, word embedding is intuitive. In graph embeddings, all of the nodes in our graph are like words and the graph is like a corpus of text. We want to understand the meaning of the node. Instead of big adjacency matrix, we want short embedding for our node.

The DeepWalk graph neural network is the best solution for graph embeddings. How do we represent a node in a graph mathematically? Is word2vec useful in mapping? Yes, it is. Each node is like a word. The neighborhood around the node is the context window, and we can extract the context for each node by sampling random walks from the graph using the skip-gram model.

Table 4.3 compares various graph embedding techniques.

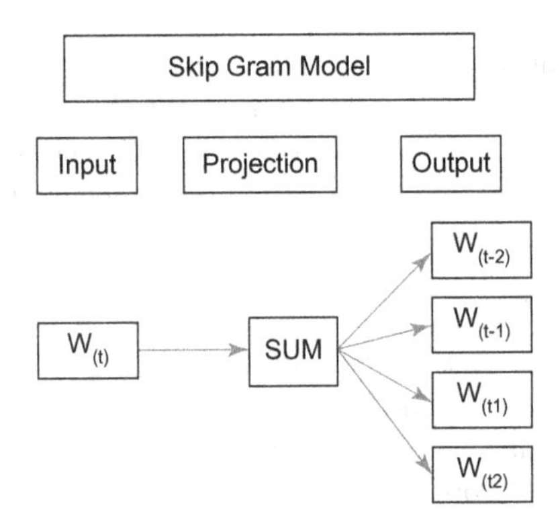

FIGURE 4.6 Skip-gram model

TABLE 4.3
Comparative Study of Techniques

Sr. No.	Model Name	Features
1	CBOW	Trains more quickly than skip-gram, and can better represent more frequent words
2	Skip-gram	Works well with small datasets, and can better represent less frequent words
3	Knowledge graph embedding	Models by embedding the entities into a low-dimensional space
4	DeepWalk [10]	Robust for different label distributions with high spectral separation

4.5 MORE EMBEDDING TECHNIQUES

There are two kinds of embeddings:

1. Monopartite (e.g., DeepWalk)
2. Multipartite (e.g., knowledge graphs)

We are trying to represent the following aspects in terms of graph embeddings [11] and related applications [12]:

1. Vertex (node) embeddings – these are useful to describe connectivity of each node.
2. Path embeddings – these represent traversals across the graph (e.g. eBay's traversal embeddings, a patient's journey to hospital).
3. Graph embeddings – with these, we can encode the entire graph into a single vector and process this vector to understand context (e.g., a molecular graph, where every molecule is represented as an individual graph).
4. Node embeddings – these consist of:
   A similarity function that measures the similarity between nodes
   An encoder function that generates the node embedding
   A decoder function that reconstructs pairwise similarity
   A loss function It measures importance of graph reconstruction.
5. Shallow graph embedding techniques – in these, the encoder function is an embedding lookup table.

Matrix factorization techniques rely on an adjacency matrix input. They are applied either directly or to a transformed input. This method is computationally intense and requires massive amounts of memory.

Random walk techniques are used to determine node co-occurrence via random walks. They learn weights to optimize similarity measures. They have a local-only perspective and assume that similar nodes are close together.

Drawbacks of shallow embeddings:

They are inefficient – no parameters are shared between nodes.
They cannot leverage node attributes.
They not suitable for large, evolving graphs.

4.6 CONCLUSION

Newer methodologies used to compress information include:

1. Neighborhood aggregation
2. Neighborhood autoencoder methods
3. Convolutional autoencoders

Clustering and community detection algorithms used to apply generic tabular data approaches like k-means. These algorithms allow capturing functional and structural roles, KNN graph based on embedding similarity etc.

Embeddings has potential to build the graph algorithm library more powerful. Node classification/semi-supervised learning can be used to predict missing node attributes link prediction by using either similarity measures (heuristics) or machine learning (ML) pipelines. Embeddings can be used wherever we encounter complex, high-dimensional data – e. g., climate analysis. Consequently, a significant goal of NLP research has been to address the demanding task of developing technologies that "understand language." In this chapter, we have studied an influential technique called single value decomposition. Truly, this is one of the goals of this chapter, illustrating the skills and knowledge required to build convenient NLP systems. It helps to build value added to long-term intelligent machines. Machines will work towards node classification, recommendation, link prediction, feature extraction and visualization.

4.7 CASE STUDY: NEO4J LAB IMPLEMENTATIONS

Two prototypes have been implemented by Neo4j [6] – DeepWalk and DeepGL:

1. DeepGL is more similar to a "hand-crafted" embedding.
2. Use graph algorithms to generate features.
3. Diffusion of values across edges, dimensionality reduction.

Python is easy to get started with for experimentation, but doesn't perform at scale.

REFERENCES

1. S. Bird, E. Klein, and E. Loper, *Natural Language Processing with Python*. O'Reilly Media, Inc. (2009).
2. Y. Goldberg, *Neural Network Methods in Natural Language Processing. (Synthesis Lectures on Human Language Technologies)*. Morgan & Claypool Publishers (2017).
3. https://dictionary.cambridge.org/dictionary/english/zebra (Retrieved on 6 March 2022)
4. R. Kibble, *Introduction to Natural Language Processing*. University of London International Programmes (2013).
5. https://www.kaggle.com/alincijov/nlp-starter-continuous-bag-of-words-cbow (Retrieved on 6 March 2022)
6. https://www.youtube.com/watch?v=oQPCxwmBiWo (Retrieved on 6 March 2022)
7. M. Naili, A. H. Chaibi, and H. H. Ben Ghezala, *Comparative study of word embedding methods in topic segmentation. Procedia Computer Science*, vol. 112, pp. 340–349, (2017).
8. D. Suleiman, and A. Awajan, *Bag-of-concept based keyword extraction from Arabic documents*, in 8th International Conference on Information Technology (ICIT), Amman, Jordan, pp. 863–869 (2017).

9. D. Suleiman, and A. Awajan, *Comparative study of word embeddings models and their usage in Arabic language applications.* 19th *International Arab Conference on Information Technology (ACIT)*, pp. 95–101, (2018).
10. M. Khosla, V. Setty, and A. Anand, *A Comparative Study for Unsupervised Network Representation Learning*, 6, pp. 1–1211 (2020).
11. Z. Chen, Y. Wang, B. Zhao, J. Cheng, X. Zhao, and Z. Duan, Knowledge graph completion: A review. *IEEE Access*, 8, 192435–192456 (2020).
12. Y.-J. Zhang, K.-C. Yang, and F. Radicchi, Systematic comparison of graph embedding methods in practical tasks. *Physical Review E* 104(4), 044315 2021).

5 Natural Language Processing with Graph and Machine Learning Algorithms-based Large-scale Text Document Summarization and Its Applications

Shaikh Ashfaq Amir, Pathan Mohd. Shafi, Vinod V. Kimbahune, and Vijaykumar S. Bidve

CONTENTS

DOI: 10.1201/9781003272649-5

5.1 INTRODUCTION

The growing amount of information available on the internet has led to an overload of text information. Researchers working on simple methods to provide accurate and precise summaries of large documents have considered various approaches to deal with the problem, and natural language processing (NLP) along with the graph data approach can provide one of the most efficient methods. Machine learning (ML)-based approaches increase the accuracy of the summarization process. The main idea is to take a document in the form of a PDF, Word document, PowerPoint presentation, images, etc. and convert it into graph data. The algorithm will then extract the meanings from the graphical information using various approaches, such as calculating the ranks of the nodes. The system will keep improving its training so that the accuracy of the summary improves. Python-based libraries can be used to read the data, and it can be converted into a Neo4j graph database or MongoDB text documents to provide the sources the Python code will use to summarize the document.

NLP and graph-based summarization of large documents use unsupervised machine learning algorithms to convert the data into graph format. Once a graph is constructed, the weight of edges is determined to extract the meaningful sentences from the document. The important challenge here is that the system needs to identify the relationships in the sentences and assign accurate values to each edge. Once the data has been represented as a graph using ML approaches, the document summary can be constructed and displayed to users as an output [1].

Some of the standard graph-based approaches to text summarization include:

1. Page Rank – this very well known algorithm was developed by Google to determine the interconnectivity of web pages with similar content.
2. LexRank – this method uses term frequency-inverse document frequency TF-IDF models and cosine similarity.
3. TextRank – This is similar to LexRank, in addition to normalization of data.

5.1.1 Types of Text Summary

The choice of text summarization approach can be based on various parameters, such as the number of documents, their type, or their purpose. Graph-based machine learning approaches provide effective solutions. Figure 5.1 shows different types of text summarization.

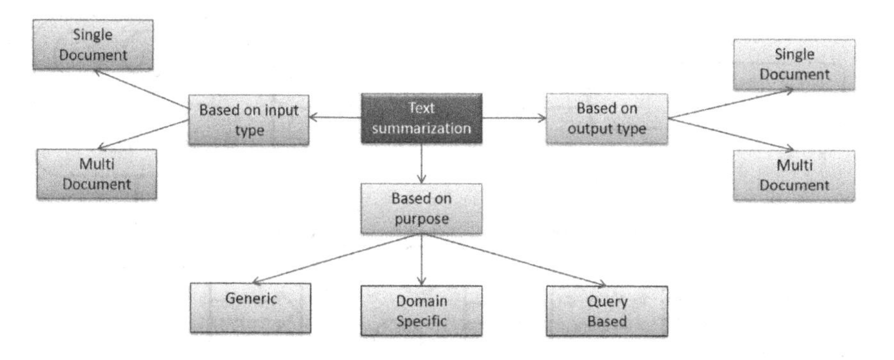

FIGURE 5.1 Types of text summary

5.2 TEXT SUMMARIZATION AND MACHINE LEARNING

Text summarization extracts the important information from large documents or collections of documents so that time can be saved. There are several ways to extract document summaries. Natural language processing using Python libraries like NLTK provides a simple extraction process.

5.2.1 What Is Graph ML?

The concept of applying machine learning to graph data is fundamental to the use of ML algorithms with graph data. Traditional algorithms that use graph-based models include PageRank, shortest path, and click identification. The problem is to convert large amounts of text data into some graph format and to store and process that graph. NoSQL database systems like Neo4j may help in this process. We can convert document text into graphs using Neo4j, but major challenges in the process include:

- How to tabularize the data (e.g., how to convert text information into node lists, how to work on node-edge-node triples) using traditional ML approaches such as linear regression and feed-forward networks
- How to construct graphs from large data sources, as the data need to be represented in the form of edges and nodes
- How to process the data for the text summarization task
- How to manage the image and table dataset in the summarization process
- How to manage and process large datasets
- How to implement ML algorithms to achieve accurate summaries

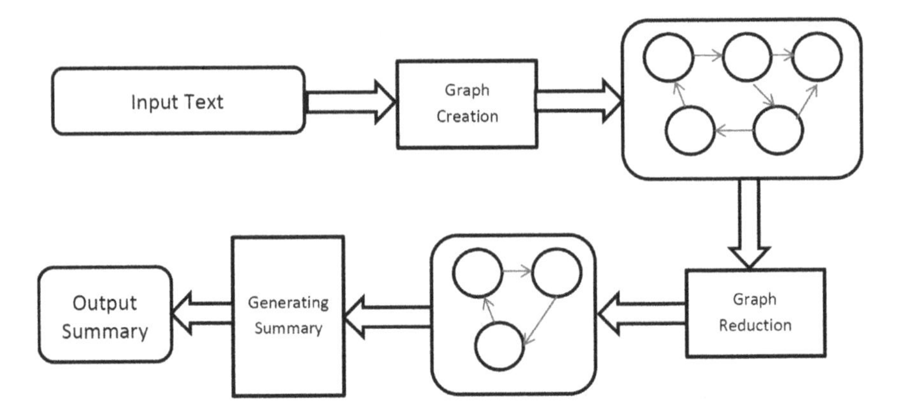

FIGURE 5.2 Simple algorithmic approach

5.2.2 Simple Algorithmic Approach

Figure 5.2 shows the simple algorithmic approach to problem-solving. In this approach, a text document is converted into graph nodes and edges, and once the relationships between them have been analyzed, and a weight can be assigned to each of them to determine their importance.

To implement the system, the data need to be pre-processed so that an accurate graph can be constructed and the meaning of the text preserved. The first step in most systems is to remove stopwords. Once this has been done, the next question is how to construct the graph. One approach is to represent verbs and nouns in the form of nodes and edges in the graph.

5.3 LITERATURE SURVEY

Kadriua and Obradovic proposed a graph-based extractive approach for summarization using edit distances and sentence overlaps to calculate sentence similarity [2]. Chen and Zhuge proposed a multi-model text and image summarization method using the DailyMain dataset and demonstrated how summarization can be achieved with text and images [3]. Krishnaveni and Balasundaram proposed a learning materials multi-document summarization method using the Dynamic Summary Generation Algorithm to provide a system learners could use for revision [4]. Moawad and Aref proposed a novel approach to summarizing single documents using a rich semantic graph reducing technique to summarize the input document's semantic graph and then generate an abstractive summary from the reduced graph. Using this approach, they showed that summarized document with 50% reduction could be achieved [5]. Lloret and Palomar conducted a literature review of human language technologies in text summarization, including how users can benefit and extract important relevant facts from large text documents [6]. Hovy and Lin proposed a system architecture for text summarization using equation summarization for topic identification, interpretation, and generation [7].

Awasthi et al. proposed several methods of text summarization, the main ones being extractive and abstractive methods which analyze text in an effective way so that the summary is less repetitive and more meaningful [8].

Nenkova and McKeown proposed an ML-based text summarization method where scoring for importance was based on the topic and other parameters [9]. Gambhir and Gupta proposed various approaches for text summarization, including automatic and human text summarization [10, 11]. Thakkar, Dharaskar, and Chandak proposed unsupervised graph-based summarization methods for automatic sentence extraction using graph-based ranking algorithms and a shortest path algorithm. [12] Bhandari et al. proposed an evaluation method for text summarization [13, 14]. Nallapati et al. proposed methods such as modeling keywords, capturing the hierarchy of sentence-to-word structure, and omitting words that are rare or unseen at training time to achieve document summary [15, 16].

5.3.1 Gap Analysis

Various text analysis techniques for summarization of large documents use NLP. The main problem with the work done to date is that all the techniques focus mainly on single documents. Multi-document summary with a high degree of accuracy presents particular challenges. Document summaries collected from various sources can be analyzed to arrive at a powerful text analysis. Most of the techniques proposed also do not address the fundamental challenge of the accuracy of the summary in terms of the points extracted from large documents and the fact that Images and tables are not addressed during the summarization process. There is therefore a need to handle images and tables in large texts, which can contribute to creating accurate summaries.

5.4 PROBLEM STATEMENT

In the case of large collections of text documents with other data embedded in them such as images and tables, there is a need to summarize them while extracting the meaningful information. NLP techniques with graph-based approaches can be used to address this problem. The proposed system can be used in e-learning, in e-newspapers, where news summaries need be extracted, and many more application areas.

5.5 SYSTEM ARCHITECTURE

Figure 5.3 shows a typical text summarization system architecture. The system takes documents from various sources, and then applies graph techniques with machine learning to produce accurate summaries. Tools like Neo4j can be used for data modeling, and once the database is constructed using machine learning, the large document text can be summarized.

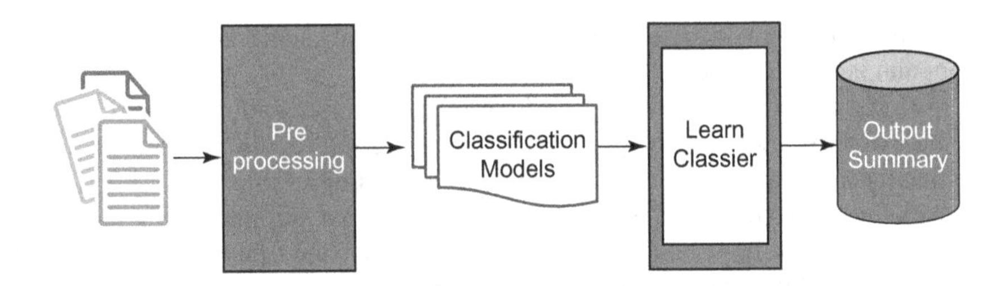

FIGURE 5.3 Architecture text summarization

5.6 GRAPH-BASED SOLUTIONS

Graph-based approaches provide a very different way to represent data using technologies like the NoSQL graph database Neo4j. The resulting graph data can then be processed using ML algorithms with weight graphs to produce highly accurate document summaries.

Text summarization results are presented as graphs in which the weight graph algorithm can identify the meaningful sentences to arrive at a detailed summary. The summary data can then be examined at any level with the help of the weight graph.

There are several ways to construct graphs for text sentences. The simple steps shown in Figure 5.4 consider how weights are assigned in a simple sentence to extract meaningful information from the text.

Figure 5.4 shows a simple approach to construct a redundant graph for each module of sentences. Initially, verbs and nouns can be used to define edges and

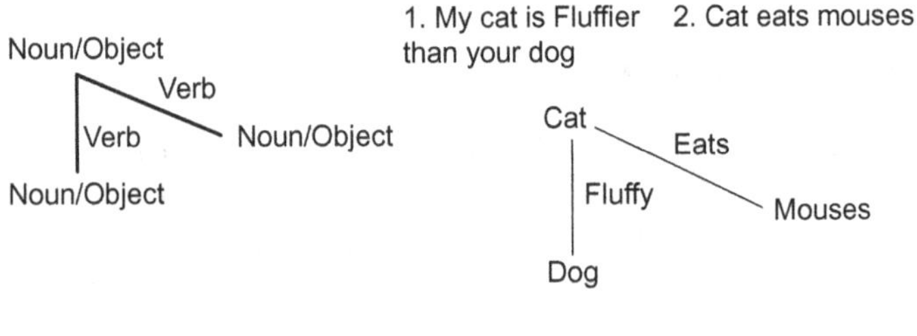

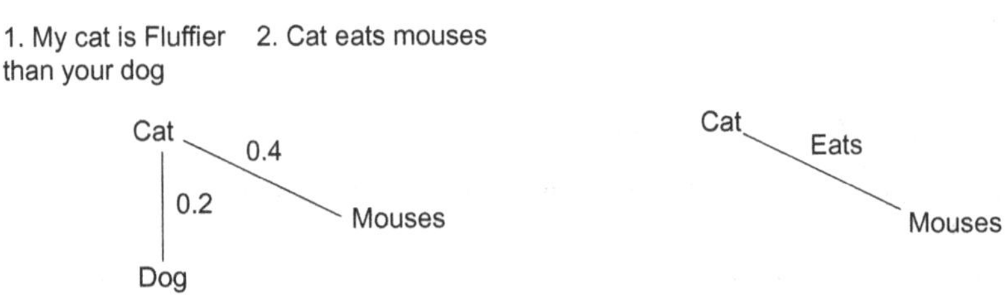

FIGURE 5.4 Graph construction from text

nodes of the graph, then the graph can be reduced by mapping the predicate to the argument. Special care needs to be taken so that the meaning of the sentence is preserved. We can then normalize the data using simple log-transformation, as shown in Figure 5.4:

$$\text{Normalization} = \log\left(\text{length}\left[\text{words 1}\right]\right) + \log\left(\text{length}\left[\text{words 2}\right]\right)$$

where words1 and words2 are the set of words in any sentence sentence1 and sentence2 respectively.

This example shows a procedure for producing a simple abstractive summary from the text in the form of a graph. However, we can use a variety of approaches to construct a graph from a large text and display it in the form of nodes and edges. A NoSQL database like Neo4j can be used for this purpose.

5.7 CONCLUSION

This chapter has explored the summarization of lengthy and multiple text documents. An integrated approach using NLP-based text summarization and graph-based algorithms can be used to provide detailed summaries of large multi-text documents for use in various application areas, such as learning, research, and corporate meeting summarization. Large documents can easily be condensed without compromising their meanings. The Sumy automatic extractive summary utility uses a variety of algorithms to summarize text documents, including LexRank, Luhn, Latent Semantic Analysis LSA, TextRank, and SumBasic. We have proposed a simple architecture for document summarization using NLP and graph methods along with machine learning algorithms to increase accuracy.

REFERENCES

1. Andhale, N., & Bewoor, L. A. (2016, August). An overview of text summarization techniques. In 2016 International Conference on Computing Communication Control and Automation (ICCUBEA) (pp. 1–7). IEEE.
2. Kadriu, K., & Obradovic, M. (2021). Extractive approach for text summarisation using graphs. *arXiv preprint arXiv:2106.10955.*
3. Chen, J., & Zhuge, H. (2018, September). Extractive text-image summarization using multi-modal RNN. In 2018 14th International Conference on Semantics, Knowledge and Grids (SKG) (pp. 245–248). IEEE.
4. Krishnaveni, P., & Balasundaram, S. R. (2021). Summarizing learning materials using graph based multi-document summarization. *International Journal of Web-Based Learning and Teaching Technologies (IJWLTT)*, 16(5), 39–57.
5. Moawad, I. F., & Aref, M. (2012, November). Semantic graph reduction approach for abstractive text summarization. In 2012 Seventh International Conference on Computer Engineering & Systems (ICCES) (pp. 132–138). IEEE.
6. Lloret, E., & Palomar, M. (2012). Text summarisation in progress: A literature review. *Artificial Intelligence Review*, 37(1), 1–41.
7. Hovy, E., & Lin, C. Y. (1999). Automated text summarization in SUMMARIST. *Advances in Automatic Text Summarization*, 14, 81–94.

8. Awasthi, I., Gupta, K., Bhogal, P. S., Anand, S. S., & Soni, P. K. (2021, January). Natural language processing (NLP) based text summarization: A survey. In 2021 6th International Conference on Inventive Computation Technologies (ICICT) (pp. 1310–1317). IEEE.
9. Nenkova, A., & McKeown, K. (2012). A survey of text summarization techniques. In *Mining Text Data* (pp. 43–76). Springer.
10. Gambhir, M., & Gupta, V. (2017). Recent automatic text summarization techniques: A survey. *Artificial Intelligence Review*, 47(1), 1–66.
11. Thakkar, K. S., Dharaskar, R. V., & Chandak, M. B. (2010, November). Graph-based algorithms for text summarization. In 2010 3rd International Conference on Emerging Trends in Engineering and Technology (pp. 516–519). IEEE.
12. Bhandari, M., Gour, P., Ashfaq, A., Liu, P., & Neubig, G. (2020). Re-evaluating evaluation in text summarization. *arXiv preprint arXiv:2010.07100.*
13. Nallapati, R., Zhou, B., Gulcehre, C., & Xiang, B. (2016). Abstractive text summarization using sequence-to-sequence rnns and beyond. *arXiv preprint arXiv:1602.06023.*
14. Erkan, G., & Radev, D. R. (2004). Lexrank: Graph-based lexical centrality as salience in text summarization. *Journal of Artificial Intelligence Research, 22,* 457–479.
15. Yousefi-Azar, M., & Hamey, L. (2017). Text summarization using unsupervised deep learning. *Expert Systems with Applications, 68,* 93–105.
16. Abualigah, L., Bashabsheh, M. Q., Alabool, H., & Shehab, M. (2020). Text summarization: A brief review. *Recent Advances in NLP: The Case of Arabic Language,* 1–15. DOI: 10.1007/978-3-030-34614-0_1.

6 Ontology and Knowledge Graphs for Semantic Analysis in Natural Language Processing

Ujwala Bharambe, Chhaya Narvekar, and Prakash Andugula

CONTENTS

DOI: 10.1201/9781003272649-6

6.1 INTRODUCTION

The scope of natural language goes beyond human communication. Across human history, it has been used to preserve cultural achievements and as a medium to pass on to future generations. Natural language processing (NLP) facilitates tools and techniques to translate human-understandable language into machine-understandable forms in order to perform tasks. NLP is defined as "a theoretically motivated range of computational techniques for analysing and representing naturally occurring texts at one or more levels of linguistic analysis for the purpose of achieving human-like language processing for a range of tasks or applications" (Liddy, 2001). NLP involves interaction with intelligent systems based on the semantics of natural language. NLP helps processing systems to decipher quantitative meaning from human language. Examples of NLP systems in everyday life include Facebook Messenger and Skype Translator, and interaction through personal voice assistants such as Siri, Google Now and Microsoft Cortana. Research in NLP has led to the use of statistical methods (e.g., machine learning [ML] and data mining) that has paved the way to exciting new directions in traditional artificial intelligence (AI). The problem of how to represent language semantics in a manner that can be processed by computers is one of the primary issues in AI research (attempting to give machines the ability to understand natural language). Semantic representation of natural language information (Helbig, 2006) is relevant for knowledge representation in developing querying and machine translation systems. To understand the semantics of natural languages in general, it is necessary to understand that the term "language" has more than one meaning, and understand each meaning in its context.

6.2 BACKGROUND

With the growing availability of interconnected data, we are witnessing an upsurge in NLP tools and applications such as word sense disambiguation, entity recognition, part of speech (POS) tagging, text classification, morphological analysis, relationship extraction, and sentiment analysis (Jurafsky et al., 2012). The availability of vast volumes of qualitative background knowledge about semantic technology helps to enhance the quality of NLP tools. Semantic representation and semantic analysis are two aspects which deal with representation of language structure and deciphering the meaning in such a representation, respectively.

6.2.1 SEMANTICS IN NLP

"Semantics" refers to the analysis of natural language text as it relates to the concept of meaning, taking into account the deep understanding of entities. It is the study of the meaning of *natural language expressions*. Traditionally, meaning has been associated with definition, intention, and reference (Jurasfsky et al., 2012): meaning implies defining an entity in a sentence, intention corresponds to describing the state of action of the subject, and reference specifies an equivalent relationship with the object in a sentence. Two important aspects of semantics in natural language are describing semantic representation with natural language, and using semantic representations to draw inferences. Semantic expression or language is expressed by denotation and connotation: in denotation, the original meaning can be found in a dictionary, whereas in connotation, meaning is implied by describing certain characteristics which are not to be found in a dictionary, but are inferred from the structure of the sentence. This process can be divided into two steps: (1) the study of individual words (lexical semantics), and (2) the study of combinations of words which are associated with the meaning of the sentence. The basis for semantic understanding is representing the meaning of expressed statements.

6.2.1.1 Meaning Representation

There are formal structures to identify the meaning of expressions. The idea is to capture specific aspects of a sentence in order to infer the meaning of the statement. To identify the meaning semantically, in general the following aspects are identified: meanings of words, knowledge of the discourse, context, and commonsense knowledge (Tiwary et al., 2008). The process of creating and assigning representations to linguistic inputs is called *semantic analysis* (Jurasfsky et al., 2012). The most important aspect of semantic analysis is meaning representation. There are certain characteristics which are considered for meaning representations. The characteristics include verifiability, unambiguity, canonical form, inference, variables, and expressiveness (Tiwary et al., 2008). Each of the characteristics has a distinctive function in representation of meaning:

(1) Verifiability – Meaning representation must be verifiable – i.e., the truth of the representation must be determinable. This could be achieved by comparing the meaning representation of the input with a repository of facts existing in a domain (i.e., representation in a knowledge base). Verifiability is the system's ability to compare the input representation to the situation that exists in the world as modeled in the knowledge base.
(2) Unambiguity – The second criterion of a meaning representation language is that needs to be unambiguous – i.e., it should enable only one possible interpretation. Ambiguity can be divided into two categories. The first is the semantic ambiguity that is inherent in language. The second is representational ambiguity, which is created by misunderstandings of the representation scheme. A related term is vagueness, which is not always distinguishable from ambiguity. A representation needs to be able to express different levels of vagueness. It is quite common for NLP to be vague due to a lack of precision.
(3) Canonical form – Multiple representations of some set of words (e.g., "Does Air India offer a flight to Mumbai?" and "Does Air India have a flight to Mumbai?") may have the same meaning. This leads to

inconsistencies and an issue with matching. The goal is for inputs that have the same meaning to be represented in the same way. The usage of canonical form is therefore required.

(4) Inference and variables – We can derive new facts that logically follow the known facts from a set of facts about the world in the knowledge base and an input representation. The ability of a system to make appropriate inferences based on the meaning representation of inputs and representation of facts in its knowledge base is referred to as *inference.* Additionally, variables should be allowed in meaningful representation languages.

(5) Expressiveness – Natural language encompasses a wide range of topics. A meaning representation language must be able to represent the meaning of a variety of types of topic. As a result, in order to be useful, a meaning representation language must be able to convey itself.

In order to address the above criteria, predicate argument structures (subject-object predicate, triple structure) are used for representation of meaning in languages. For example, "book on the table" represents a relationship between "book" and "the table" expressed though the preposition "on." The meaning representation of this phrase is expressed as on (book, table). Any language for representing meaning must be able to represent predicate argument structure. It must support the encoding of predicate argument structure with a variable number of predicates, the semantic labeling of arguments to predicates, and semantic restrictions placed on those arguments (Tiwary et al., 2008). All conventional AI meaning representation languages, such as first-order predicate calculus, semantic networks, and conceptual graphs, support the representation of argument structure. These languages serve as the foundation for ontological languages like the Resource Description Framework (RDF) and Web Ontology Language (OWL), which follow the predicate argument structure and are verifiable, unambiguous, cannibalistic, and expressive.

6.2.2 Semantic Analysis in Natural Language Processing

Semantic analysis is a branch of NLP concerned with deciphering the meaning of natural language. To us as humans, understanding natural language may appear to be a simple procedure. However, deciphering human language is a difficult challenge for machines due to the tremendous intricacy and subjectivity involved. Semantic analysis of natural language captures the meaning of a document by considering context, logical sentence structure, and grammar roles.

The semantic investigation of normal language content begins by perusing every one of the words in the content to capture the genuine significance of any text. It recognizes the text components and assigns to them to their linguistic roles. It dissects the setting of the encompassing text and investigates the text's construction to precisely disambiguate the appropriate importance of words that have more than one definition. Generally, semantic analysis in natural language processing is divided in two parts:

1. Lexical semantic analysis – This involves understanding the meaning of each lexical item (word, phrasal verb, etc.) in a text. It basically refers to fetching the dictionary meaning that a word in the text is deputed to carry.
2. Compositional semantic analysis – Although knowing the meaning of each word in a text is important, understanding the meaning of the text in its entirety is not. As a result, we strive to comprehend how individual words combine to generate the meaning of the text via compositional semantic analysis. Both lexical and compositional semantic can be supported by semantic technology, but the technology has a greater utility for compositional semantics, which is quite complex.

One of the aspects of understanding NLP is to exploit the use of semantic understanding of language which corresponds to meaning representation and deciphering the meaning.

6.3 SEMANTIC TECHNOLOGIES

Semantic technologies employ formal semantics to assist AI systems in comprehending and processing information in the same way that humans do. As a result, they can store, organize, and retrieve data based on its meaning and logical relationships (Ontotext, 2020). Semantic technologies have gained popularity in recent years, and have attracted the interest of academics. Moreover, these technologies have become a critical enabler for innovation and change in e-commerce, geo-informatics, education, e-government, agriculture, healthcare, and social networks, to name but a few domains. Semantic technologies differ fundamentally from other data technologies such as relational databases because they focus on the meaning of data rather than its structure.

Ontologies, for example, which are a key component of the semantic web, have been effectively used to create or improve systems that deal with knowledge-based tasks and processes. Moreover, ontologies for interoperability and model-based systems can address the current lack of common understanding among systems and applications. World Wide Web Consortium (W3C) ontologies are among the building blocks of the semantic web as part of its standards. In this way, users can connect one piece of data to another on the web of linked data. An ontology enables database interoperability, querying across databases, and integrating knowledge from remote and heterogeneous sources by specifying standard models for expressing data from disparate systems and databases.

So how might NLP improvements be applied to semantic technologies in practical terms? The answer is that a mixture of them can be employed in any application that deals with a lot of unstructured data, especially if dealing with related, ordered data stored in regular datasets. Obviously, the most important example at this stage is to use NLP to extract organized textual data. These data are then linked to past information in datasets and elsewhere using semantic advancements, removing any barriers between records and formal, ordered data.

6.3.1 Ontology Essentials

During the development of artificial intelligence, ontologies were created to facilitate the sharing and reuse of knowledge. Several AI research communities, including knowledge engineering, natural language processing, and knowledge representation, have been studying ontologies since the 1990s. Over the past few years, ontologies have been gaining popularity in the fields of intelligence retrieval, natural language processing, and knowledge management. Ontologies provide a common understanding of a domain that can be shared between people and systems. In addition to quantifiers, negations, intersections, and inconsistent knowledge, ontologies model several complex forms of knowledge.

Ontologies have been defined in a number of ways over the past decade, but one that most closely aligns with the essence of ontology is the following: "An Ontology is a formal explicit specification of shared conceptualization" (Gruber, 1993). A "conceptualization" is an abstract representation of some phenomenon in the world that identifies the relevant concept of that phenomenon. "Explicit" means that the types of concepts and constraints on their use are explicitly defined. The term "formal" describes the ontology as having a machine-readable format, which results in varying degrees of formality. "Shared" refers to the idea that ontology captures consensus knowledge – i.e., it does not belong exclusively to a particular individual, but is accepted by a group.

DEFINITION 1

According to Euzenat et al. (2007), for general purposes ontologies can be divided into subsets represented as a four-tuple $O = (C, P, I, T, L)$, where O refers to the *ontology*, C means the *concepts/classes* within the ontology, I means the actual *individual* instances of these classes, L means *literals*, the concrete data values, T stands for *types*, which are possible values, and P stands for *properties*, or definitions of possible relationships between instances, called object properties, or between one instance and a literal, called datatype properties. Four specific relations form part of an ontology: (1) specialization or subsumption ($\leq$), exclusion or disjointness ($\perp$), instantiation or membership ($\in$); and assignment (=). The main reasons for developing an ontology are to share a common understanding of the structure of information among people or software agents to enable reuse of domain knowledge. Ontology is generally used for information retrieval and extraction, knowledge reuse, knowledge interchange, knowledge integration, and knowledge representation.

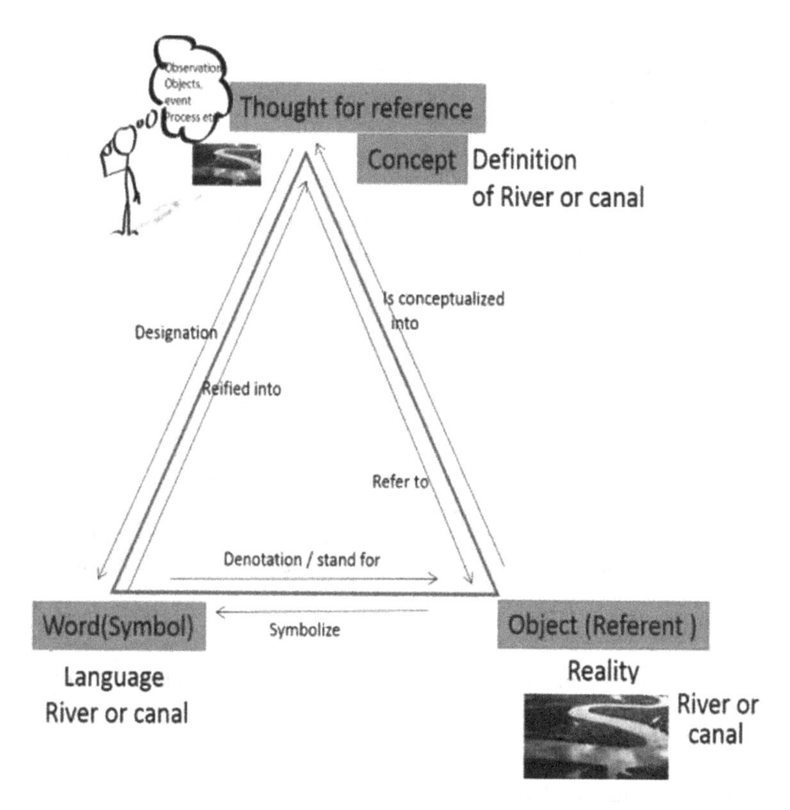

FIGURE 6.1 The ontology semiotic triangle (Ogden et al., 1925) – Ullmann's Triangle: the relations between a thing in reality, its conceptualization, and a symbolic representation of this conceptualization

The study of how things gain or convey meaning is *semiotics*. The semiotic triangle defined by Ogden et al. (1925) is composed of concept, symbol, and referent. A referent is conceptualized into a concept which is expressed as a symbol. The symbol designates the concept which refers to the referent (as explained in Figure 6.1). Ogden's triangle (a.k.a. Ullman's triangle) provides the philosophical base for conceptualizing ontology construction.

6.3.2 Formalization of an Ontology

In principle, an ontology may be described in any language, but in order to share, exchange, and map ontologies, a formal language must be chosen. The use of natural language alone is not sufficient for this as it leaves a significant amount of interpretation to the user, which means that significant aspects of the ontology may be missed. This issue can be resolved and the knowledge can be made automatically processable by a machine by expressing it as simply as possible in an adequate format. Several syntactic and semantic languages have

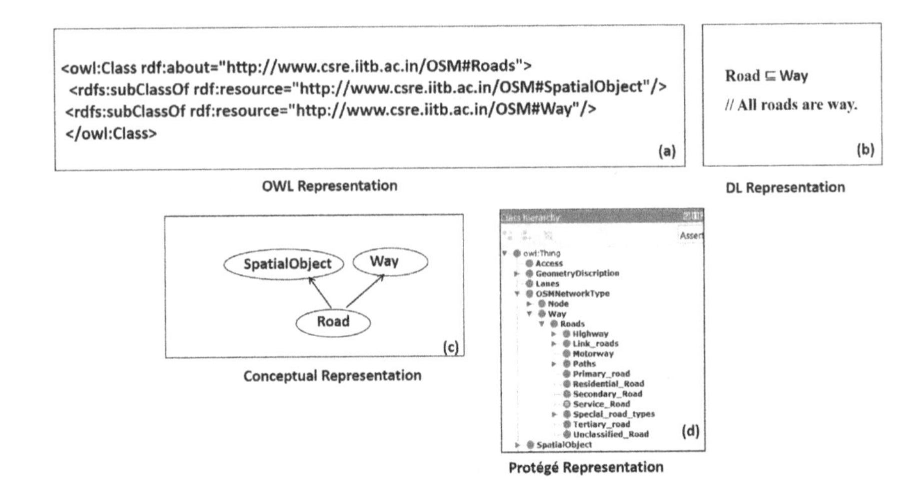

FIGURE 6.2 An example of ontology representation of road network: (a) OWL representation, (b) description logic representation, (c) conceptual representation, and (d) protégé representation

been developed and standardized for this purpose, such as RDF and OWL (see Figure 6.2).

6.3.3 Description Logics

A family of formal knowledge representation languages is known as description logics (DLs). A description logic is set of formal logic-based knowledge representation formalisms aimed at describing domain-specific knowledge in a structured and well-understood manner. In artificial intelligence, DLs are used to characterize and reason about the relevant concepts in a domain (known as terminological knowledge). Each description logic describes a language, and each language differs in expressibility versus reasoning complexity, defined by allowing or disallowing different constructs (conjunction, disjunction, negation, quantifiers, etc.) in their language. A description logic is the result of the merging of two traditions: knowledge representation and automated reasoning. Arvor et al. (2013) stated: "Description Logic allows the formal representation of knowledge by modeling the interrelationships among subject (Concept), predicate (Property) and object (Concept, Property) as axioms." Description logic and first-order logic are also comprised of two parts: the logical part that is core of the language, and the non-logical part pertaining to the domain.

The architecture of a knowledge base system based on description logics is shown in Figure 6.3. It provides facilities to set up knowledge bases, to reason about their content, and to manipulate them. A knowledge base comprises two components: the TBOX and the ABOX. The TBOX introduces the terminology

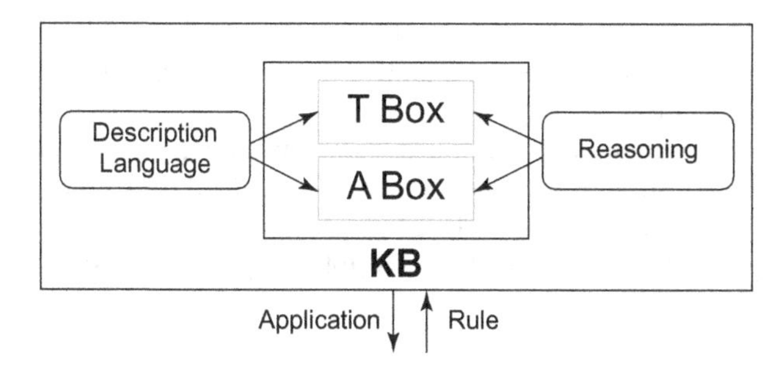

FIGURE 6.3 Architecture of a knowledge representation system based on description logics. Adapted from Baader and Nutt (2003)

– i.e., the vocabulary of an application domain – while the ABOX contains assertions about named individuals in terms of this vocabulary.

6.3.4 Ontological Languages

Even though an ontology in principle is independent of a particular language, it is necessary to choose a language to describe it. This language needs to be formal in order to share, exchange, and map ontologies (Figure 6.4).

6.3.5 Knowledge Graphs

A knowledge graph (KG) is network of interconnected descriptions of entities, whether they are physical objects or abstract concepts. In a network of entity descriptions, each entity is a part of the description of the entities related to it,

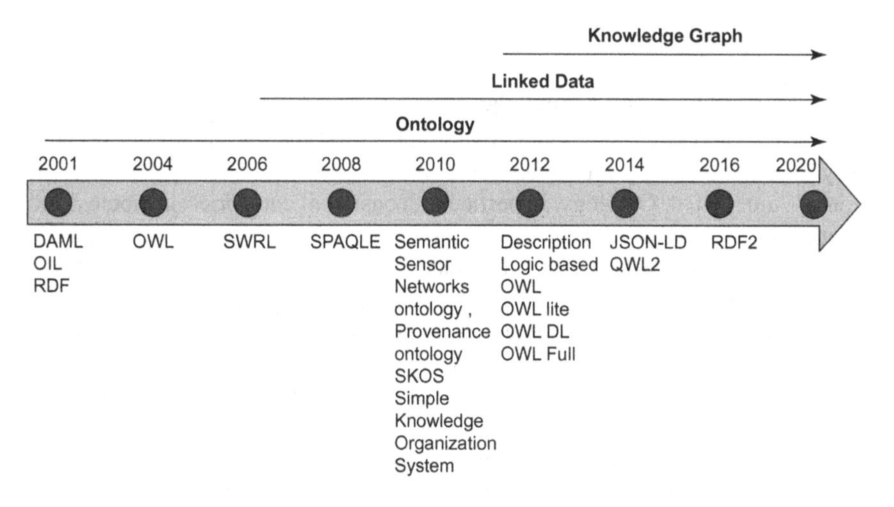

FIGURE 6.4 Timeline of semantic technologies

providing context for all of their interpretations. Descriptions have formal semantics that allow both humans and computers to process them in an efficient and unambiguous manner.

Furthermore, a knowledge graph is dynamic, meaning it may make new conclusions and reconstruct itself when new data are added over time. As a result, unlike traditional methods, a knowledge graph is neither inert nor requires manual updating. Knowledge graphs have the following characteristics (Elnagar et al., 2022):

- A KG has interrelationship.
- A KG uses techniques to extract knowledge from some source.
- There may be a schema that defines classes and relations.
- The KG supports various types of graph processing.
- A reasoner can be used to infer new facts.

DEFINITION 2

A knowledge graph G consists of schema graph Gs, a data graph G_d, and the relations R between Gs and G_d, denoted as $G = <Gs, G_d, R>$. The schema graph $Gs = <Ns, Ps\ Es>$, where Ns is a set of nodes representing classes (concepts), Ps is a set of nodes representing properties, and Es is a set of edges representing the relationships between classes in the graph Gs $E_s \subseteq N_s \times P_s \times N_s$. $G_d = <N_d, P_d, E_d>$ is a data graph in which N_d is a set of nodes stand for instances and literals, P_d is a set of nodes representing properties, and E_d is a set of edges representing the relationships between nodes in the graph G_d. Each edge (subject, predicate, object) represents the fact. N_d includes two disjoint parts: instances (N_i) and literals (Elnagar et al., 2022).

6.3.5.1 Ontology and Knowledge Graphs

The terms "ontology" and "knowledge graph" are sometimes confused because they both communicate information in a similar way by illustrating how its components are related. Ontology, in particular, consists of categories, attributes, and relationships between concepts, data, and entities. Subgraphs, properties, relationships, data, and vertices are all included in knowledge graphs (nodes). There is, however, a significant difference between them. A knowledge graph is a graph-based representation of knowledge that frequently comes from a graph database, which is a database that stores data using a graph architecture (CodeX, 2021).

Knowledge graphs combine features of several data management concepts (Ontotext, 2020): (i) structured queries can be used to explore the data in a *database*; (ii) because they can be analyzed like any other network data structure, they're called *graphs*; (iii) because they have formal semantics, *knowledge bases* can be utilized to interpret data and infer new facts.

The knowledge graphs represented in RDF are the most effective framework for linking, integrating, and reusing data because they combine expressivity: RDF(S) and OWL, two semantic web standards, support the expressive representation of numerous types of data and content, including data structure, taxonomies, and vocabularies, various types of metadata, reference data, and master data.

In terms of performance, specifications have been developed, and proven in practice, to enable the efficient management of graphs with billions of facts and properties.

In terms of interoperability, the Semantic Query Language for Databases (SPARQL) lays out a wide range of specifications for managing data, accessing data (SPARQL Protocol), and federating data (SPARQL Graph Store). By using globally unique identifiers (uniform resource identifier [URIs]), data integration and publishing can be facilitated.

In terms of standardization, to ensure that all the above requirements are met, the Open Web Platform for application development W3C community process is used.

6.3.5.2 Property Graphs

A property graph is a kind of graph model in which associations have a name (type) and some qualities in addition to being connections. Property graphs excel at demonstrating links between data in various data architectures and data formats. A property graph can be described as follows: (i) it has directed (edges have source and target vertices); (ii) it is vertex-labeled (for some kind of "label"); (iii) it is edge-labeled (for some kind of "label"); (iv) it is multi-graph (several versions of the exact same edge may exist); (v) it has self-loops (vertices can have edges to themselves), and (vii) it has sets of attribute-value pairs associated with any vertex or edge.

DEFINITION 3

A property graph is defined as the tuple $G = (V, E, L, P, U, e, l, p)$, where V is a set of nodes *id*, E is set of edge *id*, L is a set of labels, P is a set of properties, U is a set of values, e: $E \rightarrow V \times V$ maps an edge *id* to a pair of node *ids*, $V \cup E \rightarrow 2^L$ maps a node or edge *id* to a set of labels, and p: $V \cup E \rightarrow 2^{P \times U}$ maps a node or edge *id* to a set of property value pairs s (Hogan et al., 2020).

The approach of mapping a relational schema from an entity relationship diagram is analogous to using an ontology to generate a property graph schema. To do this, all concepts in the ontology must be mapped to a schema node, and all relationships must be mapped to schema edges. Because of its speed in graph traversal, data storage mechanism efficiency, and versatility in modeling domains, the labeled property graphs data model is widely used for encoding data into knowledge graphs. Real-time queries, in particular those in the context of knowledge graphs, can be extremely resource-intensive. Labeled property graphs are a way of speeding up analytical procedures on large graphs. Property graphs, also known as labeled graphs, use a property value structure that corresponds to things and describes them in a minimal fashion. The terms "edges" and "nodes" are used in this type of graph to describe interrelationships. Although both property and semantic graphs have directed labeled edges, only some property graphs allow annotations to be applied to the label.

6.3.5.3 Comparison of KGs, PGs, and Ontologies

Ontologies are known for representing domain knowledge, whereas KGs are domain-independent methodologies for knowledge representation (see Table 6.1). As a result, the number of instances statements in KGs is far higher than the

TABLE 6.1
Differentiation between Ontologies, Knowledge Graphs, and Property Graphs

Criteria	Ontologies	Knowledge Graphs	Property Graphs
Assumption	CWA (closed-world assumption)	OWA (open-world assumption)	OWA (open-world assumption)
Scope	Domain-specific	Problem-specific	Problem Specific
Size	Relatively small	Massive	Massive
Scalability	Limited scalability	Very scalable	Very Scalable
Real-time	Limited real-time capabilities	Can be generated in real time	Can be generated in real time
Generation	Mostly by humans	Automatic	Automatic
Trustworthiness	Trustworthy	Not trustworthy	Not trustworthy*
Knowledge base type	More TBOX than ABOX	More ABOX than TBOX	More ABOX than TBOX
Language	RDF, RDF3, OWL	Mostly RDF,	Neo4j graphs
Quality in terms of correctness and completeness	High quality	Questionable	Questionable
Agility	Static	Dynamic	Dynamic
Redundancy	Not likely	Very likely	Very likely
Maintenance	Burdensome	Challenging	Challenging
Security	Reasonable	Questionable	Questionable
Relevancy	High	Low	Low
Interoperability	High	Low	Low

* https://ontotext.com, https://handle.net, https://iswc2016.semanticweb.org

number of schema level statements. Knowledge graphs emphasize the instance level (ABOX) more than the concept level (TBOX). There is a greater importance to the instance (ABOX) level of knowledge graphs than the concept (TBOX) level of knowledge graphs. While ontologies are concerned with creating schematic taxonomies of concepts and relations for a specific domain, the KG schema is rather shallow, with only a minimal degree of formalization and no hierarchical structure. Because most ontology revisions are done manually by domain experts (Galkin et al., 2017), the ontology may be incomplete at times. KGs, on the other hand, are created in real time and include current data. For various reasons, KGs are very likely to evolve: KGs represent dynamic resources, and the graphs as a whole can change or disappear. On the other hand, in order to evolve, ontologies necessitate domain expert engagement, which is often an expensive and difficult process.

6.4 THE ROLE OF ONTOLOGY AND KNOWLEDGE GRAPHS IN SEMANTIC ANALYSIS

The heart of semantic technology is made up of two components. The first is based on knowledge representation and reasoning research conducted by AI in the 1970s and 1980s, and includes ontology representation languages such as RDF and OWL and inference engines such as Fact++, Pellet, and Racer. The second is based on data representation and querying with triple stores, RDF and SPARQL, which has little to do with AI. A broad definition of semantic technology encompasses a wide range of AI-based technologies. Figure 6.5 represents the intersection of AI, NLP, and semantic technologies.

Over the past decade, the science of NLP has progressed to the point that robust and scalable applications are now available in a range of fields, and current semantic web efforts are well positioned to take advantage of this advancement.

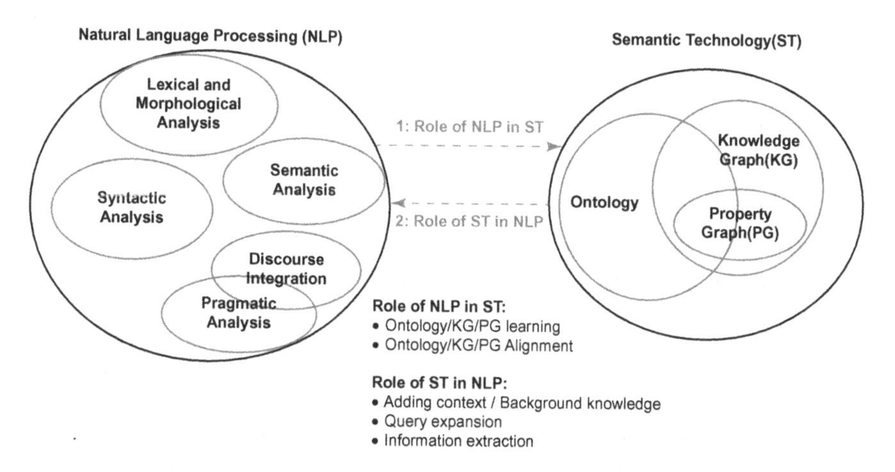

FIGURE 6.5 Relationship between natural language processing and semantic technology

While NLP experts have begun to recognize and exploit the technology's potential for providing semantics, the growth in semantic technology necessitates that experts from various domains (e.g., law, finance, agriculture, health, biology) develop their own domain-specific tools for quickly acquiring semantics for their particular domain. NLP covers a wide range of activities, from simple tasks like segmenting text into sentences and words to more advanced applications like semantic annotation and opinion mining, question answering, sentiment analysis, document analysis, information extraction, text mining, and machine translation. It is semantic technology that adds meaning, making it easier for machines to process and manipulate data. In NLP, semantics can be added to data, for instance by automatically identifying entities and relations and by recognizing which real-world entities are referenced so that URIs can be assigned to each.

The role of semantic technology can be viewed from two perspectives. First, semantic technology is used for addressing standard NLP tasks such as named entity recognition, POS tagging, machine translation, and question answering. Second, NLP is used for creating ontologies and knowledge graphs (Erekhinskaya et al., 2020). Also, the usage of semantic technology in NLP applications can be divided into two categories, first is knowledge-based NLP which doesn't include machine learning methods and the latter is called machine learning NLP demonstrating the use of AI approaches to NLP (see Table 6.2).

6.4.1 The Role of Semantic Technology in Knowledge-based NLP Applications

Traditional knowledge-based methodologies are still widely used. These methods work well when the task is easy to specify. Ontology is primarily used for sharing and reusing data, and to provide a link between user and information by logical abstraction of data and by providing notions and relationships to enable users to develop and refine their queries. Ontology has also been employed in inference mechanisms in information retrieval systems, referred to as intelligent

TABLE 6.2
Differentiation between Knowledge-based NLP Applications and ML-based Applications

Knowledge-based NLP Applications	ML NLP Applications
Based on hand-coded rules	Use statistics or other machine learning techniques
Developed by NLP specialists	Developers do not need NLP expertise
Make use of human intuition	Require large amounts of training data
Easy-to-understand results	Causes of errors are hard to understand
Development can be very time-consuming	Development is quick and easy
Changes may require rewriting rules	Changes may require re-annotation

information retrieval. Ontology's contribution to knowledge-based systems can be summarized as: (i) query expansion, (ii) information abstraction, (iii) semantic formalization, and (iv) natural language understanding (Dan et al., 2006).

1. *Query expansion* – Since traditional queries are only keywords and do not specify user intentions, ontologies have been widely used to address this problem.
2. *Information abstraction* – Ontology encodes information in terms of definitions, categorizations, hierarchy, relations, and properties. This allows for the understanding and abstraction of information by domain experts.
3. *Semantic formalization* allows for the creation of a logical, coherent representation of the conceptual structure, resulting in a computer interpretation and making it easier to understand the sort of relationship that exists between two or more concepts. Through the semantic formalization of the conceptual structure, ontology gives a clear declaration of the conceptual relationships within a particular field in the process of developing an information retrieval system.
4. *Natural language understanding* – Ontology aids in the interpretation of user requirements and their mapping to information resources. It infers the meaning of an idea by comparing the logic structures of other conceptions (Dan et al., 2006). For example, if one of the prerequisites of being concept A is that concept B is an instance of concept A, ontology can reason that concept B is an instance of concept A, and then concept B is automatically placed under concept A (Krippendorff et al., 1989). When a user's query is in the form of natural language, the information retrieval system splits the question into terms that appear in the domain ontology, in addition to NLP.

6.4.2 The Role of Semantic Technology Machine Learning NLP Applications

Figure 6.6 depicts the general architecture of an ontology-based machine learning model for NLP. It takes text as an input and pre-processes it using basic NLP approaches before applying parsing. Ontology/knowledge graph aids the ML model. Ontologies provide background knowledge that can be employed in ML models for at least two purposes: expanding or enriching the features that are used, and constraining the search for the best solution to a learning issue. Expanding or enriching features may provide knowledge to an ML model that it would not otherwise have access to without the use of ontologies. For example, the knowledge in ontologies can also be used to confine the search for solutions to optimization problems in an ML model, allowing a better solution to be found more quickly or in more generalized terms. Ontology/knowledge graph and deep learning approaches are combined to form a new technology. For example, Wang et al. (2020b) proposed K-ADAPTER, which keeps the original parameters of a

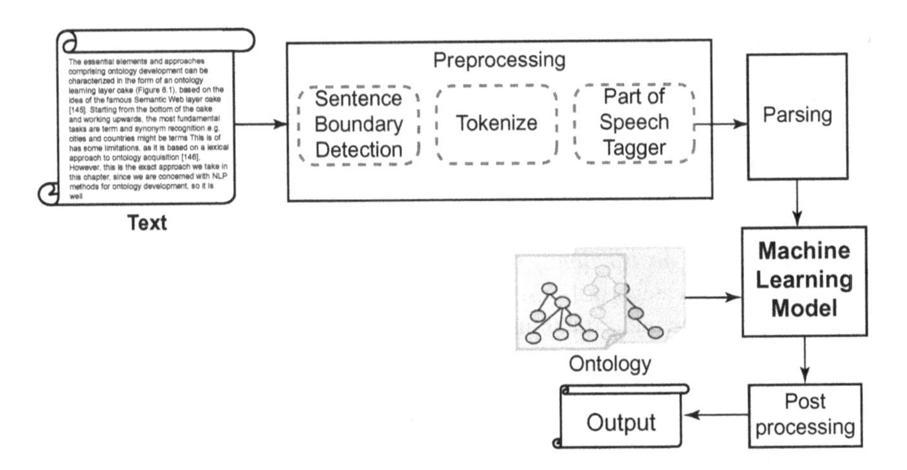

FIGURE 6.6 General architecture of an ontology-based machine learning model for NLP applications

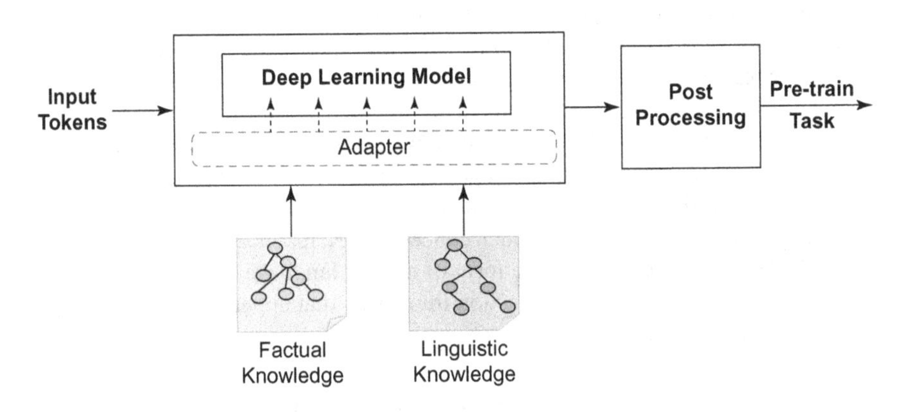

FIGURE 6.7 The K-ADAPTER method in knowledge infusion techniques

pre-trained model fixed while supporting knowledge infusion (see Figure 6.7). This proposal introduced two types of knowledge: factual knowledge from Wikipedia and Wikidata's automatically aligned text triplets, and linguistic knowledge via dependency parsing.

6.4.3 The Role of Natural Language Processing in Ontology Generation

Ontology generation refers to the task of constructing an ontology from scratch, which involves defining concepts and establishing relevant relationships among them. Based on the ideas of Berners-Lee (1999), the main aspects and methodologies that comprise ontology development can be characterized in the form of

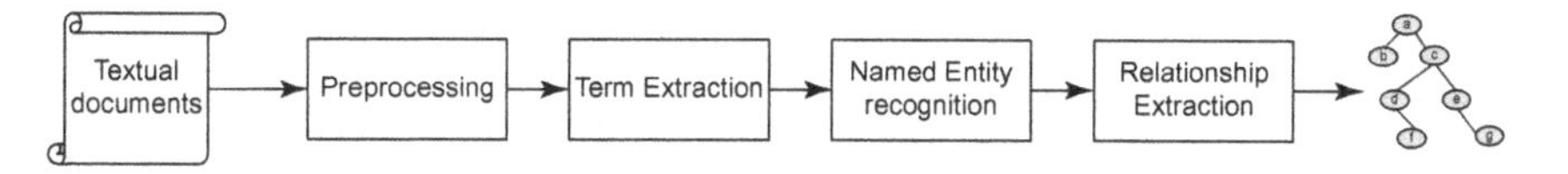

FIGURE 6.8 Automated ontology generation system

an ontology learning layer cake. The most basic tasks, starting at the bottom and working up the cake, are term and synonym recognition – e.g., cities and countries could be terms. Concepts, classes, and relationships (properties) are involved at the subsequent levels, – e.g., cities belong to countries, some cities are capital cities, and countries have capital cities. Finally, axioms such as disjointness are at the very top (something cannot be both a river and a mountain).

The first phase of the automated ontology generation system is data cleaning, where NLP pre-processing tasks such as sentence splitting, tokenization, stopword removal, lemmatization, POS tagging, and noun phrase chunking are performed. Following that, several term extraction methods are used, and named entities are extracted for concept selection (nodes). Text relations are extracted to represent properties in an ontology and edges in a knowledge graph (an example is shown in Figure 6.8). Wang et al. (2020a) demonstrated how to use pre-trained language models (e.g., Bidirectional Encoder Representations from Transformers [BERT]; Generative Pre-Trained [GPT-2/3]) to generate KGs without human supervision. Popular KGs are developed in supervised or semi-supervised settings and require humans in order to learn. Recent deep language models use pre-training to automatically acquire knowledge from large-scale corpora. The language models have been able to improve downstream NLP tasks, such as answering queries and creating code and articles, thanks to the stored information.

6.5 REVIEW OF DEVELOPMENTS IN ONTOLOGICAL SEMANTIC ANALYSIS

We can observe from a survey of semantic technology from 2015 to 2022 (see Table 6.3), that knowledge graphs play an important role in text analytics due to their potential to locate facts and comprehend their meaning, adding context, efficient querying, and explainability. KGs have been shown to be more effective at revealing higher-order interdependencies in unstructured data. Knowledge representation refers to the way in which information is modeled such that a computer program can access it autonomously to accomplish complex tasks (Opdahl et al., 2020)]. Querying such knowledge graphs necessitates specialist knowledge of query languages like SPARQL as well as a thorough comprehension of the graphs' underlying structure (Liang et al., 2021). Chen et al. (2021) illustrated a systematic review of topic analysis and development in knowledge graph research as well as different applications of knowledge graphs such as link prediction, recommendation, natural language processing, question answering, knowledge management, and entity linking. Maulud et al. (2021) provided a detailed survey

TABLE 6.3
Comparison of Semantic Analysis-based Techniques Applied in the Literature from 2015 to 2021

Authors	Techniques	Goals of Work	Technology/Tools Utilized in Research	Remarks
Lovera et al. (2021)	Knowledge graphs and description logic	Sentiment analysis	Long- and Short-term Memory, knowledge graphs, sentiment	Illustrated the traceability and explainability of the classification
Abu-Salih et al., 2021	Ontology, Knowledge graphs, social big data analytics	Semantic analysis to obtain better understanding of social content	IBM Watson Natural Language Understanding	Semantic analysis in the context of politics presented and evaluated
Dessì et al., 2021	Knowledge graphs	To represent the knowledge of scientific publications as structured graphs	NLP/ML	Automatically produced good-quality scientific knowledge graphs
Alam et al., 2021	Knowledge raphs	To develop knowledge-based algorithms for labelling semantic roles from a text	Framester, FrameNet, VerbNet, Stanford CoreNLP	Compared TakeFive performance with SRL (self-regulated learning) tools SEMAFOR, FRED, Pikes
Xin Xu et al. (2021)	NLP based on ontologies and rules	To make the interpretation of utility laws more automated	User profile ontology, social ontology	Framework tested on the spatial configuration only
Tang et al. (2021)	Knowledge graphs	To develop intelligent question answering in power systems	Intelligent question answering framework, POWER KG	Intelligent question answering evaluated in an experimental environment and compared with an expert system

(*Continued*)

TABLE 6.3 (CONTINUED)
Comparison of Semantic Analysis-based Techniques Applied in the Literature from 2015 to 2021

Authors	Techniques	Goals of Work	Technology/Tools Utilized in Research	Remarks
Ilievski et al. (2021)	Knowledge graphs	To develop reasoning with commonsense knowledge graphs	ConceptNet, ATOMIC, Wikidata, WordNet, Roget, FrameNet	Commonsense knowledge graph applied commonsense reasoning, such as question answering, resulting in improved performance.
Logan IV et al. (2021)	Knowledge graphs	To evaluate behavior using commonsense knowledge graphs	RoBERTa-large, BERT-large, ATOMIC, PIQA, ConceptNet	Created test cases for inference and commonsense question answering as these are most critical in natural language understanding
Zafar et al. (2020)	Knowledge graphs	SQA (Software Quality Assurance) with intended semantic queries with interaction	LC-QuAD, interactive question answering –option gain, interactive question answering –information gain	Interactive question answering based on the option gain, leading to better satisfaction compared to interactive question answering with information gain
Zhuang et al. (2020)	Ontology building	To develop aspect-based sentiment analysis with semi-automated ontology building	Two-stage hybrid model	Ontology built for the restaurant and laptop domains
García-Díaz et al. (2020)	Ontology and description logic	To develop sentiment analysis based on aspects pertaining to infectious diseases	Word embeddings and linguistic features used in deep learning	Evaluated sentiments about infectious diseases like zika and chikungunya in Latin America in texts written in Spanish with aspects extracted from a domain ontology

(Continued)

TABLE 6.3 (CONTINUED)
Comparison of Semantic Analysis-based Techniques Applied in the Literature from 2015 to 2021

Authors	Techniques	Goals of Work	Technology/Tools Utilized in Research	Remarks
Ahmadnia et al. (2020)	Machine translation, knowledge graphs	To retain source-language semantic relations in target-language translations	Freebase, OpenNMT	Evaluated a method for English–Spanish translation, with promising results
Dörpinghaus et al. (2019)	Knowledge graphs	To use context data for knowledge expression and extraction	Bayesian Ontology Language	Tested biomedical knowledge graphs using various data as contexts to each other
Gunasekara et al. (2019)	Text generation	To reduce the computational cost of using semantic natural language production in chatbots.	OWL with natural language understanding	Used OWL verbalizers and an application programming interface-based approach to generate text responses for chatbots
Cavar et al. (2018)	Deep NLP, knowledge graphs	To provide linguistically informed, detailed analyses of case law	Partial Directed Acyclic Graph, PACER	Mapped case law documents, opinions and the holding, to KGs, allowing users to search documents via graph similarity
Atzeni et al. (2018)	Translation using ontology	To translate natural language commands to object-oriented source code	RDF dataset, OpenJDK, CodeOntology	Translated NLP commands to Java code

(*Continued*)

TABLE 6.3 (CONTINUED)
Comparison of Semantic Analysis-based Techniques Applied in the Literature from 2015 to 2021

Authors	Techniques	Goals of Work	Technology/Tools Utilized in Research	Remarks
Okba et al. (2017)	Ontology	To develop semantic machine translation to translate a given text from a source language to another	OWL-XML	Evaluated English–French disambiguation based on semantic interpretation
Hixon Ben et al. (2015)	Knowledge graphs	To develop knowledge acquisition from conversations and dialogs	WordNet, KNowBot, Pesticide Properties DataBase PPDB,	KNOWBOT learned helpful, task-driven relationships from dialogs
Rehman et al. (2015)	Ontology	To facilitate teaching and learning of NLP.	Protégé	Helped teachers to concentrate on a specific problem and domain knowledge in detail
Ismail (2015)	Ontology and rich semantic graphs	To generate Arabic text from rich semantic graphs using ontology	Arabic domain ontology	Used rich semantic graphs in abstractive text summarization for Arabic text

of semantic analysis in NLP. Gesese et al. (2021) presented a comprehensive survey of KG embedding models with literals with various applications of KGs in the area of AI. KGs can be used to support decision-making processes and to improve machine learning applications such as question answering, recommender systems, and relation extraction. Franco et al. (2020) presented a systematic survey of intelligent question answering using ontology. We can observe a surge in commonsense reasoning, labeling semantic roles, and sentiment analysis using knowledge graph natural language generation approaches in 2020–2021 due to their capability to turn data into intelligence. Semantic analysis is chiefly used for translation, intelligent question answering, aspect-based sentiment analysis, ontology generation, labeling semantic roles, knowledge expression and extraction, KG embedding, and dialog systems.

6.6 SUMMARY

This chapter has attempted to address aspects of natural language processing, semantic analysis, semantic technology, ontology and languages of ontology. Furthermore, difference between knowledge graph and property graph are explained. This chapter presents the significant roles of ontologies, knowledge graphs in natural language processing. We have examined numerous applications that use ontology for NLP. We have found that using ontologies to drive a succession of NLP applications that are all based on the same knowledge domain or similar ones is incredibly advantageous because it keeps the applications in sync. Moreover, ontologies provide an additional benefit of having multiple layers of representation, which can streamline the application of NLP to similar problems.

REFERENCES

Abu-Salih, B., Wongthongtham, P., Zhu, D., Chan, K. Y., & Rudra, A. (2021). Semantic data discovery from social big data. In *Social Big Data Analytics* (pp. 89–112). Springer. https://doi.org/10.1007/978-981-33-6652-7_4

Ahmadnia, B., Dorr, B. J., & Kordjamshidi, P. (2020). Knowledge graphs effectiveness in neural machine translation improvement. *Computer Science*, 21(3). (pp. 89–112). https://doi.org/10.7494/csci.2020.21.3.3701

Alam, M., Gangemi, A., Presutti, V., & Reforgiato Recupero, D. (2021). Semantic role labeling for knowledge graph extraction from text. *Progress in Artificial Intelligence*, 10(3), 309–320.

Atzeni, M., & Atzori, M. (2018). Translating natural language to code: an unsupervised ontology-based approach. In 2018 IEEE First International Conference on Artificial Intelligence and Knowledge Engineering (AIKE) (pp. 1–8). IEEE. 26–28 September 2018, Laguna Hills, California, USA. https://doi.org/10.1109/aike.2018.00009

Arvor, D., Durieux, L., Andrés, S., & Laporte, M. A. (2013). Advances in geographic object-based image analysis with ontologies: A review of main contributions and limitations from a remote sensing perspective. *ISPRS Journal of Photogrammetry and Remote Sensing*, 82, 125–137. https://doi.org/10.1016/j.isprsjprs.2013.05.003

Baader, F., & Nutt, W. (2003). Basic description logics. In *The Description Logic Handbook: Theory, Implementation, and Applications* (pp. 43–95). Cambridge University Press, New York, NY.

Berners-Lee, T., Connolly, D., & Swick, R. R. (1999). Web architecture: Describing and exchanging data. *W3C Nota*, 7, 7.

Cavar, D., Herring, J., & Meyer, A. (2018). Case law analysis using deep NLP and knowledge graphs. In Proceedings of the LREC. Miyazaki, Japan.

Chen, X., Xie, H., Li, Z., & Cheng, G. (2021). Topic analysis and development in knowledge graph research: A bibliometric review on three decades. *Neurocomputing*, 461, 497–515. https://doi.org/10.1016/j.neucom.2021.02.098.

CodeX (2021). Understanding Ontologies and Knowledge Graphs. https://medium.com/codex/understanding-ontologies-and-knowledge-graphs-4664afc4f961.

Dan, W.U., & Hui-lin, W.A.N.G. (2006). Role of ontology in information retrieval. *Journal of Electronic Science and Technology*, 4(2), 148–154.

Dessì, D., Osborne, F., Recupero, D. R., Buscaldi, D., & Motta, E. (2021). Generating knowledge graphs by employing natural language processing and machine learning techniques within the scholarly domain. *Future Generation Computer Systems*, 116, 253–264.

Dörpinghaus, J., & Stefan, A. (2019). Knowledge extraction and applications utilizing context data in knowledge graphs. In 2019 Federated Conference on Computer Science and Information Systems (FedCSIS) (pp. 265–272). IEEE. Leipzig University, Leipzig, Germany. https://doi.org/10.15439/2019f3

Elnagar, S., Yoon, V., & Thomas, M. A. (2022). An automatic ontology generation framework with an organizational perspective. *arXiv preprint arXiv:2201.05910.*

Erekhinskaya, T., Strebkov, D., Patel, S., Balakrishna, M., Tatu, M. and Moldovan, D. (2020). June. Ten ways of leveraging ontologies for natural language processing and its enterprise applications. In Proceedings of the International Workshop on Semantic Big Data (pp. 1–6). Portland, Oregon. https://doi.org/10.1145/3391274.3393639

Euzenat, J. and Shvaiko, P. (2007). *Ontology Matching* (Vol. 18). Springer. https://doi.org/10.1007/978-3-540-49612-0

Franco, W., Avila, C. V. S., Oliveira, A., Maia, G., Brayner, A., Vidal, V. M. P., & Pequeno, V. M. (2020). Ontology-based question answering systems over knowledge bases: A survey. In *ICEIS* Vol. 1, pp. (532–539). SCITEPRESS. ISBN 978-989-758-423-7.

Galkin, M., Auer, S., Vidal, M.E. and Scerri, S. (2017). Enterprise knowledge graphs: A semantic approach for knowledge management in the next generation of enterprise information systems. In *ICEIS* (Vol. 2, pp. 88–98). SciTePress. ISBN 978-989-758-248-6. https://doi.org/10.5220/0006325200880098

García-Díaz, J. A., Cánovas-García, M., & Valencia-García, R. (2020). Ontology-driven aspect-based sentiment analysis classification: An infodemiological case study regarding infectious diseases in Latin America. *Future Generation Computer Systems*, 112, 641–657. https://doi.org/10.1016/j.future.2020.06.019

Gesese, G. A., Biswas, R., Alam, M., & Sack, H. (2021). A survey on knowledge graph embeddings with literals: Which model links better literal-ly?. *Semantic Web*, 12(4), 617–647. https://doi.org/10.3233/sw-200404

Gruber, T.R. (1993). A translation approach to portable ontology specifications. *Knowledge Acquisition*, 5(2), 199–220. https://doi.org/10.1006/knac.1993.1008

Gunasekara, L., & Vidanage, K. (2019). UniOntBot: Semantic natural language generation based API approach for chatbot communication. In 2019 National Information Technology Conference (NITC) (pp. 1–8). IEEE. Colombo, Sri Lanka. https://doi.org/10.1109/nitc48475.2019.9114440

Helbig, H. (2006). *Knowledge Representation and the Semantics of Natural Language.* Springer.

Hixon, B., Clark, P., & Hajishirzi, H. (2015). Learning knowledge graphs for question answering through conversational dialog. In Proceedings of the 2015 Conference of the North American Chapter of the Association for Computational Linguistics: Human Language Technologies (pp. 851–861). Denver, Colorado, USA. https://doi.org/10.3115/v1/n15-1086

Hogan, A. (2020, June). Knowledge graphs: Research directions. In *Reasoning Web International Summer School* (pp. 223–253). Springer.

Ilievski, F., Szekely, P., & Zhang, B. (2021). Cskg: The commonsense knowledge graph. In European Semantic Web Conference (pp. 680–696). Springer. https://doi.org/10.1007/978-3-030-77385-4_41

Ismail, S. S., Aref, M., & Moawad, I. F. (2015). A model for generating Arabic text from semantic representation. In 2015 11th International Computer Engineering Conference (ICENCO) (pp. 117–122). IEEE. https://doi.org/10.1109/icenco.2015.7416335

Jurafsky, D., & Manning, C. (2012). Natural language processing. *Instructor*, 212(998), 3482.

Krippendorff, K., Barnouw, E., Gerbner, G., Schramm, W., Worth, T. L., & Gross, L. (1989). International encyclopedia of communication. In *Content Analysis: An Introduction to Its Methodology* (Vol. 1, pp. 403–407). Oxford University Press, New York, NY.

Liang, S., Stockinger, K., de Farias, T. M., Anisimova, M., & Gil, M. (2021). Querying knowledge graphs in natural language. *Journal of Big Data*, 8(1), 1–23. https://doi.org/10.1186/s40537-020-00383-w

Liddy, E. D. (2001). *Natural Language Processing.* In Encyclopedia of Library and Information Science, 2nd Ed. Marcel Decker, Inc, New York.

Logan, IV, Y. R. R. L., & Singh, S. (2021). *Deriving Behavioral Tests from Common Sense Knowledge Graphs.* Association for the Advancement of Artificial Intelligence.

Lovera, F. A., Cardinale, Y., Buscaldi, D., Charnois, T., & Homsi, M. N. (2021). *Deep Learning Enhanced with Graph Knowledge for Sentiment Analysis.* In DeepOntoNLP/X-SENTIMENT@ ESWC, CEUR Workshop Proceedings, Hersonissos, Greece.

Maulud, D. H., Zeebaree, S. R., Jacksi, K., Sadeeq, M. A. M., & Sharif, K. H. (2021). State of art for semantic analysis of natural language processing. *Qubahan Academic Journal*, 1(2), 21–28.

Ogden, C. K., & Richards, I. A. (1925). *The Meaning of Meaning: A Study of the Influence of Language Upon Thought and of the Science of Symbolism* (Vol. 29). Brace. https://doi.org/10.1038/111566b0

Okba, K., Hamza, S., Hind, B., Amira, A., & Samir, B. (2017). Semantic natural language translation based on ontologies combination. In 2017 8th International Conference on Information Technology (ICIT) (pp. 315–321). IEEE. https://doi.org/10.1109/icitech.2017.8080019

Ontotext (2020) What Is Semantic Technology? www.ontotext.com/knowledgehub/fundamentals/semantic-web-technology/.

Opdahl, A. L. (2020). Knowledge graphs and natural-language processing. In *Big Data in Emergency Management: Exploitation Techniques for Social and Mobile Data* (pp. 75–91). Springer.

Rehman, Z., & Kifor, S. (2015). Teaching natural language processing (NLP) using ontology based education design. In Balkan Region Conference on Engineering and Business Education (Vol. 1, No. 1, pp. 206–214). Lucian Blaga University of Sibiu, Romania. https://doi.org/10.1515/cplbu-2015-0024

Tang, Y., Han, H., Yu, X., Zhao, J., Liu, G., & Wei, L. (2021). An intelligent question answering system based on power knowledge graph. In 2021 IEEE Power & Energy Society General Meeting (PESGM). https://doi.org/10.1109/pesgm46819.2021.9638018

Tiwary, U. S., & Siddiqui, T. (2008). *Natural Language Processing and Information Retrieval*. Oxford University Press, Inc.

Wang, C., Liu, X., & Song, D. (2020a). Language models are open knowledge graphs. *arXiv preprint arXiv:2010.11967.*

Wang, R., Tang, D., Duan, N., Wei, Z., Huang, X., Cao, G., Jiang, D., & Zhou, M. (2020b). K-adapter: Infusing knowledge into pre-trained models with adapters. *arXiv preprint arXiv:2002.01808.*

Xu, X., & Cai, H. (2021). Ontology and rule-based natural language processing approach for interpreting textual regulations on underground utility infrastructure. *Advanced Engineering Informatics*, 48, 101288. https://doi.org/10.1016/j.aei.2021.101288

Zafar, H., Dubey, M., Lehmann, J., & Demidova, E. (2020). IQA: Interactive query construction in semantic question answering systems. *Journal of Web Semantics*, 64, 100586. https://doi.org/10.1016/j.websem.2020.100586

Zhuang, L., Schouten, K., & Frasincar, F. (2020). SOBA: Semi-automated ontology builder for aspect-based sentiment analysis. *Journal of Web Semantics*, 60, 100544. https://doi.org/10.2139/ssrn.3502455

7 Ontology and Knowledge Graphs for Natural Language Processing

Jayashree Prasad, Rahesha Mulla, Namrata Naikwade, B. Suresh Kumar, and Suresh Shanmugasundaram

CONTENTS

7.1 INTRODUCTION

Artificial intelligence (AI) has become an essential part of our lives, being used in healthcare, automobile, banking and finance, education, social media, etc. It uses machine learning (ML) and natural language processing (NLP). NLP helps to automatically process and analyze meaning in text or audio speech. The use of NLP is growing day by day due to its ability to handle huge, complex, inconsistent data. With explainable artificial intelligence, researchers can develop tests, improve the approaches used to build AI systems and make them more transparent and understandable for system users [1].

DOI: 10.1201/9781003272649-7

Natural language processing is a branch of machine learning that deals with how machines understand human languages. The textual form of language is a widespread problem domain for NLP applications. When working with text data, it is essential to transform the raw text into a form that can be understood and used by ML algorithms. This step is called text pre-processing. Various techniques are involved in pre-processing, including stemming, lemmatization, parts of speech (POS) tagging, and dependency parsing.

7.1.1 Ontology

Ontology in the context of metaphysics is the study of things. An ontology is a set of rules that describe how things work [2]. It involves working with more general questions about what exists in nature. It provides general/formal representation of knowledge within a given subject area, such as philosophy, library science, scientific research, etc., and helps to define structure and relationships between elements. Ontology creation involves POS tagging and phrase chunking to extract terms and noun phrases. However, creating ontologies manually can be difficult and time-consuming [3]. It describes concepts within a particular domain, the relationships between them, and their common properties.

7.1.1.1 The Core Ideas of Ontology

In philosophy, ontology is defined as the study of things in general. It is derived from the Latin word *ontologia*, meaning "science of being," and was coined by the German philosopher Jacob Lorhard (Lorhardus). However, in artificial intelligence, ontology is a description of the semantics of symbols.

Here is some basic terminology used in ontology:

- *Stemming* – In linguistic morphology, stemming is the process of reducing inflected words to their root word, known as a stem. Stemmers or stemming programs are used to perform this task.
- *Lemmatization* – This is a process used to remove inflectional endings [4] by returning to the root of a word, known as a lemma.
- *POS tagging* – This is also known as defining word classes or morphological classes, or lexical tagging to describe the way words are used in a sentence. The main parts of speech are noun (N), verb (V), adjective (ADJ), adverb (ADV), preposition (P), determiner (DET), interjection (INT), pronoun (PRO), and conjunction (CON), as shown in Table 7.1. POS tagging involves assigning appropriate labels to words to resolve lexical ambiguity. A POS-tagged corpus can be used for linguistic observations, as training and testing corpus for automatic POS taggers, and for text cleaning, feature engineering tasks, and word sense disambiguation.
- *Phrase chunking* – Chunking is the process of extracting phrases from unstructured text. Instead of simply using tokens, it is a good way to analyze phrases to derive the actual meaning of the text, such as treating "silver coin" as a single chunk rather than "silver" and "coin" as two

TABLE 7.1
POS Examples

Sr. No.	Parts of Speech	Descriptions	Tags	Examples
1	Noun	Object/entity	N	bottle, car, hat, money, table
2	Verb	Action/activity	V	eat, play, study, work
3	Adjective	An attribute of noun	ADJ	red, slow, short, few
4	Adverb	Qualifier of adjective	ADV	well, softly, beautifully
5	Preposition	Word governing/preceding a noun	P	by, to, of
6	Determiner	Modifier/reference to a noun	DET	a, the, this, that, those
7	Interjection	An abrupt remark	INT	oh, hey, ouch
8	Pronoun	Alternate for a noun	PRO	I, me, mine, myself
9	Conjunction	Connects clauses	CON	although, because, but, besides

separate words. Chunking takes POS tags as input and provides chunks/blocks as output. A standard set of chunk tags are noun phrase (NP), verb phrase (VP), adjective phrase (ADJP), adverb phrase (ADVP), and prepositional phrase (PP). Chunking is very important when we wish to perform entity extraction or entity detection. NP chunking can be used to extract structured data from unstructured data by searching for chunks conforming to individual noun phrases, as follows:

Sentence → NP, P
NP → DET, N (examples: the, gold)
NP → proper noun (example: Smith)
NP → NP, CON, NP (examples: Smith and John, the moon and the sky)
VP → V, NP (example: saw the pineapple)
VP → V, P, NP (example: went to forest, sat on the grass)

Let's take the example sentence "I found the silver coin."

Figure 7.1 depicts segmentation and labeling in the chunking process.

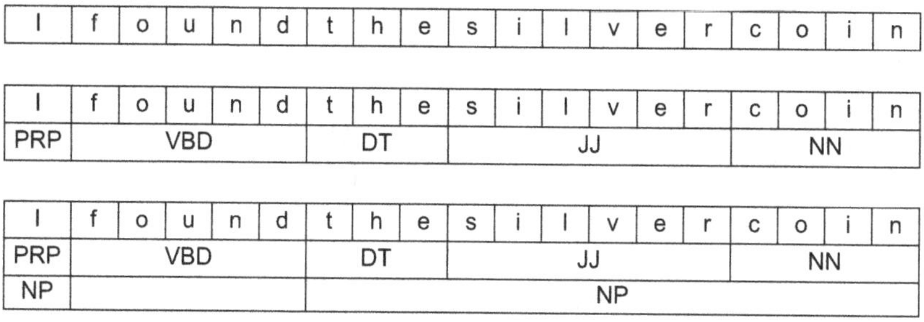

<table>
<tr><td>I</td><td>f</td><td>o</td><td>u</td><td>n</td><td>d</td><td>t</td><td>h</td><td>e</td><td>s</td><td>i</td><td>l</td><td>v</td><td>e</td><td>r</td><td>c</td><td>o</td><td>i</td><td>n</td></tr>
</table>

<table>
<tr><td>I</td><td>f</td><td>o</td><td>u</td><td>n</td><td>d</td><td>t</td><td>h</td><td>e</td><td>s</td><td>i</td><td>l</td><td>v</td><td>e</td><td>r</td><td>c</td><td>o</td><td>i</td><td>n</td></tr>
<tr><td>PRP</td><td colspan="5">VBD</td><td colspan="3">DT</td><td colspan="6">JJ</td><td colspan="4">NN</td></tr>
</table>

<table>
<tr><td>I</td><td>f</td><td>o</td><td>u</td><td>n</td><td>d</td><td>t</td><td>h</td><td>e</td><td>s</td><td>i</td><td>l</td><td>v</td><td>e</td><td>r</td><td>c</td><td>o</td><td>i</td><td>n</td></tr>
<tr><td>PRP</td><td colspan="5">VBD</td><td colspan="3">DT</td><td colspan="6">JJ</td><td colspan="4">NN</td></tr>
<tr><td>NP</td><td colspan="5"></td><td colspan="13">NP</td></tr>
</table>

FIGURE 7.1 Segmentation and labeling in chunking

We can create a chunk parser with grammar specified as: Find DT, followed by JJ and NN,

where DT = optional determiner, JJ = number of adjectives, NN = number of nouns.

In computational linguistics, IOB tags are used to format chunks, where:

I = inside, O = outside, and B = begin
B-NP defines the beginning of a noun phrase.
I-NP defines that the word is inside the current noun phrase.
O defines the end of the sentence.

A major limitation of IOB tagging is that it does not permit any nesting.

The chunk structure that appears in a file with one token per line is:

I PRP B-NP
found VBD O
the DT B-NP
silver JJ I-NP
coin NN I-NP

The tree here is a set of connected nodes that are labeled. Each labeled node is reachable by a unique path from the root.

This representation of chunks with one token per line gives the advantage that being constituent, they can be manipulated effectively.

Figure 7.2 shows the representation of chunks using IOB tags, and Figure 7.3 shows the representation of chunks using trees.

<table>
<tr><td>I</td><td>f</td><td>o</td><td>u</td><td>n</td><td>d</td><td>t</td><td>h</td><td>e</td><td>s</td><td>i</td><td>l</td><td>v</td><td>e</td><td>r</td><td>c</td><td>o</td><td>i</td><td>n</td></tr>
<tr><td>PRP</td><td colspan="5">VBD</td><td colspan="3">DT</td><td colspan="6">JJ</td><td colspan="4">NN</td></tr>
<tr><td>B-NP</td><td colspan="5">O</td><td colspan="3">B-NP</td><td colspan="6">I-NP</td><td colspan="4">I-NP</td></tr>
</table>

FIGURE 7.2 Representation of chunk: tag approach

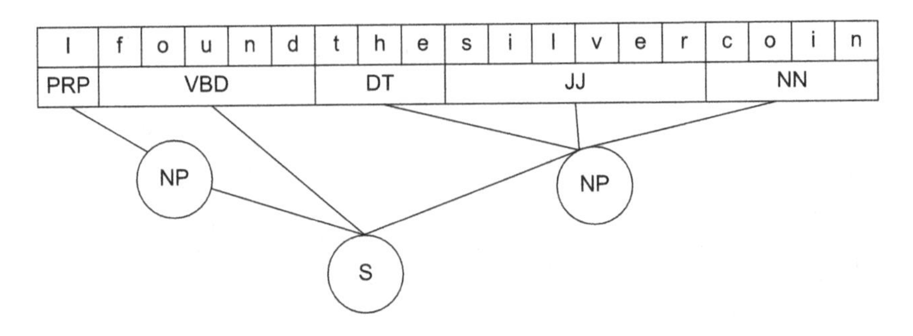

FIGURE 7.3 Representation of chunk: tree structure

TABLE 7.2
Commonly Used Named Entities

Serial No.	Named Entities	Examples
1	Date	Jan., 2022-01-31
2	Time	5.45 p.m.
3	Location	AT & T Bell Lab USA
4	Person	Smith, Robert, Jenny
5	Organization	World Wide Fund for Nature, UNICEF

Named Entity Recognition: Named entity recognition (NER) is the NLP task [5]. Generally, named entities are definite Noun-Phrases (NP). Table 7.2 shows commonly used named entities.

A NE recognition system involves identification of NE boundaries and their types.

In addition, independent sentences in NLP can be referred to as variable terms, aggregation terms, operator expressions, modifier terms, and quantifier phrases [6].

7.2 NATURAL LANGUAGE PROCESSING

Natural language processing is not a recent area of study, but it is getting more attention due to increasing technological involvement, increased human–computer interactions supporting applications with natural languages, and due to the development of big data. Such data demands powerful computing algorithms. NLP uses computers to process natural language in written (text) or spoken (audio) format. NLP has evolved into symbolic NLP, statistical NLP, and natural NLP. NLP is needed in the following situations.

7.2.1 Dealing with Huge Amounts of Unstructured Data

Natural language processing helps computers communicate with humans in their own language and scales other language-related tasks. For example, NLP makes it possible for computers to read text, hear speech, interpret it, measure sentiment, and determine which parts are important.

Today's machines can analyze more language-based data than humans, without fatigue and in a consistent, unbiased way. Considering the staggering amount of unstructured data generated every day, from medical records to social media, automation will be critical to fully analyze text and speech data efficiently.

7.2.2 Structuring Data to Support Intelligent Systems

Human language is highly complex and diverse. There are infinite ways humans express his/her thoughts, emotions. There are a number of languages and language variations (dialects). However, each language follows a particular set of grammar and syntax. Normally, humans make grammatical mistakes in writing or spoken form. Spoken form also inherits words from other languages.

7.2.3 Challenges with NLP

- *Words, phrases and homonyms* – In natural language, the same words and phrases may express different meanings in particular contexts. At the same time, handling homonyms (words that have the same pronunciation but different meanings) are challenging in speech-based applications.
- *Dictionary form/synonyms* – Synonyms also require proper contextual understanding. However, people use synonyms to represent or express different meanings within their own vocabulary. When building an NLP application, we need to incorporate possible meanings for a particular word and its synonyms.
- *Ambiguity* – Ambiguity in NLP refers to sentences and phrases that potentially have two or more possible interpretations. It can be at the lexical level or at the semantic or syntactic level.
- *Erroneous data* – Wrongly spelled, pronounced, or used words affect the performance of text analysis. Although they can be handled and corrected with a spell checker or auto corrector, this will not ensure correct interpretation of the meaning, or intention of a person.
- *Domain-specific language* – Industries use different language forms for communication. A model needed for healthcare would be very different from one used for a student enterprise system. Building models suitable for a particular domain demands in-depth, domain-specific knowledge.
- *Low-resource languages* – Most applications use highly resourced languages with the availability of corpora, lexical information, and higher rates of occurrence on the web, etc. However, the majority of regional languages lack these resources.

Supervised and unsupervised learning with a deep learning approach is used for natural language modeling. The most crucial aspect is syntactic and semantic learning in the context of machine learning approaches. NLP demands large collections of linguistic data known as corpora. A corpus can be defined as a collection of language data. It is composed of written texts, transcriptions of speech, or a combination of speech and transcriptions. According to McEnery [7] corpora fall into three broad categories:

1. *Monolingual corpora* – these consist of data from a single language.
2. *Comparable corpora* – these include a range of monolingual corpora in various languages.
3. *Parallel corpora* – these include original texts in one language with translations of them into one or more different languages.

Data pre-processing is an essential step. It mainly includes data cleaning and data transformation [8]. To process and analyze huge amounts of unstructured corpus data, NLP follows five different stages: lexical analysis, syntax analysis, semantic analysis, disclosure, and pragmatic analysis (see Figure 7.4).

NLP is important because it helps resolve ambiguity in language and adds useful numeric structure to the data for many downstream applications, such as speech recognition or text analytics. Table 7.3 presents machine learning frameworks for NLP.

NLP combines computational linguistics and rule-based models. NLP tasks include:

- *Speech recognition* – This converts voice/speech data into text form. Speech recognition is used in applications that respond to voice-based instructions or questions. What make speech recognition challenging

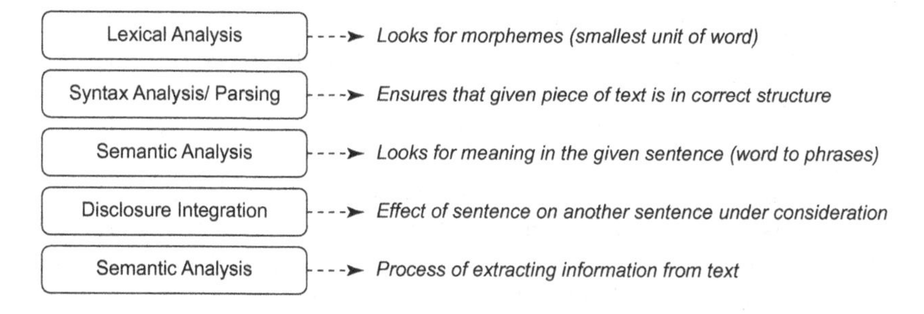

FIGURE 7.4 Stages in NLP

TABLE 7.3
Machine Learning Frameworks for NLP

Serial No.	Frameworks	Notable Applications/Approaches
1	PyTorch	Classification, tagging, and text generation.
2	SpaCy	Named entity recognition
3	Stanford coreNLP	Sentiment analysis, bootstrapped pattern learning
4	TensorFlow	Text processing with tokenization
5	Keras	Deep learning, compatible with both convolutional neural networks and recurrent neural networks
6	Chainer	Supports deep learning and recurrent neural network-based language models
7	Gensim	Sentiment analysis and document modelling, word embedding
8	Sci-Kit Learn	Regression and classification problems, baseline machine learning algorithms

are factors such as speed, pronouncing words together, changes in emphasis and intonation, varying accents, and often improper grammar.
- *Part of speech tagging* – This is the process of determining the part of speech of a specific word or chunk of text, taking into account its use and context.
- *Word sense disambiguation* – This is the selection of the meaning of a word with multiple meanings through a process of semantic analysis that determines the meaning that makes the most sense in a given context. For example, word sense disambiguation helps to distinguish the meanings of the verb "make" in "make the grade" (achieve) versus "make a bet" (place).
- *Named entity recognition* – This identifies words or phrases as useful entities, for example "Kentucky" as a location or "Fred" as a man's name.
- *Coreference resolution* – This is the task of identifying if and when two words refer to the same entity. The most common example is determining the person or object to which a certain pronoun refers (e.g., "she" = "Mary"), but it can also involve identifying a metaphor or an idiom in the text (e.g., an instance in which "bear" isn't an animal, but a large, hairy person).
- *Sentiment analysis* – This extracts subjective qualities from text. NLP relies heavily on sentiment analysis in processing online reviews [9].
- *Text to speech* – This is the opposite of speech recognition, being task of presenting structured information as natural language.
- *Information extraction* – This uses pattern matching rules based on syntactic features and semantic features [10].

Some of the notable advantages and disadvantages of NLP are listed in Table 7.4.

TABLE 7.4
Advantages and Disadvantages of NLP

Advantages	Disadvantages
Using NLP is less expensive and time-efficient than using human resources.	Training can be time-consuming. If a new model needs to be developed without the use of a pre-trained model, it can take weeks before achieving a high level of performance.
NLP offers better customer service in businesses.	
Machine learning-based approaches enable easy use of NLP.	Being dependent on ML, NLP reliability sometimes raises questions.

7.3 ONTOLOGY AND KNOWLEDGE GRAPHS FOR NLP

7.3.1 Ontology

Ontologies are commonly mentioned in the context of knowledge graphs. Ontologies help to formalize the representation of the entities or things in the graph. They can contain multiple taxonomies, each with its own unique definition. Because knowledge graphs and ontologies are represented in a similar way – through nodes and edges – and are based on resource description framework (RDF) triples, they lean toward similar visualizations. The procedure of forming a new ontology or refining an existing one with minimal expert assistance is known as ontology learning [11].

Ontologies are semantic data models that provide descriptions of types and structures of instances/objects. Ontologies are considered as a generalized data model because they work on general types of objects having common properties. The entities are represented by the nodes of the graph, and the relationships are represented by the arcs [12].

There are three main components to an ontology:

- *Classes* – the unique types of things that exist in data.
- *Relationships* – properties that relate two classes.
- *Attributes* – properties that describe an individual class.

A knowledge graph contains facts and explicit knowledge of how instance data relate to each other. Let's consider Tables 7.5, 7.6, and 7.7.

TABLE 7.5
Person

Name	Gender	Age	Address	Mother Tongue	Vaccination
Namrata	Female	23	Maharashtra	Marathi	Yes
Rahesha	Female	31	Karnataka	Kannada	Yes
Jayashree	Female	36	Gujarat	Gujarati	No
Rajesh	Male	40	Uttar Pradesh	Hindi	Yes

TABLE 7.6
Address

State	District	City
Maharashtra	Pune	Kothrud
Karnataka	Belgaum/Belgavi	Karoshi
Gujarat	Ahmedabad	Walsad
Uttar Pradesh	Ayodhya	Rudauli

TABLE 7.7
Vaccination

Vaccination Status	Name of Vaccine	First Dose	Second Dose	Eligible for booster
Yes	Co-vaccine	Yes	No	No
Yes	Co-vaccine	Yes	Yes	Yes
No	Not applicable	No	No	No
Yes	Covi-shield	Yes	Yes	Yes

These are the ontological relationships between the classes person, address, vaccination, and booster:

i. person→has name→person
ii. person→has age→person
iii. person→ has gender→person
iv. person→lives at→address
v. person→knows language→person
vi. address→ located in→address
vii. person→has vaccination→vaccination
viii. vaccination→has name→vaccination
ix. vaccination→is eligible for booster→booster

Figure 7.5 represents an ontology in graph format.

7.3.2 Knowledge Graphs

Knowledge graph is becoming increasingly interesting to represent structural relations between entities [13]. Knowledge graphs have proven their usefulness

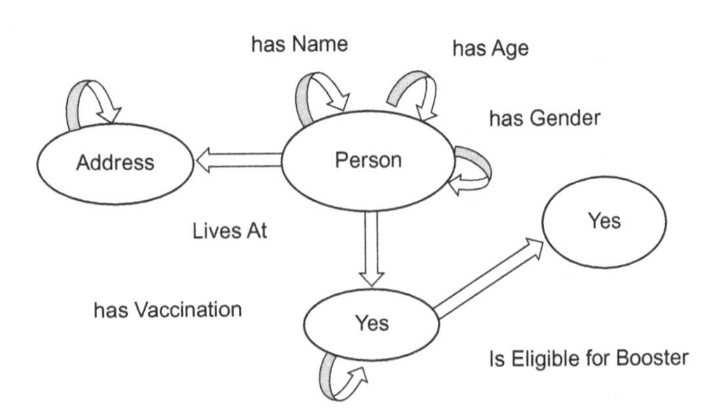

FIGURE 7.5 Ontology in graph format

in wide variety of applications in semantic search and understanding of natural language processing [14]. Different applications of machine learning use structured knowledge in the form of graphs to generate explanations [15]. A knowledge graph, also known as a semantic network, depicts the interactions between a network of real-world elements, such as objects, events, situations, concepts, or things. The term "knowledge graph" comes from the fact that this information is frequently kept in a graph database and represented as a graph structure. Traditional knowledge graph quality assurance systems can be divided into semantic parsing, information retrieval with textual query [16], and embedding [17, 18].

Nodes, edges, and labels are the three fundamental components of a knowledge graph: for example, a node can be a person and vaccination. The relationship between the nodes is defined by an edge: for example, a person is eligible for a booster dose of vaccination.

A knowledge graph is created by applying an ontology to a set of individual data points/instances:

knowledge graph = ontology + data

Let's consider the ontological relationship person→lives at→address.

This can be depicted as shown in Figure 7.6.

Despite the availability of numerous large-scale knowledge graphs, the content of a single knowledge graph is frequently inadequate, especially when it comes to domain-specific applications [19]. An historical knowledge graph with a description of earlier forms of the ontology in a single graph reduces the storage space and data processing required [20]. Very important, when

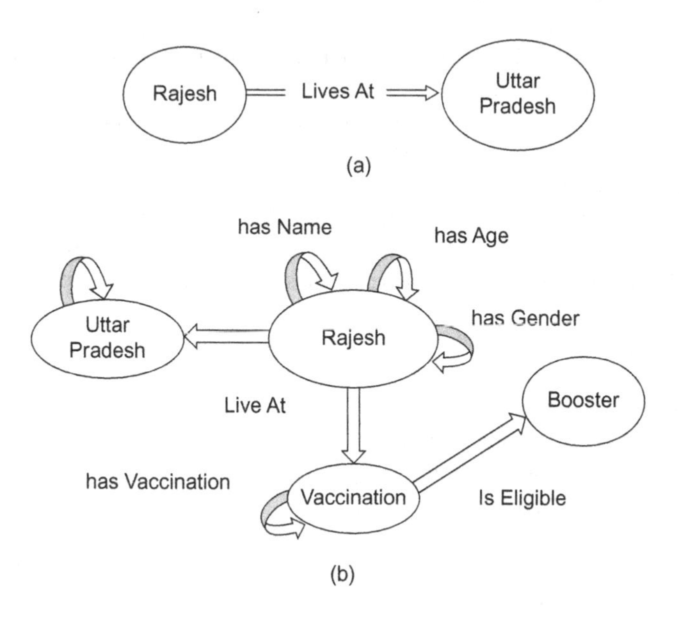

FIGURE 7.6 Ontological graph for (a) single ontological relation, and (b) an instance

developing dynamic knowledge graph using technologies from the semantic web, then concepts and instances that are defined using ontologies plays significant role [21].

7.4 ONTOLOGICAL LANGUAGES

Semantic web technologies have received increased attention in artificial intelligence and computer science more generally. Knowledge graphs are essential in semantic webs, in addition to ML and NLP [12]. Ontology has found applications in the computer science field and is getting more attention due to the huge development of semantic web technologies. It is used to support applications in the domains of NLP and ML, including intelligent chatbots, question-and-answer forums, and language translators:

- *2CycL* – This was developed for the Cyc project, and is based on first-order predicate calculus.
- *W3C Rule Interchange Format (RIF)* – A rule (IF-THEN construct) is one of the fundamental concepts in computer science. RIF is the language used for combining ontologies and rules. It aims to developing a web standard for exchanging rules.
- *Open Biomedical Ontologies (OBO)* – These are used for various biological and biomedical ontologies.
- *Web Ontology Language (OWL)* – This was developed for using ontologies over the World Wide Web, and has emerged as a standard language for representing knowledge in semantic webs.

Linguistics-based applications are adopting semantic web technologies to enhance functionality. Let's look at an example of OWL, based on RDF [17]. Providing basic users with accurate and efficient ways to query large knowledge graphs is difficult. The Resource Document Framework publishing format seeks to address this [22].

In our example, we need to define a class of things – say, "Employee" – with some properties such as "name," "address," "company_name," "designation," and "salary." The RDF syntax to describe the class person and related properties is:

```
<Class ID = "Employee">
<Property ID = "name"/>
<Property ID = "address"/>
<Property ID = "company_name"/>
<Property ID = "designation"/>
<Property ID = "salary"/>
```

Given instance can be described as follows: Smith Jones lives in the United States and works for IBM Ltd. He is a Senior Manager, and a Senior Manager gets a salary of $1L.

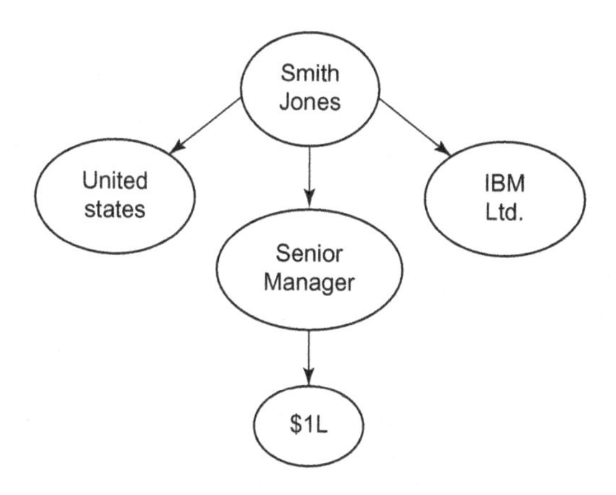

FIGURE 7.7 RDF graph

<Person ID = "Employee">
<name>Smith Jones</name>
<address>United States</address>
<company_name>IBM Ltd.</company_name>
<designation>Senior Manager</designation>
<salary>$1L</salary>

The RDF graph for this is shown in Figure 7.7.

Protégé is an open-source graphical user interface and knowledge management system that allows users to model and edit ontologies. It supports ontologies in frames as well as in OWL frameworks. It provides a graphical user interface and an application programming interface, an editor for logical OWL expressions, wizards to handle complex tasks, and direct access to high-performance classifiers. It provides various features such as multi-user support, support for multiple file formats (Clips, XML, Resource Document Framework, and OWL), and form generation.

To query RDF datasets, structured query languages such as SPARQL provide a powerful tool [23]. Although a certain number of NLP tools are available, there is a limit on those that can be used for knowledge extraction [24].

7.5 CONCLUSION

This chapter has given an overview of the basic ideas of an ontological approach to natural language. This included an introduction to ontology and fundamental aspects of ontologies. There are a number of potential benefits in using an ontological approach in linguistics: it facilitates representing data more generally, it can be used to generate new knowledge, and it can reuse existing knowledge. Ontology allows formal modeling of semantic and grammatical relationships in a precise way.

The significance of POS tagging for language processing is that it gives a significant amount of information about words and their neighbors. Tagging for natural languages is the same process as tokenization for machine languages. Taggers are essential, and play a crucial role in speech recognition, NL parsing, information retrieval, etc.

REFERENCES

1. Futia, G., & Vetrò, A. (2020). On the integration of knowledge graphs into deep learning models for a more comprehensible AI: Three challenges for future research. Information, 11(2), 122.
2. Jiang, W., Wang, Y., Hu, J., Guan, L., & Zhu, Z. (2021, April). Construction of substation engineering design knowledge graph based on "ontology seven-step method". In 2021 4th International Conference on Energy, Electrical and Power Engineering (CEEPE), Chongqing, China, (pp. 957–962). IEEE.
3. Erekhinskaya, T., Strebkov, D., Patel, S., Balakrishna, M., Tatu, M., & Moldovan, D. (2020, June). Ten ways of leveraging ontologies for natural language processing and its enterprise applications. In Proceedings of the International Workshop on Semantic Big Data, Oregon, Portland, (pp. 1–6).
4. Govindarajan, U. H., Trappey, A. J., & Trappey, C. V. (2019). Intelligent collaborative patent mining using excessive topic generation. Advanced Engineering Informatics, 42, 100955.
5. Jaradeh, M. Y., Oelen, A., Farfar, K. E., Prinz, M., D'Souza, J., Kismihók, G., ... & Auer, S. (2019, September). Open research knowledge graph: next generation infrastructure for semantic scholarly knowledge. In Proceedings of the 10th International Conference on Knowledge Capture (pp. 243–246).
6. Zheng, W., Cheng, H., Yu, J. X., Zou, L., & Zhao, K. (2019). Interactive natural language question answering over knowledge graphs. Information Sciences, 481, 141–159.
7. McEnery, T., & Gabrielatos, C. (2006). English corpus linguistics. The handbook of English linguistics, 33–71.
8. Dou, J., Qin, J., Jin, Z., & Li, Z. (2018). Knowledge graph based on domain ontology and natural language processing technology for Chinese intangible cultural heritage. Journal of Visual Languages & Computing, 48, 19–28.
9. Yan, X., Jian, F., & Sun, B. (2021). SAKG-BERT: Enabling language representation with knowledge graphs for chinese sentiment analysis. IEEE Access, 9, 101695–101701.
10. Xu, X., & Cai, H. (2021). Ontology and rule-based natural language processing approach for interpreting textual regulations on underground utility infrastructure. Advanced Engineering Informatics, 48, 101288.
11. de Oliveira, N. R., Medeiros, D. S., & Mattos, D. M. (2020, October). A syntactic-relationship approach to construct well-informative knowledge graphs representation. In 2020 4th Conference on Cloud and Internet of Things (CIoT), NITEROI, Brazil, (pp. 75–82). IEEE. doi: 10.1109/CIoT50422.2020.
12. de Castro Fernández, A. S. (2022). Semantic Web and Knowledge Graphs: History and Evolution.
13. Chen, X., Xie, H., Li, Z., & Cheng, G. (2021). Topic analysis and development in knowledge graph research: A bibliometric review on three decades. Neurocomputing, 461, 497–515.

14. Abdelaziz, I., Dolby, J., McCusker, J., & Srinivas, K. (2021, December). A toolkit for generating code knowledge graphs. In Proceedings of the 11th on Knowledge Capture Conference, virtual event, USA, (pp. 137–144).
15. Tiddi, I., & Schlobach, S. (2022). Knowledge graphs as tools for explainable machine learning: A survey. Artificial Intelligence, 302, 103627.
16. Shekarpour, S., Marx, E., Auer, S., & Sheth, A. (2017, February). RQUERY: rewriting natural language queries on knowledge graphs to alleviate the vocabulary mismatch problem. In Thirty-First AAAI Conference on Artificial Intelligence. San Francisco, California USA. https://doi.org/10.1609/aaai.v31i1.11131
17. Zou, X. (2020, March). A survey on application of knowledge graph. Journal of Physics: Conference Series, 1487(1), 012016. IOP Publishing.
18. Varma, S., Shivam, S., Jamaiyar, R., Anukriti, A., Kashyap, S., & Sarkar, A. (2020, December). Link prediction using semi-automated ontology and knowledge graph in medical sphere. In 2020 IEEE 17th India Council International Conference (INDICON), New Delhi, India, (pp. 1–5). IEEE.
19. Xiang, Y., Zhang, Z., Chen, J., Chen, X., Lin, Z., & Zheng, Y. (2021). OntoEA: Ontology-guided entity alignment via joint knowledge graph embedding. ACL|Findings, Association for Computational Linguistics arXiv preprint arXiv:2105.07688, pp. 1117–1128.
20. Cardoso, S. D., Da Silveira, M., & Pruski, C. (2020). Construction and exploitation of an historical knowledge graph to deal with the evolution of ontologies. Knowledge-Based Systems, 194, 105508.
21. Akroyd, J., Mosbach, S., Bhave, A., & Kraft, M. (2021). Universal digital twin: A dynamic knowledge graph. Data-Centric Engineering, 2. E14. doi:10.1017/dce.2021.10.
22. Bakhshi, M., Nematbakhsh, M., Mohsenzadeh, M., & Rahmani, A. M. (2022). SParseQA: Sequential word reordering and parsing for answering complex natural language questions over knowledge graphs. Knowledge-Based Systems, 235, 107626.
23. Zheng, W., Cheng, H., Zou, L., Yu, J. X., & Zhao, K. (2017, November). Natural language question/answering: Let users talk with the knowledge graph. In Proceedings of the 2017 ACM on Conference on Information and Knowledge Management, Singapore,(pp. 217–226).
24. Xia, P., Qin, G., Vashishtha, S., Chen, Y., Chen, T., May, C., ... & Van Durme, B. (2021). Lome: Large ontology multilingual extraction. Association for Computational Linguistics, EACL, arXiv preprint arXiv:2101.12175, pp. 149–159.

8 Perfect Coloring by HB Color Matrix Algorithm Method

A. A. Bhange and H. R. Bhapkar

CONTENTS

8.1 INTRODUCTION

Graph coloring is the most popular element in graph theory, due to its abundant applications in numerous fields. In computer engineering, it is used in data mining, networking, image segmentation, clustering, etc. In electrical engineering, it is used in coding theory and networking. Also, it is used in many real-life applications such as Sudoku, mobile networking, aircraft management, etc. There are basically three types of coloring: point coloring, line coloring, and face coloring [1]. In point coloring, the points are assigned colors so that no two adjoint points receive the same color. The least number of such colors is the chromatic number of the graph. Line coloring assigns different colors to the lines of the graphs so that no two adjoint lines will receive the same color. Face coloring assigns separate colors to adjoint faces of the graph. The four-color theorem is the base of all graph coloring problems [2]. Bhapkar and Salunke proved the important four-color theorem using the pivot region number of the graph [3]. Basically,

DOI: 10.1201/9781003272649-8

the solution to graph coloring problems can be found using three methods: the hybrid method, the heuristic method, and the metaheuristic method. The hybrid methods are the most widely used as they require very little time for execution. In the heuristic approach, RLF and DSATUR are popular methods. The local search method and population-based method are the most widely used among the metaheuristic methods [4]. Santoso et al. proposed a graph coloring algorithm using an adjacency matrix [5]. Bhange and Bhapkar invented the HB color matrix algorithm for graph coloring, which is based on assignments in the matrix using comparison among elements [6]. Also, they defined a new type of coloring – perfect coloring, which is a combination of point, line, and face coloring [7]. Graph coloring found numerous applications in the recent COVID-19 pandemic predictions, being used in decision-making and calculating mortality rates and the impact on the education sector, etc. [8–10]. The concept of corona products is used in virus graphs [11].

In this chapter, we will define the perfect HB color matrix for any planar graph. The perfect HB color matrix (PHBCM) algorithm is developed, and a Python program is coded using that algorithm. Also, we will calculate the perfect chromatic (PC) number for a few standard graphs using the PHBCM algorithm.

In 2020, Ramachandran and Deepika proposed a new matrix algorithm using an adjacency matrix. The sum of each row of the matrix is calculated, and the row with the maximum sum is chosen. If there is a tie in the maximum sums, then the maximal null matrix is chosen. If there is also a tie in the maximal null matrix, then the row with a maximum degree is selected. Finally, the color is assigned to a vertex corresponding to the row [12].

In 2017, Mohan et al. calculated the total coloring of the corona product of any two graphs G and H, where they considered H as either a cycle, complete, or bipartite graph. They proved that the total coloring of the corona product of any graph with a cycle graph C_n is Δ+1, where Δ is the degree of the resultant graph after the corona product. Also, the total coloring of the corona product with a complete graph K_n is Δ+1. The same result is obtained for a corona product with bipartite graphs [13].

In 2018, Geetha et al. proposed a survey of total coloring after 2010. They proved the result of total coloring conjecture for non-planar graphs like circulant graphs, product graphs, Sierpinski graphs, cubic graphs, graphs with degree constraints, etc. They also surveyed the results of complexities of total coloring [14]. In 2018, Vighnesh proved the total coloring conjecture for some groups of graphs like line graphs, double graphs, and deleted lexicographic products. If the total coloring of the graph is Δ+1, it is a type I graph, whereas if the total coloring is Δ+2, it is type II. Therefore, the author proved that for any graph H, the deleted lexicographic product and line graph $L(K_n)$ is of type I. Any double graph is type I if G is type I, and the double graph is type II if G is type II [15].

In 2020, Vighnesh et al. proved the total coloring conjecture for core satellite graphs, cocktail parts graphs, modular product of paths, and Shrikhande graphs. Core satellite graphs are total colorable with Δ+1 if the core and all the satellite cliques have total coloring of Δ+1 i.e., they are type I. Cocktail party graphs with n vertices $n \geq 3$ have total coloring of $\Delta+1$. A strong product is the union of Cartesian and direct products. The combination of strong product edges and edges corresponding to the non-adjacent vertices is the modular product. The Shrikhande graph is a type I graph [16].

8.2 PRELIMINARIES

8.2.1 HB Color Matrix

A HB color matrix of any graph is a matrix of 0's and ∞'s, depending on adjacency of elements of the graph. The matrix will have a value of 0 if the corresponding elements are not adjoint, otherwise its value is ∞. Depending upon the elements of the graph, there are three types of HB color matrices:

1. Vertex HB color matrix (VHBCM)
2. Edge HB color matrix (EHBCM)
3. Region HB color matrix (RHBCM)

8.2.2 Perfect Coloring

A function $f: P(G) \cup L(G) \cup R(G) \rightarrow C$ is said to be perfect coloring of the graph G if $f(x) \neq f(y)$ for any two adjoint or incident elements $x,y \in P(G) \cup L(G) \cup R(G)$. And the PC number $\chi^{P}(G)$ is the least colors needed to assign colors to any graph using perfect coloring [17, 18].

8.3 RESULTS

8.3.1 Perfect HB Color Matrix

Consider a graph H with m points or vertices $P_1, P_2, P_3 \ldots P_m$, n lines or edges l_{m+1}, $l_{m+2}, l_{m+3} \ldots l_{m+n}$, and r faces $f_{m+n+1}, f_{m+n+2}, f_{m+n+3} \ldots f_{m+n+r}$. A perfect HB color matrix of graph H is denoted by $C_p(H) = (m_{ij})_{(m+n+r)X(m+n+r)}$, with the following conditions:

$$m_{ij} = \infty \begin{cases} \text{if } p_i \text{ and } p_j \text{ are adjoint vertices,} \\ \text{if } i = j, \\ \text{if } l_i \text{ and } l_j \text{ are adjoint lines or edges,} \\ \text{if } f_i \text{ and } f_j \text{ are adjoint faces,} \\ \text{if } p_i \text{ and } l_j \text{ are adjoint vertex and edge,} \\ \text{if } p_i \text{ are vertices forming faces } f_j, \\ \text{if } l_i \text{ are edges forming faces } f_j \end{cases}$$

$m_{ij} = 0$, otherwise.

8.3.1.1 Example of a PHBCM

Consider a graph K with four vertices, six edges, and three regions, as shown in Figure 8.1. The PHBCM of this graph is shown in Figure 8.2.

8.3.1.2 Properties of a PHBCM

1. A PHBCM is a symmetrical matrix with diagonal elements ∞.
2. The 0 element in the matrix is assigned to any two non-adjoint elements.
3. The ∞ element in the matrix is assigned to any two adjoint elements.
4. If any row or column of PHBCM is with all ∞ elements, then that element is adjoint to rest of all elements.

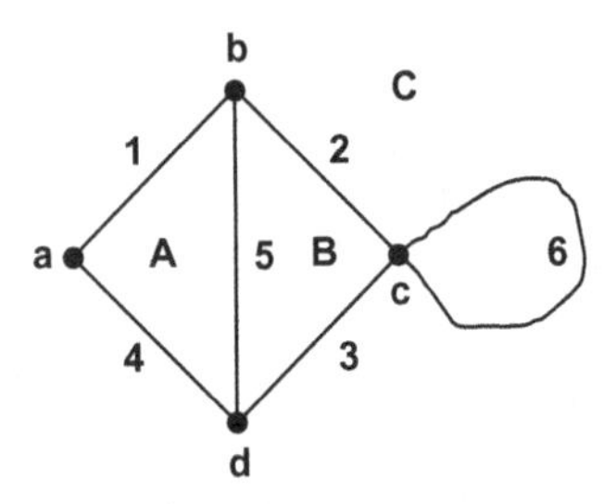

FIGURE 8. 1 Graph K

	a	b	c	d	1	2	3	4	5	6	A	B	C
a	∞	∞	0	∞	∞	0	0	∞	0	0	∞	0	∞
b	∞	∞	∞	∞	∞	∞	0	0	∞	0	∞	∞	∞
c	0	∞	∞	∞	0	∞	∞	0	0	∞	0	∞	∞
d	∞	∞	∞	∞	0	0	∞	∞	∞	0	∞	∞	∞
1	∞	∞	0	0	∞	∞	0	∞	∞	0	∞	0	∞
2	0	∞	∞	0	∞	∞	∞	0	∞	∞	0	∞	∞
3	0	0	∞	∞	0	∞	∞	∞	∞	∞	0	∞	∞
4	∞	0	0	∞	∞	0	∞	∞	∞	0	∞	0	∞
5	0	∞	0	∞	∞	∞	∞	∞	∞	0	∞	∞	0
6	0	0	∞	0	0	∞	∞	0	0	∞	0	0	∞
A	∞	∞	0	∞	∞	0	0	∞	∞	0	∞	∞	∞
B	0	∞	∞	∞	0	∞	∞	0	∞	0	∞	∞	∞
C	∞	∞	∞	∞	∞	∞	∞	∞	0	∞	∞	∞	∞

FIGURE 8.2 PHBCM of graph K

Theorem 8.1: The null graph N_n with n vertices will contain exactly two ∞'s in each row of its PHBCM.

Proof: Consider a null graph N_n with n isolated vertices without edges. As per the property of PHBCM, the diagonal elements of a matrix will have ∞. Also, the open region is adjoint to every vertex of the null graph. So the column corresponding to the open region will have ∞ everywhere. Hence the proof.

Theorem 8.2: If in the PHBCM of a simple graph H a row or column is having all ∞'s, then graph H is a line graph, star graph, comb graph, or a tree.

Proof: Consider a simple graph H, which is either a line graph, star graph, comb graph, or a tree. The elements of the graph like edges and vertices are adjoint to an open region. Hence the row or column corresponding to the open region will have all over ∞ in its PHBCM. Hence the proof.

Theorem 8.3: If C_n is an n vertex circular graph, then there are exactly two rows or columns with all ∞'s in its PHBCM.

Proof: Consider the circular graph C_n with n vertices. There are two regions, an open region and a closed region, in the circular graph. These two regions are adjoint to each other and to every edge and vertex of the graph. Hence the rows corresponding to these two regions in the PHBCM of the circular graph will have all over ∞. Hence the proof.

8.3.2 Algorithm of Perfect Coloring by HB Color Matrix Method

Consider a set $S(H) = \{u_1, u_2, u_3, \ldots u_{m+n+r}\}$ with m vertices $v_1, v_2, v_3 \ldots v_m$, n edges $e_1, e_2, e_3 \ldots e_n$, and r faces $f_1, f_2, f_3 \ldots f_r$ of the graph H. The following is an algorithm for perfect coloring using the HB color matrix method for the graph H, and sequence of elements considered here is chromatic.

Step 1: Plot the perfect HB color matrix $C_p(H)$ of the graph H. Make the assignments in the upper triangular matrix of $C_p(H)$. So consider only the upper triangle of $C_p(H)$ and let it be $M(H)$.

Step 2: Choose the element u_1 from the first row of matrix $M(H)$. Search for cell $(u_1, u_r) = 0$ for least r, where $r = 2, 3, 4 \ldots m+n+r$. If the least of r is some s, then assign identical colors i.e., colorl to u_1 and u_s.

1. If there exists the least t such that $(u_1, u_{s+t}) = 0$ and $(u_s, u_{s+t}) = 0$, then assign the same color to u_s and u_{s+t} i.e., color 1. If there is least p so that $(u_1, u_{s+t+p}) = 0$, then verify the values of cells (u_s, u_{s+t+p}) and (u_{s+t}, u_{s+t+p}).
   (a) If either of them is ∞, then cross out $(u_1, u_{s+t+p}) = 0$.
   (b) If all are 0, then assign color 1 to u_{s+t+p}.
   Continue in this way for all 0 values of row 1.
2. If $(u_1, u_{s+t}) = \infty$ and $(u_s, u_{s+t}) = 0$, then cross out the 0, or if $(u_1, u_{s+t}) = 0$ and $(u_s, u_{s+t}) = \infty$, then cross out the 0 of the respective places.
3. If $(u_1, u_{s+t}) = \infty$ and $(u_s, u_{s+t}) = \infty$, then u_1 and u_{s+t} will have separate colors.

Step 3: Implement a similar process for the elements u_2 of the second row, then for $u_3, u_4 \ldots u_{m+n+r}$

Step 4: If all 0's of the perfect HB color matrix M(H) are either assigned or strikethrough, then verify whether or not colors have been assigned to all elements. If any elements have not been assigned a color, then assign colors to them using previously unused colors. And if any row contains all ∞'s, then the corresponding elements must have different colors than the previous color.

8.4 ILLUSTRATION OF THE PERFECT HB COLOR MATRIX METHOD

Consider the house graph H with five vertices: *p*, *q*, *r*, *s*, *t*, six edges *a*, *b*, *c*, *d*, *e*, *f*, and three regions r_1, r_2, and r_3 (see Figure 8.3).

Step 1: Plot a PHBCM of the graph using adjacency of the elements of the matrix. The cell element is ∞ for adjoint elements, and 0 for non-adjoint elements. Consider only the upper triangular part of the matrix as this matrix is symmetrical, as shown in Figure 8.4.

Step 2: Consider the first row of the matrix – i.e., the row for vertex *p*. Now, search for the first 0 in this row. The first 0 is at cell (*p*, *r*). Make an assignment at (*p*, *r*). Assign the same color, e.g., color 1 (red), to the vertices *p* and *r*. Strike out the column corresponding to *r* (see Figure 8.5(a)).

(a) Compare the cells (*p*, *s*) and (*r*, *s*). As (*p*, *s*) = 0 and (r, s) = ∞, assignment can't be made at (*p*, *s*). Cross out the 0 at (*p*, *s*) (see Figure 8.5(a)).

(b) The next 0 is at (*p*, *c*), but there is no 0 at (*r*, *c*), hence no assignment can be made at (*p*, *c*). Cross out the 0 at (*p*, *c*) (see Figure 8.5(a)).

(c) The cells (*p*, *d*) and (*r*, *d*) have the values 0 and ∞ respectively, hence no assignment can be made at (*p*, *d*). Cross out the 0 at (*p*, *d*) (see Figure 8.5(a)).

(d) Both the cells (*p*, *e*) and (*r*, *e*) having a value of 0, hence assignment can be made at cell (*p*, *e*), as shown in Figure 8.5(b), which means

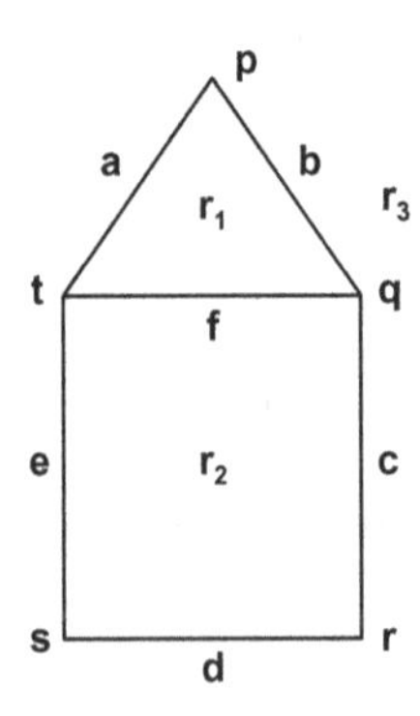

FIGURE 8.3 House graph H

M(H) =

	p	q	r	s	t	a	b	c	d	e	f	r_1	r_2	r_3
p	∞	∞	0	0	∞	∞	∞	0	0	0	0	∞	0	∞
q	–	∞	∞	0	∞	0	∞	∞	0	0	∞	∞	∞	∞
r	–	–	∞	∞	0	0	0	∞	∞	0	0	0	∞	∞
s	–	–	–	∞	∞	0	0	0	∞	∞	0	0	∞	∞
t	–	–	–	–	∞	∞	0	0	0	∞	∞	∞	∞	∞
a	–	–	–	–	–	∞	∞	0	0	∞	∞	∞	0	∞
b	–	–	–	–	–	–	∞	∞	0	0	∞	∞	0	∞
c	–	–	–	–	–	–	–	∞	∞	0	∞	0	∞	∞
d	–	–	–	–	–	–	–	–	∞	∞	0	0	∞	∞
e	–	–	–	–	–	–	–	–	–	∞	∞	0	∞	∞
f	–	–	–	–	–	–	–	–	–	–	∞	∞	∞	0
r_1	–	–	–	–	–	–	–	–	–	–	–	∞	∞	∞
r_2	–	–	–	–	–	–	–	–	–	–	–	–	∞	∞
r_3	–	–	–	–	–	–	–	–	–	–	–	–	–	∞

FIGURE 8.4 Upper triangular perfect HB color matrix for house graph H

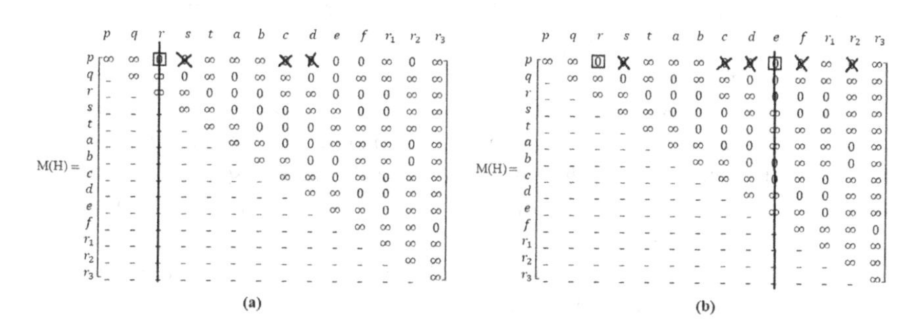

FIGURE 8.5 Assignment in first row of PHBCM of house graph H

same (red) color can be assigned to edge e. Strike out the column corresponding to e (Figure 8.5(b)).

(e) Compare the cells (p, f), (r, f) and (e, f). They have the values 0, 0, and ∞ respectively, hence assignment can't be made at cell (p, f). Cross out the 0 at (p, f) (see Figure 8.5(b)).

(f) Compare the cells (p, r_2), (r, r_2), and (e, r_2). They have the values 0, ∞, and ∞ respectively, hence assignment can't be made at cell (p, r_2). Cross out the 0 at (p, r_2) (Figure 8.5(b)).

Step 3: As all 0's of row 1 are covered, search for first the 0 in row 2. The first 0 in row 2 is at cell (q, s). Make an assignment at (q, s) as shown in Figure 8.6(a). Assign color 2 (blue) to vertices q and s. Strike out the column corresponding to s (Figure 8.6(a)).

(a) Both the cells (q, a) and (s, a) have the value 0, hence assignment can be made at cell (q, a), as shown in Figure 8.6(b), which means the

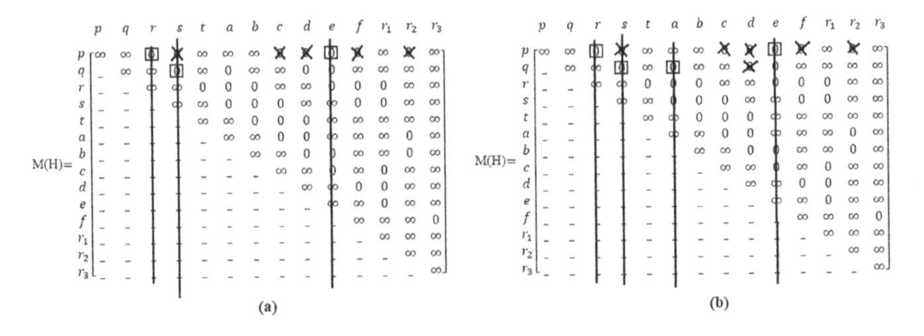

FIGURE 8.6 Assignment in second row of PHBCM For house graph H

same (blue) color can be assigned to edge *a*. Strike out the column corresponding to *a* (see Figure 8.6(b)).

(b) The next 0 is at (*q*, *d*).Compare the cells (*q*, *d*), (*s*, *d*), and (*a*, *d*). They have the values 0, ∞, and 0 respectively, hence assignment can't be made at cell (*q*, *d*). Cross out the 0at (*q*, *d*) (see Figure 8.6(b)).

Step 4: As the colors are assigned to vertices *r* and *s*, cross out all the 0's of the rows corresponding to *r* and *s* and directly consider the row corresponding to vertex *t*.

(a) Make an assignment at (*t*, *b*). Give color 3 (green) to vertex *t* and edge *b*. Strike out the column corresponding to *b* (see Figure 8.7(a)).

(b) The cells (*t*, *c*) and (*b*, *c*) have the values 0 and ∞ respectively, hence no assignment can be made at (*t*, *c*). Cross out the 0 at (*t*, *c*) (see Figure 8.7(a)).

(c) Compare the cells (*t*, *d*) and (*b*, *d*). Both these cells have values of 0, so assignment can be made at cell (*t*, *d*), as shown in Figure 8.7(b), which means the same (green) color can be assigned to edge *d*. Strike out the column corresponding to *b* (see Figure 8.7(b)).

(d) As the assignments have been made for edges *a* and *b*, cross out the remaining 0's of the rows corresponding to *a* and *b* and consider the row corresponding to *c* for further assignments.

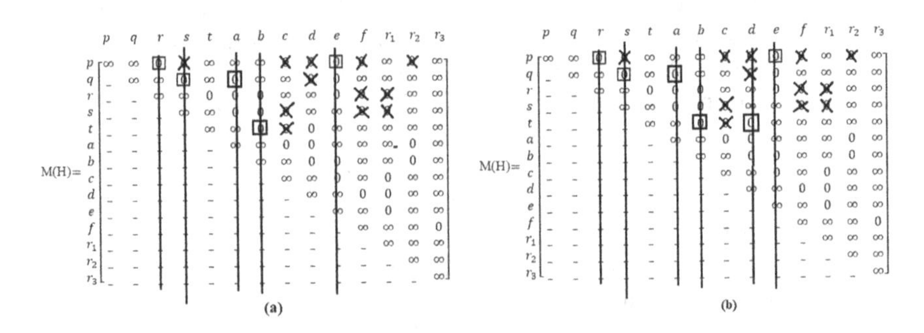

FIGURE 8.7 Assignment in fifth row of PHBCM for house graph H

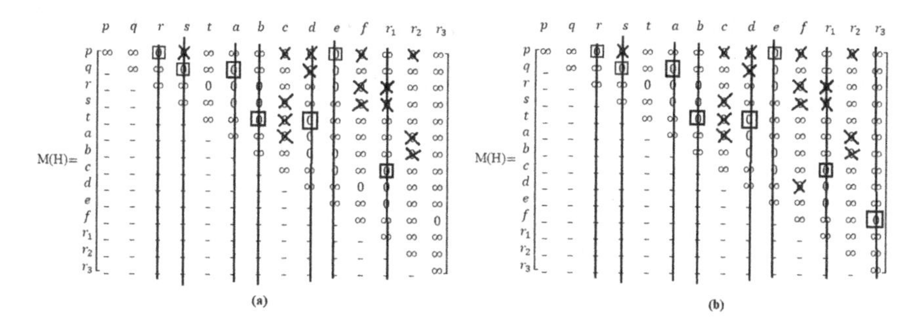

FIGURE 8.8 Assignment in eighth and eleventh row of PHBCM For graph H

(e) Make an assignment at (c, r_1) (see Figure 8.8(a)). The same color, color 4 (yellow), is assigned to edge c and region r_1. Strike out the column corresponding to r_1 (see Figure 8.8(a)).

(f) Skip the rows with edges d and e as colors are already assigned to them, and cross out the 0's in rows d and e (see Figure 8.8(b)). Consider the first 0 of the row corresponding to edge f, and make an assignment at cell (f, r_3) (see Figure 8.8(b)). Hence edge f and region r_3 will have color 5 (orange).

(g) All the 0's of column r_2 are all crossed out without any assignment, hence no color is assigned to region r_2 (see Figure 8.8(b)). Assign a separate color to it, color 6 (pink).

The resultant graph after perfect coloring is shown in Figure 8.9. The house graph is having PC number 6.

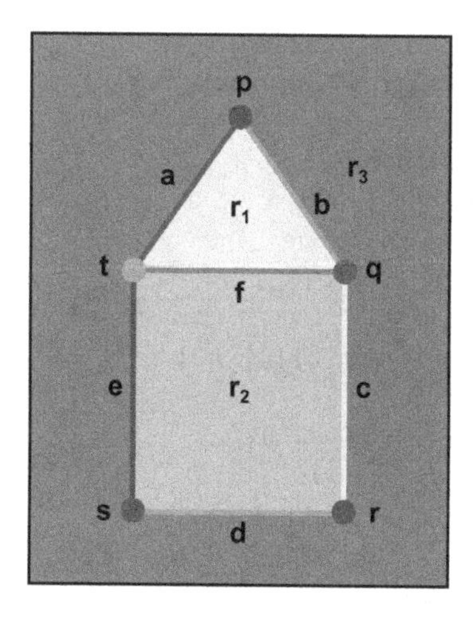

FIGURE 8.9 House graph H after perfect coloring

8.5 PYTHON PROGRAM FOR GRAPH COLORING BY PHBCM

The code for the python program using the PHBCM algorithm is as follows:

```
1  import numpy as np
2
3  name = input("Enter name of the graph: ")
4  column = int(input("enter the no of columns: "))
5  arr = np.zeros((column, column), dtype=np.int64)
6  i = y = 0
7  for _ in range(column):
8      lis = []
9      lis = input(f"enter {_} row:").split(" ")
10     for x in range(y, column):
11         arr[_][x] = int(lis[i])
12         i += 1
13     y += 1
14     i = 0
15
16 # print(arr)
17
18 row = []
19 flag = 0
20 z = 2
21 x = 0
22
23 final_row =[]
24 while x <= column- 1:
25     for _ in range(x, column):
26         if not len(row) and not arr[x][_]:
27
28             row.append(_)
29             arr[x][_] = z
30             for c in range(_):
31                 if arr[c][_] == 0:
32
33                     arr[c][_] = 1
34
35         elif arr[x][_] == 0:
36             for y in row:
37                 if arr[y][_] == 0:
38                     arr[y][_] = 1
39                 else:
40                     flag = 1
```

```
41              if flag == 1:
42                  arr[x][_] = 1
43 
44              else:
45                  row.append(_)
46                  arr[x][_] = z
47                  for c in range(_):
48                      if arr[c][_] == 0:
49 
50                          arr[c][_] = 1
51              flag = 0
52      z += 1
53      x += 1
54 
55      for b in row:
56          for n in range(column - b):
57              arr[b][n + b] = 1
58      final_row.extend(row)
59      row = []
60 
61  l = []
62  for b in range(column);
63      for v in range(column - b):
64          if b not in final_row:
65              if arr[b][v + b] != 1:
66                  break
67          else:
68              break
69      else:
70          l.append(b)
71          for n in range(column - b):
72              arr[b][n + b] = z
73          z += 1
74 
75  # print(arr)
76 
77  p = 1
78  print("Name of graph is {}".format(name))
```

```
78  print("Name of graph is {}".format(name))
79  print("Number of vertices are {}".format(column))
80  for b in range(column):
81      no_chng = 1
82      j = 0
83      nan = 'vertex'
84      if b not in 1:
85          nan = 'vertices'
86          j = 1
87      for n in range(column - b):
88          if arr[b][n + b] != 1.
89              if no_chng:
90                  print("Assign colour{} to {} {}".format(p, nan,
    b+1), end="")
91              if j :
92                  print(' {}'.format(n + b + 1), end="")
93              no_chng = 0
94      print("")
95      if not no_chng:
96          p += 1
97  print("Chromatic number is {}".format(p-1))
98
```

The output is shown in Figures 8.10, 8.11, and 8.12.

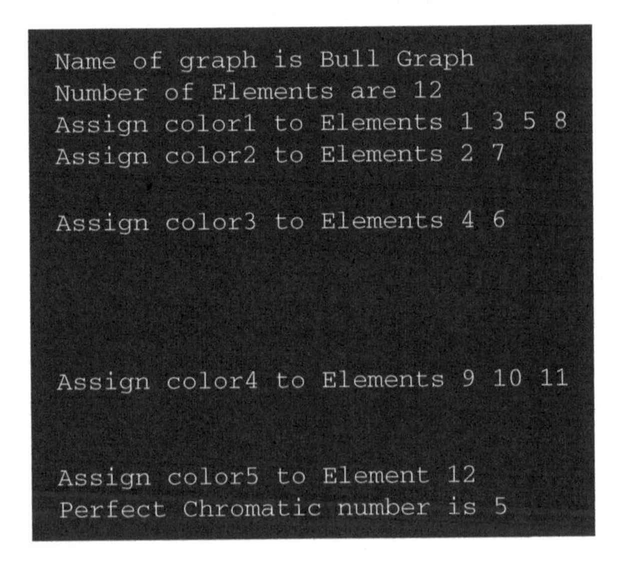
Name of graph is Bull Graph
Number of Elements are 12
Assign color1 to Elements 1 3 5 8
Assign color2 to Elements 2 7
Assign color3 to Elements 4 6
Assign color4 to Elements 9 10 11
Assign color5 to Element 12
Perfect Chromatic number is 5

FIGURE 8.10 Output for bull graph

```
Name of graph is Cycle Graph C5
Number of Elements are 12
Assign color1 to Elements 1 3 9
Assign color2 to Elements 2 4 10


Assign color3 to Elements 5 6 8

Assign color4 to Element 7




Assign color5 to Element 11
Assign color6 to Element 12
Perfect Chromatic number is 6
```

FIGURE 8.11 Output for cycle graph C_5

```
Enter name of the graph: Wheel Graph W4
Number of Elements are 18
Assign color1 to Elements 1 3 11
Assign color2 to Elements 2 4 10


Assign color3 to Elements 5 6 8

Assign color4 to Elements 7 9 15 17




Assign color5 to Elements 12 14
Assign color6 to Elements 13 16




Assign color7 to Element 18
Perfect Chromatic number is 7
```

FIGURE 8.12 Output for wheel graph W_4

TABLE 8.1
PC Numbers of a Few Standard Graphs

Sr. No.	Name of Graph	No. of Vertices	PC No.
1	Diamond graph D_n	n+2 (n≥6)	n+3
2	Null graph N_n	n (n≥1)	2
3	Friendship graph F_n	2n+1 (n≥2)	2n+2
4	Tadpole graph $T_{3n,m}$	3n+m (n≥1)	5
5	Corona graph C_{3n}	3n (n≥1)	5
6	Ladder rung graph L_n	2n (n≥1)	4
7	Path graph P_n	n (n≥2)	4
8	Complete graph K_4	4	9

8.6 THE PERFECT CHROMATIC NUMBERS FOR SOME STANDARD GRAPHS USING THE PHBCM ALGORITHM METHOD

The PC numbers of a few types of graphs calculated using the PHBCM algorithm method are shown in Table 8.1.

8.7 CONCLUSION

This chapter has defined the perfect HB color matrix algorithm method to calculate the perfect chromatic numbers of graphs. The method has been illustrated for a house graph. The PC number for the house graph is 6. The chapter also provided Python code using the PHBCM algorithm, and showed the outputs of the program for a bull graph, cycle graph C_5, and wheel graph W_4. Along with this, the PC numbers for a few standard graphs using the PHBCM algorithm method were defined.

REFERENCES

1. Narsingh D. (2003) *Graph Theory with Applications To Engineering and Computer Science*, Prentice–Hall of India, 88–111.
2. Appel K., Haken W. (1977) Every planar map is four colorable, *Bulletin of American Mathematical Society*, 82, 711–712.
3. Bhapkar H. R., Salunke J. N. (2014) Proof of four colour map theorem by using PRN of graph, *Journal of Bulletin of Society for Mathematical Services and Standards*, 3(2), 35–42.
4. Manouchehr Z. (2020) *A New Vertex Coloring Heuristic and Corresponding Chromatic Number Algorithmica*. Springer, 1–20.
5. Santoso K. (2019) Vertex colouring using the adjacency matrix, *IOP Conf. Series: Journal of Physics*, 1211, 1–6.

6. Bhange A. A., Bhapkar H. R. (2021) Colouring of graphs by HB colour matrix algorithm method, *Journal of Physics: Conference Series*,1743, 1–8.
7. Bhange A. A., Bhapkar H. R. (2020) Perfect coloring of the graph with its kinds, *Journal of Physics: Conference Series*,1663, 1–9.
8. Bhapkar H. R., Mahalle P. N., Shinde G. R., Mahmud M. (2021) Rough sets in COVID-19 to predict symptomatic cases. In: K. C. Santosh and A. Joshi (eds.) *COVID-19: Prediction, Decision-making, and Its Impacts, Lecture Notes on Data Engineering and Communications Technologies* 60, 57–68.
9. Bhapkar H. R., Mahalle P. N., Dey N., & Santosh K. C.(2020) Revisited COVID-19 mortality and recovery rates: Are we missing recovery time period, *Journal of Medical Systems*, 44(12), 202.
10. Shinde G. R., Majumder S., Bhapkar H. R., Mahalle P. N. (2022) Impact of COVID-19 pandemic on education sector. In *Quality of Work-Life During Pandemic, Studies in Big Data*,100. Springer,Singapore.
11. Bhapkar H. R., Mahalle P. N., Dhotre P. S. (2020) Virus graph and COVID-19 pandemic: A graph theory approach. In Hassanien A. E., Dey N., Elghamrawy S. (eds.) *Big Data Analytics and Artificial Intelligence Against COVID-19: Innovation Vision and Approach. Studies in Big Data*, 78. Springer international publishing.
12. Ramachandran T., Deepika, N.(2020) Vertex coloring of graphs using adjacency matrix, *International Journal of Engineering Research and Applications*,10(4), 1–5.
13. Mohan S. Geetha J., Somasundaram, K.(2017) Total coloring of the corona product of two graphs, *Australasian Journal of Combinatorics*, 68(1), 15–22.
14. Geetha, J., Narayanan, N., Somasundaram, K. (2018) Total coloring-A survey. *ArXiv: 1812.05833v1,1-23.*
15. Vighnesh R., Geetha J., Somasundaram K. (2018) Total coloring conjecture for certain classes of graphs, *Algorithms*,11(10), 161, 1–7.
16. Vighnesh R., Mohan S., Geetha J., Somasundaram K. (2020) Total colorings of core-satellite, cocktail party and modular product graphs, *TWMS Journal of Applied and Engineering Mathematics*, 10(3), 778–787.
17. Bhange A. A., Bhapkar H. R. (2019) α, β Colouring of graphs and related aspects, *Journal of Emerging Technologies and Innovative Research*, 6(4), 661–663.
18. Bhange A. A., Bhapkar H. R. (2020) Perfect coloring of corona product of cycle graph with cycle, path and null graph, *Advances in Mathematics: Scientific Journal*, 9(12), 10839–10844.

9 Cross-lingual Word Sense Disambiguation Using Multilingual Co-occurrence Graphs

Neha Janu, Anjali Singh, Meenakshi Nawal, Sunita Gupta, Tapesh Kumar, and Vijendra Singh

CONTENTS

DOI: 10.1201/9781003272649-9

9.1 INTRODUCTION

Words' meanings vary depending on the context in which they are used. Human languages are also ambiguous, since many words may be understood in a variety of ways based on the contexts in which they appear. Word sense disambiguation (WSD) is the process of determining which meaning of a word is denoted by its use in a certain context in natural language processing (NLP). Figure 9.1 shows a basic WSD model. One of the first problems that every NLP system confronts is lexical ambiguity, whether it is syntactic or semantic. Syntactic ambiguity of words can be solved with high-precision part of speech (POS) taggers. The challenge of resolving semantic ambiguity, on the other hand, is called word sense disambiguation. It is more difficult to resolve semantic ambiguity than it is to resolve syntactic ambiguity.

Consider the two distinct definitions of the word "bark":

1. He heard a short bark of laughter.
2. Beavers feed on leaves and the living bark of trees.

noindent

Here, "bark" has two different meanings:

1. A sound made by someone laughing or coughing
2. The tough protective outer sheath of a tree

noindent

If WSD can resolve the ambiguity, the correct meanings of the preceding phrases may be assigned. In a given context, WSD automatically attributes the most acceptable meaning to an uncertain term. WSD is useful in a variety of NLP applications where such problems arise, such as question answering, information retrieval, machine translation, and dialogues [1].

Large-scale lexical resources like the *Oxford Advanced Learner's Dictionary* were available in the 1980s, and information extracted automatically from these

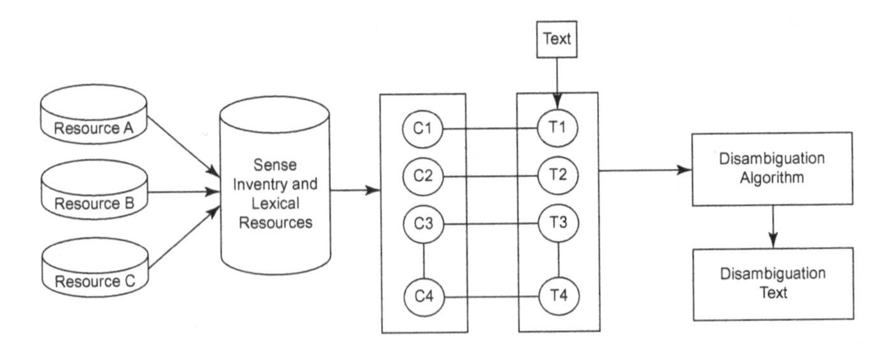

FIGURE 9.1 Basic WSD model

resources replaced hand coding; nonetheless, WSD remained dictionary-based or knowledge-based. WSD became a fundamental issue to which machine learning techniques with supervision might be applied when the statistical revolution swept across computational linguistics in the 1990s [2]. As supervised approaches reached the point of diminishing returns in the 2000s, researchers turned their focus to domain adaptation, mixed methods, coarser-grained senses, and unsupervised and semi-supervised and graph-based techniques for knowledge-based systems.

9.2 EVALUATION OF WSD

The following two inputs are required for WSD evaluation:

1. *Language dictionary* – The dictionary, which is used to specify the senses to be disambiguated, is the initial input for WSD assessment.
2. *Test corpus* – WSD also requires a large, well-annotated test corpus with the goal of defining correct senses. Test corpora can be divided into two categories:
   (a) *Lexical sample* is a type of corpus used in systems when the meaning of a tiny sample of words has to be disambiguated.
   (b) *All-words corpora* are utilized in systems which seek to clarify all the words in a chunk of flowing text.

The use of all-words corpora is seen as a more realistic method of evaluation. The goal of Senseval is to assess the merits and shortcomings of such programs in terms of various words, linguistic variations, and languages [3]. Senseval has five versions: Senseval_1 (released in 1998), Senseval_2 (released in 2001), Senseval_3 (released in 2004), SemEval_2007 (released in 2007), and Semeval_2010 (released in 2010).

9.2.1 Types of WSD

There are four types of WSD:

- *Classic monolingual WSD* assessment tasks rely on semi-supervised/supervised classification with sense corpora that have been manually annotated and employ WordNet as the sense inventory [4].
- *Cross-lingual WSD* evaluation looks at WSD in two or more languages at the same time. Unlike multilingual WD tasks, the sense inventory is generated on the basis of a concurrent corpus, such as the Europarl Parallel Corpus, rather than giving sense-annotated samples manually for each sense of a polysemous term [5].
- *Multilingual WSD* is WSD across two or more languages [6], and its evaluation activities use their respective sense inventories, such as WordNet, or a bilingual sense inventory, such as BabelNet.

- *Word sense induction and disambiguation* is a combined task evaluation in which the sense inventory is first inducted from a predetermined training dataset of polysemous words and the sentences in which they occurred, then the sense inventory is inducted from the sentences in which they appeared, and then WSD is conducted on a separate testing dataset [7].

9.2.2 Difficulties in Word Sense Disambiguation

This chapter discusses the typical and conventional description of WSD, defined as an explicit and separate disambiguation procedure for a dataset of word senses. In lexical semantics, words are generally believed to have a different and finite collection of senses, and there is a significant reduction in the complexity of word meanings. WSD is difficult for a variety of reasons, some of which we will now address.

9.2.2.1 Differences between Dictionaries

One issue with word sense disambiguation is defining individual words' senses, because various thesauruses and dictionaries differ in how they divide words into distinct meanings. Some academics have proposed utilizing a specific lexicon and its set of senses to address this problem. In general, however, study findings based on broad sense differences have outperformed those based on limited ones [8]. The majority of researchers are still working on fine-grained WSD. The most common method of study regarding WSD is to use WordNet as an English sense inventory resource. WordNet is a computer lexicon which uses sets of synonyms for encoding. *Roget's Thesaurus* and Wikipedia are two more resources utilized for disambiguation. For multilingual WSD, BabelNet has recently been employed [9].

9.2.2.2 Part of Speech Tagging

In tests, sense tagging and POS tagging have been shown to be inextricably linked, with one possibly constraining the other. The topic of whether these tasks should be addressed together or separated remains unresolved, although scientists are increasingly inclined to deploy them independently (e.g., to disambiguate text in the SemEval/Senseval challenges, chunks of speech are given as input). Both disambiguating and tagging with words are involved in WSM POS tagging.

9.2.2.3 Inter-judge Variance

WSD systems are typically tested by having them perform a particular task, then comparing their performance to that of a human. Assigning parts of speech to text is very simple, but teaching individuals to tag sensations is considerably more complex.

9.2.2.4 Pragmatics

Few artificial intelligence (AI) researchers claim that parsing meanings out of words is impossible without commonsense ontology. Pragmatics is the term for this language problem. According to experts, knowing commonsense information is required to detect word senses correctly. Furthermore, when cataphoras or anaphoras are present in a text, it is often necessary to use common sense to decipher terms such as pronouns.

9.2.2.5 Sense Inventories and Task-dependent Algorithms

A sense inventory that is task-independent is not a logical concept. Every activity necessitates the self-categorization of a word's meaning into task-relevant senses. Furthermore, various applications may require totally different algorithms. The difficulty of selecting target words arises in machine translation. The "senses" are terms in the target language that frequently correlate to major sense/meaning disparities in the native/source language (e.g., "bank" might be translated as "finance bank" or as "river's edge").

9.2.2.6 Sense Discreteness

Finally, the concept of "word sense" is nebulous and contentious. The majority of people can agree about coarse-grained homograph discrepancies (e.g., "pen" as enclosure or writing device). However, when it comes to fine-grained polysemy, there are disputes. In principle, word sense is indefinitely changeable and context-dependent. It is difficult to break down into separate or distinctive sub-meanings. This is known as the discreteness of sense.

9.3 APPROACHES TO WORD SENSE DISAMBIGUATION

Deep *approaches* and shallow methods are the two primary approaches to WSD:

- *Deep methods* imply access to a vast corpus of global information. Outside relatively narrow fields, computer-readable versions of such corpora of knowledge do not exist. Therefore, these techniques are typically not regarded to be particularly effective in practice [10].
- *Shallow methods* focus on the surrounding words rather than trying to grasp the content. By using a training corpus of words labeled with their respective senses, a computer can mechanically generate these rules. WSD is usually approached in major four ways:
    1. Dictionary- and knowledge-based methods
    2. Semi-supervised or minimally supervised methods
    3. Unsupervised methods
    4. Supervised methods

9.3.1 Dictionary and Knowledge-based Methods

These approaches rely on knowledge resources such as WordNet, thesauruses, and machine-readable dictionaries (MRDs). For disambiguation, they may utilize grammatical rules and/or hand-coded rules. Many dictionaries, such as the *Collins Dictionary*, *Oxford English Dictionary*, thesauruses that include synonymy information (such as *Roget's Thesaurus*), and the *Longman Dictionary of Ordinary Contemporary English*, have been made accessible in MRD format in recent years [11]. MRD formats provide a collection of definitions, meanings, and typical use examples, but a thesaurus offers a detailed guide to synonymy between the semantic network and most word meanings [12]. A dictionary-based method, the Lesk algorithm, is considered fundamental. The foundation of Lesk is the concept that words in a text are linked to one another, and that this relationship can be observed in the meanings and definitions of the terms. The dictionary senses of pairs of words that highly overlap in their meanings are used to disambiguate two (or more) terms. When disambiguating "pine cone," for example, the related senses include "tree" and "evergreen" (at least according to one dictionary) [11].

9.3.2 Supervised Methods

The premise behind supervised techniques is that the context can give enough data to disambiguate words on its own, and as a result, logic and common sense are regarded as superfluous. WSD has probably been subjected to every machine learning algorithm known to man, and related approaches such as ensemble learning have proven to be very effective techniques so far, owing to their ability to cope with the feature space's high dimensionality. However, because these supervised techniques rely on large quantities of manual sense-labeled corpora for use in training, which are time-consuming and costly to generate, they face a new knowledge acquisition bottleneck [13]. These techniques include the naïve Bayesian classifiers method, the decision tree and decision list method, the support vector machine method, and the neural network method [14, 15].

9.3.3 Semi-Supervised Methods

In Semi-supervised methods employ a secondary source of information as seed data. Most WSD methods employ semi-supervised learning that permits both labeled and unlabeled input due to a lack of training data. For word sense disambiguation, this approach employs human languages' "one sense per discourse" and "one sense per collocation" characteristics. Words in most discourses and collocations tend to have only one sense based on observation.

9.3.4 Unsupervised Methods

These use raw, unannotated corpora, avoiding (nearly entirely) external information. For WSD researchers, the most difficult problem is unsupervised learning. The fundamental premise is that the same meaning occurs in the same situations [16]. Therefore, senses may be inferred from a text by grouping occurrences of words according to some measure of context similarity, a process known as word sense discrimination or induction. The nearest inducted clusters/senses can then be categorized as new instances of a term.

9.4 GRAPH-BASED CROSS-LINGUAL WORD SENSE DISAMBIGUATION

Parallel corpora offer a novel way to integrate the benefits of unsupervised and supervised methods, as well as a way to make use of textual translation correspondences. WSD methods that are cross-lingual disambiguate by labeling target terms with the correct translation to clear up any ambiguity.

Graph Learning is useful in the case of languages with scarce resources [17]. Graph learning is a successful upgrade to current meta-learning methods that allows for better and more stable learning, as well as setting a new state of the art for certain languages while performing on a par with others, using just a small quantity of labeled data [18]. Graph learning is a new multidisciplinary area that combines graph analytics with deep learning.

9.4.1 MultiMirror Model

A model developed by Luigi Procopio et al. [10], MultiMirror is a multilingual WSD sense projection approach to word alignment based on a new neural discriminative model. This model is capable of jointly aligning all source and target tokens with each other at the same time, beating its competitors across multiple language combinations when given a pair of parallel phrases as input. It utilizes pre-trained contextual embedding, specifically multilingual BERT [19], to create continuous representations of each token. It then concatenates the two phrases using a special token, [SEP], to separate them and two additional tokens, [CLS] and [SEP], to surround the entire sequence. It further divides the input tokens into subwords to fit the mBERT input structure. Using this method, subwords can interact with one another and produce a representation that is contextualized not just in the sentence in which they appear, but also in the translation. Finally, to allow token-level contextualization, MultiMirror uses an extra six-layer transformer encoder that closely resembles the design of mBERT[1]. Essentially, it takes the existing representations of each token as input and outputs of a series of token_level_out h_{ul} having l + k vectors of dimension 768 each. It then categorizes each potential alignment individually now that each token has a fully contextualized representation. It begins by computing the tensor, $H \in R^{l*k*768}$, where H_{ij} is the vector generated by the element-wise product of h_{ui} and h_{vj}. Following that, the word alignment matrix $A \in R^{l*k}$ is generated, with A_{ij} representing the probability of aligning *ui* to *vj*: here, matrices W1 and W2 $\in R^{768 \times 768}$, while W3 $\in R^{768 \times 1}$.

9.4.2 UHD Model

Silberer et al. [20] have presented a graph-based method for cross-lingual WSD. They begin by creating a multilingual co-occurrence graph for each target word based on matching instances identified in parallel corpora for the target term. Translation edges, labeled with the target word's interpretations as observed in relevant situations, connect multilingual nodes. They next calculate the Minimum

Spanning Tree, which is used to choose the most relevant words in context to disambiguate a particular test instance, using a modified PageRank method to identify the nodes that reflect the target word's multiple meanings. Finally, the incoming translation edges of the selected context words provide translations.

9.4.3 Co-occurrence Graphs for WSD in the Biomedical Domain

Any system attempting to handle documents in the field of biology faces challenges. To address them, Duque et al. [21] offer a novel unsupervised graph-based approach. The technique given here uses a co-occurrence graph relying on the notion that there are consistent documents – i.e., there is a strong tendency for ideas in a text to be connected together. Because this is not always true for all of the concepts in a text, statistical analysis is employed to identify those that do not meet this hypothesis. This approach to building a co-occurrence graph has been successfully used in a variety of WSD applications, including cross-lingual WSD [22], suggesting that a similar approach might produce useful outcomes in domain-specific word sense disambiguation as well. The method may also be used to investigate the consequences of adding the latest potential beneficial elements to WSD tasks in the field of biology, such as multilingual [23]. In this paper, the co-occurrence graphs utilized in the disambiguation procedure now include information from multilingual corpora in order to see if smaller multilingual corpora may achieve similar results to those obtained with large monolingual corpora.

9.4.4 WSD Based on Word Similarity Calculation Using Weighted Voronoi Regions from a Knowledge Graph

Dongsuk et al. [24] present a novel WSD approach that uses the similarity between a term in the input document and an ambiguous word to produce the context of an ambiguous word. They also offer a novel word similarity computation technique built on BabelNet's semantic network structure to complement the WSD method. They have tested the suggested techniques on the English WSD datasets SemEval-2015 and SemEval-2013. According to experimental data, the suggested WSD approach considerably outperforms the baseline WSD method. Furthermore, in the Semeval-13 dataset, this WSD system beats the previous best WSD systems and the current best unsupervised knowledge WSD system.

9.4.5 Graph Convolutional Networks for WSD

Discriminative characteristics, words, parts of speech, and semantic categories from all left and right units around the ambiguous word are used in Zhang et al.'s [25] WSD approach based on graph convolutional networks (GCNs). Words, components of speech, semantic categories, and sentences are represented as nodes in the WSD network. Edges are inserted between words, parts of speech, semantic classes, and sentences, in that order. The WSD graph is processed using GCN, and the semantic class of an unclear word is determined using the softmax function.

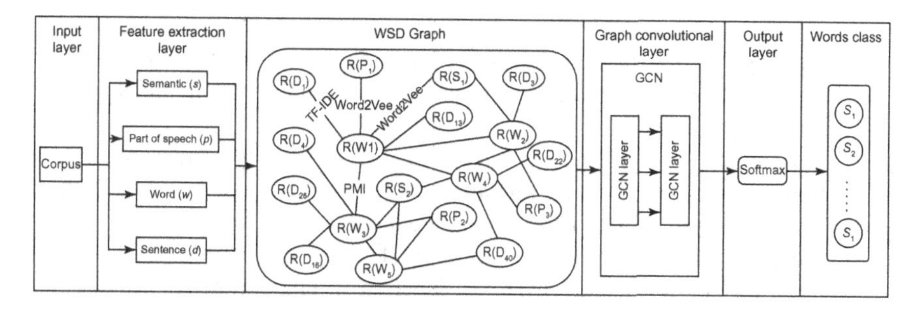

FIGURE 9.2 Graph convolutional network for WSD

Figure 9.2 shows a graph convolutional network WSD model. Experimental findings demonstrate that GCN outperforms Long Short-Term Memory (LSTM), Convolutional Neural Network (CNN), CNN + BiDirectional Long Short-Term Memory (BiLSTM), and CNN + LSTM in WSD. GCN can improve information transmission between WSD graph nodes and extract disambiguation information more efficiently. It can provide higher WSD accuracy by using minimal convolutional layers, thus reducing the amount of computation required.

9.4.6 The Context Expansion Approach in Graph WSD

Abdalgader et al. [26] propose an improved version of a famous unsupervised graph-based WSD method that leverages all possible semantic information from a lexical resource to enhance graph–semantic connections in order to identify the anticipated meanings of words.

9.4.7 WSD Using WordNet Knowledge Graphs

Sequential contextual similarity matrix multiplication (SCSMM) is a unique knowledge-based WSD technique developed by Abdalgader, K., and Al Shibli, A. [26]. To utilize the benefits of human understanding about terms, a document's primary theme in disambiguating terms, and local context between successive terms, the SCSMM algorithm chains document context, semantic similarity, and heuristic knowledge.

9.5 APPLICATIONS OF WSD

Word sense disambiguation [18] is used in nearly every language technology application, such as:

- *Machine translation* – The most obvious use of WSD is machine translation, often known as MT. The lexical choice for words with various translations for different meanings is handled by WSD in MT. In the target language, the emotions in MT are represented as words.

- *Information retrieval* (IR) – IR technology essentially aids users in locating the information they seek, but it does not directly deliver the answers to questions. WSD is used to address ambiguities in an IR system's inquiries [17].
- *Text mining and information extraction* – WSD is used in most applications to carry out accurate text analysis, for example to aid intelligence collecting systems in correctly flagging terms.
- *Lexicography* – Because contemporary lexicography is based on corpora, lexicography and WSD can function in tandem. WSD provides rough empirical sense classifications as well as statistically significant contextual markers of sense through lexicography.

9.6 CONCLUSIONS AND FUTURE SCOPE

Artificial intelligence is a burgeoning and crucial field in computer science. Its use and applicability may be seen not just in computer science and its applications, but also in a wide range of other fields, including engineering, fundamental sciences, literature, and social studies. It has the potential to transform the research process completely. WSD is an indispensable field in AI. Words with many meanings/senses exist in all human languages, and picking the correct/intended meaning of a phrase is critical for accurate text comprehension. WSD methods are used to accomplish this. WSD is now used in a variety of fields, including information retrieval, automated answering machines, information extraction, speech reconstruction, and machine translation, adopting a variety of approaches.

Techniques are shifting towards automatic learning. The majority of the work that has been done in WSD has focused on English through supervised, knowledge-based, and semi supervised approaches. Future work in this field will be able to focus on other languages, such as Gujarati, Marathi, or Hindi.

REFERENCES

1. Manning, C., & Schutze, H. (1999). *Foundations of Statistical Natural Language Processing*. MIT Press.
2. Stevenson, M., & Wilks, Y. (2001). The interaction of knowledge sources in word sense disambiguation. *Computational Linguistics*, *27*(3), 321–349.
3. Specia, L., Nunes, M. D. G. V., Stevenson, M., & Ribeiro, G. C. B. (2006). Multilingual versus monolingual WSD. In Proceedings of the Workshop on Making Sense of Sense: Bringing Psycholinguistics and Computational Linguistics Together, Trento, Italy.
4. Lefever, E., & Hoste, V. (2010). Semeval-2010 task 3: Cross-lingual word sense disambiguation. In 5th International workshop on Semantic Evaluation (SemEval 2010) (pp. 15–20). Association for Computational Linguistics (ACL), Uppsala, Sweden.
5. Moro, A., Raganato, A., & Navigli, R. (2014). Entity linking meets word sense disambiguation: a unified approach. *Transactions of the Association for Computational Linguistics*, 2, 231–244.

6. Specia, L., Nunes, M. D. G. V., Stevenson, M., & Ribeiro, G. C. B. (2006). Multilingual versus monolingual WSD. In Proceedings of the Workshop on Making Sense of Sense: Bringing Psycholinguistics and Computational Linguistics Together, Trento, Italy.
7. Agirre, E., & Soroa, A. (2007, June). Semeval-2007 task 02: Evaluating word sense induction and discrimination systems. In Proceedings of the Fourth International Workshop on Semantic Evaluations (semeval-2007) (pp. 7–12).
8. Pradhan, S., Loper, E., Dligach, D., & Palmer, M. (2007, June). Semeval-2007 task-17: English lexical sample, srl and all words. In Proceedings of the Fourth International Workshop on Semantic Evaluations, Prague, Czech Republic (SemEval-2007) (pp. 87–92).
9. Locke, W. N. (1955). Speech typewriters and translating machines. *PMLA*, *70*(2), 23–32.
10. Procopio, L., Barba, E., Martelli, F., & Navigli, R. (2021). Multimirror: Neural cross-lingual word alignment for multilingual word sense disambiguation. In Proceedings of the Thirtieth International Joint Conference on Artificial Intelligence, IJCAI-21, Montreal (pp. 3915–3921).
11. Lucy, V. (1990). Using an on-line dictionary to disambiguate verbal phrase attachment. In Proceedings of the 2nd IBM Conference on NLP, Paris, France (pp. 347–359).
12. Lesk, M. (n.d.). Automatic sense disambiguation: How to tell a pine cone from an ice cream. In Proceedings of the SIGDOC Conference (pp. 24–26).
13. Lee, Y. K., Ng, H. T., & Chia, T. K. (2004, July). Supervised word sense disambiguation with support vector machines and multiple knowledge sources. In Proceedings of SENSEVAL-3, the Third International Workshop on the Evaluation of Systems for the Semantic Analysis of Text (pp. 137–140).
14. Gallant, S. I. (1991). A practical approach for representing context and for performing word sense disambiguation using neural networks. *Neural Computation*, *3*(3), 293–309.
15. Leacock, C., & Chodorow, M. (1998). Combining local context and WordNet similarity for word sense identification. *WordNet: An Electronic Lexical Database*, *49*(2), 265–283.
16. Brown, P. F., Della Pietra, S. A., Della Pietra, V. J., & Mercer, R. L. (1991). A statistical approach to sense disambiguation in machine translation. In Speech and Natural Language: Proceedings of a Workshop Held at Pacific Grove, California, February 19-22, 1991.
17. Manning, C. D., Raghavan, P., & Schutze, H. (2008). *Introduction to Information Retrieval?* Cambridge University Press. Ch, 20, 405–416.
18. Grishman, Ralph. (2010). Information Extraction. 10.1002/9781444324044.ch18.
19. Jacob Devlin, Ming-Wei Chang, Kenton Lee, and Kristina Toutanova. 2019. BERT: Pre-training of Deep Bidirectional Transformers for Language Understanding. In Proceedings of the 2019 Conference of the North American Chapter of the Association for Computational Linguistics: Human Language Technologies, Volume 1 (Long and Short Papers), pages 4171–4186, Minneapolis, Minnesota. Association for Computational Linguistics.
20. Silberer, C., & Ponzetto, S. P. (2010). UHD: Cross-lingual word sense disambiguation using multilingual co-occurrence graphs. In Erk K, Strapparava C, editors. Proceedings of the 5th International Workshop on Semantic Evaluation; 2010 Jul 15–16; Uppsala, Sweden. Stroudsburg: ACL; 2010. p. 134–137. ACL (Association for Computational Linguistics).

21. Duque, A., Stevenson, M., Martinez-Romo, J., & Araujo, L. (2018). Co-occurrence graphs for word sense disambiguation in the biomedical domain. *Artificial Intelligence in Medicine*, *87*, 9–19.
22. Duque, A., Araujo, L., & Martinez-Romo, J. (2015). CO-graph: A new graph-based technique for cross-lingual word sense disambiguation. *Natural Language Engineering*, *21*(5), 743–772.
23. Duque, A., Martinez-Romo, J., & Araujo, L. (2016). Can multilinguality improve biomedical word sense disambiguation?. *Journal of biomedical informatics*, *64*, 320–332.
24. Dongsuk O, Sunjae Kwon, Kyungsun Kim, and Youngjoong Ko. 2018. Word Sense Disambiguation Based on Word Similarity Calculation Using Word Vector Representation from a Knowledge-based Graph. In *Proceedings of the 27th International Conference on Computational Linguistics*, pages 2704–2714, Santa Fe, New Mexico, USA. Association for Computational Linguistics.
25. Zhang, Chun-Xiang & Liu, Rui & Gao, Xue-Yao & Yu, Bo. (2021). Graph Convolutional Network for Word Sense Disambiguation. Discrete Dynamics in Nature and Society. 2021. 1–12. 10.1155/2021/2822126.
26. Abdalgader, K., & Al Shibli, A. (2021). Context expansion approach for graph-based word sense disambiguation. *Expert Systems with Applications*, *168*, 114313.

10 Study of Current Learning Techniques for Natural Language Processing for Early Detection of Lung Cancer

Vanita D. Jadhav and Lalit V. Patil

CONTENTS

10.1 INTRODUCTION

Lung malignancy is a principal cause of death globally. Lung abnormalities are a very dangerous issue in humans. Early detection of lung abnormalities is critical for reducing risk and enabling quick and successful treatment. For lung cancer diagnosis, chest X-rays, computer tomography (CT), magnetic resonance imaging (MRI), and positron emission tomography (PET) scans are the most common tests.

DOI: 10.1201/9781003272649-10

These tests help to examine a doubtful region that may be cancerous. A major sign of lung cancer is introverted pulmonary nodules. These nodules are round, and reside in the lung parenchyma. There are two types of nodules: cancerous and non-cancerous.

For pulmonary nodule detection, a CT scan is the best and most accurate technique compared to other techniques. CT scanning arranges several 2D slices to obtain a 3D chest image. For radiologists, reading these numerous CT slices manually is a big challenge because this task is time- and effort-consuming.

Medical staging of lung cancer is critical for determining a diagnosis and building therapy judgments. In today's medical care, doctors usually define the clinical stage of lung tumors. Clinical staging differs from pathological staging despite the adoption of various modern diagnostic techniques with excellent sensitivity and specificity. Improper lung cancer medical staging can lead to unsatisfactory treatment decisions and, as a result, poor outcomes.

Computer tomography is a significant examination technique for lung cancer patients because it offers valuable information about prime cancer sites and lymph nodes. In addition, the reports provide radiologists with readings on the CT images. Natural language processing (NLP) offers beneficial tools and approaches for communicating this essential information in clinical situations. The free-text nature of the scanning data creates issues when examining it for research and quality enhancement. Similarly, obtaining this data manually wastes time and money.

Because it has better specificity and sensitivity than other techniques, CT scanning is the best method for detecting lung nodules. CT scanning employs multiple detectors to generate a number of 2D slices that may be arranged to create a 3D chest image. The time and effort involved in manually reading these are among the main reasons for the development of computer-assisted automatic lung cancer detection systems.

The major goal of this scanning is to define various types of nodule margins, because margin characteristics are the most important elements in assessing cancer risk. The system suggested in this chapter can assist radiologists in quickly and accurately classifying nodule margin types, which aids in the determination of tumor, nodes, and metastases (TNM) stage and patient life expectancy.

We aimed to use NLP approaches to construct an information extraction system that would automatically extract valuable information from CT reports to improve clinical staging.

10.2 RATIONALE AND SIGNIFICANCE OF THE STUDY

- Lung cancer is a primary cause of death globally.
- The initial stage of detection is important because it is easier to treat abnormal tissue at that point.
- Initial diagnosis of cancer focuses on identifying symptomatic patients so that they can receive effective treatment.

- If cancer is detected in later stages, the chances of survival are less, the problems associated with treatment will be exacerbated, and the cost of care will be higher.
- Cancer cannot be treated effectively when it is in the advanced stages, since there are very few treatments that can completely cure cancer.
- When lung cancer is in its early stages, it is extremely difficult to detect.
- Utilizing a machine learning (ML) approach for early lung cancer diagnosis makes it easier to detect near-imperceptible changes.
- For radiologists, manually reading multiple CT slices is a big challenge because the task is time and effort-consuming.
- For these reasons, there is a need for the development of accurate techniques for early-stage lung cancer detection.

10.3 MOTIVATION

Keeping track of developments in the course of the disease makes it easier to spot them on later occasions and reduces the odds of making errors.

This is where technology and our system come into play. It uses machine learning techniques to detect early-stage lung cancer, which it makes it easier to teach the computer to detect near-imperceptible changes. Our approach is entirely based on data exploration of various cancer cases, ranging from early-stage to late-stage lung cancer.

10.4 LEARNING TECHNIQUES

For the detection of lung cancer in the earliest stages, several machine learning processes were applied, including neural networks and the naive Bayes, k-nearest neighbors (KNN), support vector machine (SVM), adaptive boosting (AdaBoost), and random forest algorithms. Machine learning is a form of data analysis that uses artificial intelligence (AI) to create analytical models. It is based on the principle that machines can learn from data, recognize patterns, and make decisions with little or no human participation.

Machine learning is a branch of AI defined as the ability of a machine to mimic smart human behavior. AI methods are used to support humans in carrying out complicated tasks and solving complex problems.

In the real world, image recognition is a popular application of machine learning. Machine learning is used in search engines, to tailor recommendations on websites, for email spam filters, to enable banking software to detect suspicious transactions, etc.

Machine learning is classified into three types: supervised ML, unsupervised ML, and reinforcement ML. In supervised ML, algorithm is trained on labeled data. Unsupervised ML uses unlabeled data, which means that no human work is required to make the dataset machine-readable, enabling the program to work on much larger datasets. Reinforcement ML is based on the way people study facts in their day-to-day lives.

Deep learning is an ML technique that is modeled after how humans learn. Various deep learning procedures such as mask regions with convolutional neural networks (R-CNN), U-Net, Faster R-CNN, visual geometry group (VGG), and you only look once (YOLO) were used to train the convolutional neural networks to find lung nodules.

The entities and relationships in CT reports were annotated initially as the gold standard method for improving the information extraction (IE) system. Three main parts of the IE system were then developed and evaluated using the annotated CT reports.

10.4.1 Data Annotation

In medical practice, doctors generally stage patients using the TNM staging system, which is currently in its eighth edition. The staging system includes precise criteria for three features of lung cancer: tumor (T), nodule (N), and metastases (M). A CT scan can't possibly offer all of the information needed to stage lung cancer. Other diagnostic methods used by clinicians to stage patients include PET and MRI scans, and biopsies. The clinicians identified 19 questions to answer based on the CT results. In addition, there were three questions about the tumors' form, density, and size. All 22 questions are shown in Table 10.1.

10.4.2 Word Embedding

Word embedding is an unsupervised technique that maps words to real-valued vectors to extract semantic and grammatical information from a corpus. We used word2vec [1] to apply the word embedding method to the Chinese Wikipedia corpus for convolution neural network (CNN) and recurrent neural network (RNN) models in this investigation.

10.4.3 NER Process

Named-entity recognition (NER) is a crucial technique for determining the forms and bounds of the entities under scrutiny, which may then be used to drive other NLP activities. Deep learning NER methods that have recently been developed outperform older methods without the need for tedious feature engineering.

10.4.4 Relation Classification Process

The task of establishing semantic connections among pairs of entities, which can then be used to assemble the relevant things organized to produce better off semantics, is known as relation classification (RC). Although classic RC approaches have delivered satisfactory results, deep learning RC methods have provided more effective solutions to the problem of hand-crafting features.

We can easily incorporate entity-to-entity relation criteria into the model using these strategies to boost prediction performance.

TABLE 10.1
Lung Cancer Diagnostic and Staging Questions

	Question	Type of Answer	Stage
1	Is it possible to see the tumor via bronchoscopy?	Yes/No	TX
2	What's the tumor's largest dimension?	Numerical	T1–4
3	Is there any evidence that the tumor has spread to the bronchus?	Yes/No	T1
4	Is there any evidence that the tumor has spread to the pleura?	Yes/No	T2
5	Is there an atelectasis or obstructive pneumonitis that spreads to the hilar area, affecting either a portion of the lung or the entire lung?	Yes/No	T2
6	Is there a second tumor nodule connected with the primary tumor in the same lobe?	Yes/No	T3
7	Is the tumor invading the major blood vessels?	Yes/No	T4
8	Is there any evidence that the tumor has spread to the vertebral body?	Yes/No	T4
9	Is there a secondary tumor nodule (s) in a different ipsilateral lobe to the original tumor?	Yes/No	T4
10	Are there any lymph node metastases in the region?	Yes/No	N0
11	Are there metastases in the ipsilateral hilar lymph nodes, including direct extension involvement?	Yes/No	N1
12	Are there metastases in the mediastinal lymph nodes on the ipsilateral side?	Yes/No	N2
13	Is there any indication of metastases in the subcarinal lymph nodes?	Yes/No	N2
14	Are there metastases in the mediastinal lymph nodes on the other side?	Yes/No	N3
15	Are there metastases in the hilar lymph nodes on the contralateral side?	Yes/No	N3
16	Is there any evidence of metastases in the lymph nodes of the supraclavicular region?	Yes/No	N3
17	Is there a distinct tumor nodule in the opposite lobe?	Yes/No	M1a
18	Is the tumor accompanied by pleural nodules?	Yes/No	M1a
19	Is there a pleural or pericardial effusion that is malignant?	Yes/No	M1a
20	What's the tumor's shape like?	Text	NA
21	What is the tumor's density like?	Text	NA
22	What is the extent of the tumor's enhancement?	Text	NA

10.4.5 Prediction Performance Step

It is not sufficient to use the mined triples to acquire the solutions to the questions posed in Table 10.1: further analysis is required. To reply to the question of whether there is metastasis in ipsilateral mediastinal lymph nodes, for example, we must first ascertain whether the patient has a prime tumor and a mediastinal lymph node metastasis, and then determine their relative positions.

10.5 RELATED WORK

The book *Automatic Extraction of Lung Cancer Staging Information from Computed Tomography Reports: Deep Learning Approach* by Hu et al. (2021) described an IE system that can mine information about cancer staging from CT reports efficiently and accurately [1]. PhuPaing et al. (2020) proposed an automated nodule detection approach using a 3D chain coding algorithm and an optimized random forest algorithm. Their paper presented a region growing algorithm, a 3D chain code algorithm, and an optimized random forest classifier [2]. Marcelo et al. (2020) described their small pulmonary nodules classification, which mined 3D texture and margin sharpness features from the Lung Image Database Consortium (LIDC) using machine learning algorithms [3]. Amer et al. (2019) proposed a computer-aided design (CAD) system using CT scan images comprising a two-level thresholding technique, morphological operations, a neural network, and SVM [4]. A paper by Johora et al. (2018), "Lung Cancer Detection Using Marker Controlled Watershed with SVM," used the gray level co-occurrence matrix to mine features from lung CT scans [5]. The papers "A Novel Approach to CAD System for the Detection of Lung Nodules in CT Images" by Javaid et al. (2016) and "Auto Diagnostics of Lung Nodules Using Nominal Features Extraction Technique" by Peña et al. (2016) described efficient and accurate detection carried out by extending the 2D approach into 3D [6, 7].

Mekali and Girijamma (2016) suggested pulmonary nodule classification based on the size and volume of the nodules using a chain code algorithm for border reconstruction [8].

Peña et al. (2016) presented a neuro-fuzzy classifier for finding lung nodules in CT scans using thresholding and morphological operations for nodule segmentation [7]. Jin et al. (2016) proposed a convolution neural network for nodule detection [9] Aggarwal et al. (2015) described the abstraction of features and classification of lung nodules in CT scans using thresholding and morphological operations for nodule segmentation and an artificial neural network (ANN) for classification [10]. Punithavathy et al. (2015) proposed a method for the automatic detection of lung cancer by analyzing statistical texture features using thresholding and morphological operations for nodule segmentation and morphological closing for border reconstruction [11]. Kaur et al. (2015) proposed a CAD system using a back-propagation network and an ANN [12]. Kulkarni and Panditrao (2014) described the classification of lung cancer stages by means of image processing techniques [13]. Chen et al. (2014) proposed a rolling ball algorithm for border reconstruction [14].

Shan and Rezaei (2021) proposed a lung cancer diagnosis method by means of an ANN optimized by the improved thermal exchange optimization (ITEO) algorithm using mathematical morphology for segmentation, the ITEO algorithm to optimize feature selection, and an ANN optimized by ITEO for picture classification [15, 16]. Venkatesan et al. (2021) described nodule discovery with a CNN using Apache Spark and graphics processing unit (GPU) frameworks to implement a Gaussian noise removal technique and a deep model trained by means of the CNN Apache Spark environment [17]. Li et al. (2020) described the use of multi-resolution CNNs to find lung nodules in X-ray images Their method used lung field segmentation for pre-processing and multi-resolution patch-based CNNs trained to find lung nodules [18].

The paper by Heng et al. (2020), "Deep Learning Assisted predict Of Lung Cancer On Computed Tomography Images Using The Adaptive Hierarchical Heuristic Mathematical Model (AHHMM)," described the use of deep learning-assisted AHHMM and a modified k-means algorithm [19]. In "Deep-learning Framework to Detect Lung Abnormality – a Study with Chest X-ray and Lung CT Scan images," Bhandary et al. (2020) used morphological and watershed segmentation for nodule segmentation and an ensemble feature technique to categorize lung CT scans [20]. Shakeel et al. (2020) proposed a method for "Automatic Lung Cancer Detection from CT Image Using Improved Deep Neural Network and Ensemble Classifier" [21]. In their paper "Lung Cancer Detection from CT Image Using Improved Profuse Clustering and Deep Learning Instantaneously Trained Neural Networks," Shakeel et al. (2019) described the use of the weighted mean histogram equalization approach for noise removal and the improved profuse clustering technique for segmentation [22]. Reddy et al. (2019) described "Recognition of Lung Cancer Using Machine Learning Mechanisms with Fuzzy Neural Networks" [23]. Bhatia et al. (2019) described a method for detecting lung cancer using deep learning methods, along with XGBoost and random forest for classification [24].

Makaju et al. (2018) described a lung cancer detection method using CT images where pre-processing was carried out using median and Gaussian filters, detection used watershed segmentation, and classification of nodules as cancerous or non-cancerous was accomplished using SVM [25]. The paper by Faisal et al. (2018), "An Evaluation of Machine Learning Classifiers and Ensembles for Early-stage Prediction of Lung Cancer," described the implementation of pre-processing for data cleaning using different classifiers such as neural networks, instance decision trees, gradient boosted trees, the naive Bayes algorithm, and SVM [26]. The study by Singh and Gupta (2018), "Performance Analysis of Various Machine Learning Based Approaches for Detection and Classification of Lung Cancer in Humans," discussed various denoising and thresholding methods [27]. The paper by Alam and Hossan (2018), "Multi-stage Lung Cancer Detection and prediction using multi-class SVM Classifier," described the enhancement and segmentation of images via a multi-class SVM classifier [28]. A summary of the literature is given in Table 10.2.

TABLE 10.2
Summary of Literature

Author Name and Year	Approach/methodology	Parameters Considered	Limitations
Hu et al. (2021)	Named entity recognition algorithm, relation classification method, post-processing approach used to recognize named entities	Location, size, density, enhancement, shape	Margin feature not extracted
PhuPaing et, al. (2020)	3D chain coding, optimized random forest	2D and 3D geometric features	TNM stage not detected, life expectancy not calculated
Marcelo et al. (2020)	KNN, MLP, random forest	3D texture and margin sharpness features	TNM stage not detected
Amer et al. (2019)	Thresholding technique, morphological operations, multi-layer feed-forward neural network	Statistical features, gradient features, and textural features	More work required for differentiating cancerous and non-cancerous lung nodules
Johora et al. (2018)	Marker-controlled watershed segmentation, SVM	Area, perimeter, eccentricity	Very few features extracted
Javaid et al. (2016)	Morphological closing, k-means clustering, morphological opening, SVM	2D and 3D features	Average time required to detect nodule too high
Mekali and Girijamma (2016)	Iterative thresholding, Freeman chain code algorithm, region growing algorithm	Shape, size, volume	Margin features not extracted
Peña et al. (2016)	3D blob algorithm, SVM	Diameter, area, radius, circularity, elongation	Relatively high false positive rate
Jin et al. (2016)	CNN	Size, region of interest, shape	Very few features extracted

(Continued)

TABLE 10.2 (CONTINUED)
Summary of Literature

Author Name and Year	Approach/methodology	Parameters Considered	Limitations
Aggarwal et al. (2015)	Linear discriminate analysis, optimal thresholding	Geometric, statistical and gray level characteristics	Optimum accuracy not achieved
Punithavathy et al. (2015)	Morphological operators, fuzzy clustering	Statistical texture features	Very few features extracted
Chen et al. (2014)	Rolling ball algorithm, adaptive threshold binarization	Shape, area	Margin features not extracted
Shan and Rezaei (2021)	Mathematical morphology used for segmentation, ITEO algorithm used for feature selection, ANN used for image classification	Contrast, correlation, homogeneity, entropy, energy	Convolutional features not extracted.
Venkatesan et al. (2021)	Gaussian noise removal technique, deep model trained using CNN	Geometric features, textural features	Dataset enrichment using data augmentation required
Li et al. (2020)	Lung segmentation, rib suppression, multi-resolution patch-based CNNs	Radiological features	Margin type classification not done
Yu et al. (2020)	Deep learning, aided adaptive hierarchical heuristic mathematical model, modified k-means algorithm	Spectral-related features	Margin type classification not done.
Bhandary et al. (2020)	Morphological segmentation and watershed segmentation	Deep and handcrafted features	Life expectancy not calculated

(Continued)

TABLE 10.2 (CONTINUED)
Summary of Literature

Author Name and Year	Approach/methodology	Parameters Considered	Limitations
Shakeel et al. (2020)	Improved deep neural network and ensemble classifier, as well as multilayer brightness-preserving technique for pre-processing	Geometric features	TNM stage not determined
Shakeel et al. (2019)	Weighted mean histogram equalization approach for noise removal, segmentation with the help of profuse clustering method, neural network trained using deep learning	Spectral features	Margin features not extracted
Reddy et al. (2019)	Machine learning approaches	Area, perimeter, peculiarity, entropy, contrast, association	Margin features not extracted
Bhatia et al. (2019)	XGBoost and random forest used for classification	Pre-processed features	Life expectancy not calculated
Makaju et al. (2018)	Median filter and gaussian filter for pre-processing, watershed segmentation, and SVM for classification	Perimeter, area, centroid, eccentricity, diameter, mean intensity	Optimum accuracy not achieved
Faisal et al. (2018)	Pre-processing used to clean the data, different classifiers such as SVM, decision tree, naive Bayes	Geometric features	Margin features not extracted
Singh and Gupta (2018)	Denoising methods, thresholding methods, KNN, SVM, decision tree classifier	Textural and statistical features	Life expectancy not calculated
Alam and Hossan (2018)	Image enhancement, segmentation, multi-class SVM	Vitality, entropy, mean, standard deviation, homogeneity, smoothness	Margin features not extracted

10.6 DISCUSSION

The goal of these studies is to use machine learning and deep learning to detect lung cancer. The majority of the work has used CT images, with only a handful of studies using X-ray imaging, and lung cancer detection is carried out with both technologies using the following methods:

Image acquisition – The acquisition of images is the initial step. Images provide crucial data for detecting lung disease. X-rays, CT scans, histopathology, and sputum smear microscopy images are all examples of images that could be employed. This stage produces photos, which will be used to train the model later.

Pre-processing – Here, the image is enhanced, then image processing is completed using thresholding, de-noising, binarization, zero centering, and normalization. Data augmentation is applied to the images to increase the quantity of available data. Feature extraction is conducted using deep learning models to find important features. The output of this phase is a set of improved images which will be used in further training.

Training – Three aspects are evaluated in this phase: the DL algorithms used, transfer learning applications, and ensemble practice. Deep belief networks, recurrent RNNs, and multi-layer perceptron (MLP) neural networks are among the deep learning techniques employed. These processes have quite different learning styles. "Transfer learning" is the process of passing information from one model to another model. Ensemble classification allows for the use of many models during classification. Both transfer learning and ensemble assessment are used to reduce training time and improve classification accuracy.

Classification – In this phase, the trained model predicts the class of an image – cancerous or non-cancerous – using methods including KNN, neural networks, SVM, gradient boosted tree, decision tree, multinomial random forest classifier, stochastic gradient descent, and MLP classifiers for classification. Work executed using deep learning methods achieves higher accuracy than machine learning methods.

10.7 CONCLUSION

Early detection of lung cancer can improve effectiveness of treatment and improves patients' chances of survival. This chapter has presented a comprehensive survey of numerous learning methods to classify lung malignancies using CT images. Researchers utilize a variety of classifiers, including multinomial random forest classifier, SVM, ensemble classifier, neural network, MLP, gradient boosted tree, naive Bayes, decision tree, and k-nearest neighbors. The results of the general survey conducted in this study show that deep learning-based approaches achieve more accuracy than machine learning-based approaches. To assist appropriate clinical staging, information extraction systems can be used routinely to extract relevant information from CT reports using NLP approaches.

REFERENCES

1. D. Hu, H. Zhang, S. Li, and Y. Wang (2021) *Automatic Extraction of Lung Cancer Staging Information from Computed Tomography Reports: Deep Learning Approach*, JMIR Publications.
2. M. PhuPaing, and K. Hamamoto (2020) "Automatic Detection of Pulmonary Nodules using 3-dimensional Chain Coding and Optimized-random-forest", *Applied Science*. 10(7), 2346.
3. A. F. Marcelo, C. Oliveira, and A. P. Machado (2020) "Using 3D texture and margin sharpness features on classification of small pulmonary nodules", *Computer Science, Medicine*, 2377–5416.
4. H. M. Amer, F. E. Z. Abou-Chadi, S. S. Kishk, and I. Marwa (2019) "A CAD System for the Early Detection of Lung Nodules Using Computed Tomography Scan Images", *IJOE*, 15(4), 40-51.
5. F. T. Johora, M. H. Jony, Md. S. Hossain, and H. K. Rana (2018) "Lung cancer detection using marker controlled watershed with SVM", *Journal of Science and Engineering*, 5(1).
6. M. Javaid, M. Javid, M. Z. U. Rehman, and S. I. A. Shah (2016) "A novel approach to CAD system for the detection of lung nodules in CT images", *Computer Methods and Programs in Biomedicine*, 135, 125–139.
7. D. M. Peña, S. Luo, and A. M. S. Abdelgader (2016) "Auto diagnostics of lung nodules using minimal characteristics extraction technique", *Diagnostics*. 6(1): 13.
8. V. Mekali, and Girijamma H.A (2016) "Solitary pulmonary nodules classification based on tumor size and volume of nodules", 2nd International Conference on Applied and Theoretical Computing and Communication Technology (iCATccT), Bangalore, India.
9. X. Y. Jin, Y. C. Zhang, and Q. L. Jin (2016) "Pulmonary nodule detection based on CT images using convolution neural network", 9th International Symposium On Computational Intelligence and Design (ISCID), Hangzhou.
10. T. Aggarwal, A. Furqan, and K. Kalra (2015) "Feature extraction and LDA based Classification of lung nodules in chest CT scan images", International Conference on Advances in Computing, Communications and Informatics (ICACCI), Kochi.
11. K. Punithavathy, M. M. Ramya, and S. Poobal (2015) "Analysis of statistical texture Features for automatic lung cancer detection in PET/CT images", International Conference on Robotics, Automation, Control and Embedded Systems (RACE), Chennai.
12. J. Kaur, N. Garg, and D. Kaur (2015) "An automatic CAD system for early detection of lung tumor using back propagation network", International Conference on Medical Imaging, m-Health and Emerging Communication Systems (MedCom). Greater Noida, India.
13. A. Kulkarni, and A. Panditrao (2014) "Classification of lung cancer stages on CT scan images using image processing", IEEE International Conference on Advanced Communications Control and Computing Technologies. Ramanathapuram, India
14. N. Chen, G. Liu, Y. Liao, C. Ou, and Y. Yu (2014) "Research on computer-aided diagnosis of lung nodule", IEEE Workshop on Electronics, Computer and Applications, Ottawa.
15. M. P. Paing, and S. Choomchuay (2017) "Classification of margin characteristics from 3D pulmonary nodules", IEEE Biomedical Engineering International Conference (BMEiCON). Hokkaido, Japan.
16. R. Shan, and T. Rezaei (2021) "Lung cancer diagnosis based on an ANN optimized by improved TEO algorithm", *Hindawi, Computational Intelligence and Neuroscience* 2021.

17. N. J. Venkatesan, D. R. Shin, and C. S. Nam (2021) "Nodule Detection with Convolutional Neural Network Using Apache Spark and GPU Frameworks", *Applied Science. 11*(6), 2838.
18. X. Li, L. Shen, X. Xie, S. Huang, Z. Xie, X. Hong, and J. Yu (2020) "Multi-resolution Convolutional networks for chest X-ray radiograph-based lung nodule Detection", *Artificial Intelligence in Medicine* 103, 101744.
19. Y. Heng, Z. Zhou, and Q. Wang (2020) "Deep learning assisted predict of lung cancer on computed tomography images using the adaptive hierarchical heuristic mathematical model", *IEEE Access*, 8, 86400–86410.
20. A. Bhandary, G. A. Prabhu, V. Rajinikanth, K. P. Thanaraj, S. C. Satapathy, D.E. Robbins and N. S. Raja (2020) "Deep-learning framework to detect lung abnormality: A study with chest X-Ray and lung CT scan images", *Pattern Recognition Letters* 129, 271–278.
21. P. M. Shakeel, M. A. Burhanuddin, and M. I. Desa (2020) "Automatic lung cancer detection from CT image using improved deep neural network and ensemble classifier", *Neural Computing and Applications* 1–14.
22. P. M. Shakeel, M. A. Burhanuddin, and M. I. Desa (2019) "Lung cancer detection from CT image using improved profuse clustering and deep learning instantaneously trained neural networks", *Measurement*, 145, 702–712.
23. U. Reddy, B. Reddy, and B. Reddy (2019) *Recognition of Lung Cancer Using Machine Learning Mechanisms with Fuzzy Neural Networks.* Traitement du Signal.
24. S. Bhatia, Y. Sinha, and L. Goel (2019) *Lung Cancer Detection: A Deep Learning Approach in Soft Computing for Problem Solving* (pp. 699–705). Springer.
25. S. Makaju, P. W. C. Prasad, A. Alsadoon, A. K. Singh, and A. Elchouemi (2018) "Lung cancer detection using CT scan images", *Procedia Computer Science* 125, 107–114.
26. M. I. Faisal, S. Bashir, Z. S. Khan, and F. H. Khan (2018) "An evaluation of Machine learning classifiers and ensembles for early-stage prediction of lung cancer", 3rd International Conference on Emerging Trends in Engineering, Sciences and Technology (ICEEST), India.
27. G. A. P. Singh, and P. K. Gupta (2018) "Performance analysis of various machine Learning based approaches for detection and classification of lung cancer in humans", *Neural Computing and Applications.*
28. J. Alam, S. Alam, and A. Hossan (2018) "Multi-stage lung cancer detection and prediction using multi-class svm classifier", International Conference on Computer, Communication, Chemical, Material and Electronic Engineering (IC4ME2). University of Rajshahi-6205, Bangladesh.

11 A Critical Analysis of Graph Topologies for Natural Language Processing and Their Applications

Meenakshi Nawal, Sunita Gupta, Neha Janu, and Carlos M. Travieso-Gonzalez

CONTENTS

DOI: 10.1201/9781003272649-11

11.1 INTRODUCTION

Graphs have always been an important part of natural language processing (NLP) applications. Graphs are used in question answering, machine translation based on syntax, abstract meaning illustration, etc. Graph theory, NLP, and information retrieval are well-studied disciplines. Conventionally, these fields have been considered to be separate, with different applications, algorithms, and end-users, but current study shows that they are closely connected. A large variety of NLP and information salvage applications achieve effective results using graphs. Natural language processing is incomplete without graphs and their topologies. NLP includes text, text construction or formation, speech or conversation, grammar rules, machine interpretation, and extraction of knowledge. The topologies and algorithms of graphs have played a vital role in modeling these sorts of problems and arriving at solutions.

11.1.1 Natural Language Processing

NLP is a part of artificial intelligence (AI), where computers examine, comprehend, and extract meaning from human language in a useful and smart way. By using NLP, designers can form and build knowledge to carry out tasks such as translation, relationship abstraction, automatic summarization, topic subdivision, and sentiment analysis. NLP allows developers and businesses to produce software that can recognize and comprehend human languages. NLP can be used in many ways, such as for spam detection, conversational interfaces, text composition, sentiment analysis, question answering, automatic summarization, and part of speech (POS) identification. Information from text documents can be extracted and stored as graphs. This permits numerous use cases, such as content based recommendations, natural language searches, and examining document similarity.

11.1.2 Tools and Libraries for NLP

Open source NLP libraries and tools provide the building blocks for many real-world applications.

Apache OpenNLP is a machine learning (ML) toolkit that features entity extraction, tokenizers, part of speech tagging, parsing, coreferencing, sentence segmentation, etc.

Stanford NLP is a set of NLP tools to enable POS tagging, sentiment analysis, named entity recognition, coreference resolution systems, etc.

MALLET is a Java package offering information extraction, document classification, clustering, topic modeling, etc.

Natural Language Toolkit (NLTK) is a Python library that offers modules for NLP components like classification, tagging, text processing, stemming, parsing, tokenization, and semantic reasoning. More than one implementation is available for each application, and users can select the most appropriate algorithm or procedure. It supports several languages. It is difficult to use some of its advanced functionality as all data is represented as strings. Compared to other tools, NLTK is slow. It is a good tool for testing, investigation, and for applications which require a specific combination of algorithms.

TextBlob is an NLTK extension that provides a simple way of accessing many NLTK functions. It offers functionality from its pattern library. It is a good tool for beginners for learning purposes. It is used in the creation of applications that do not need to offer very high performance. It is good for smaller projects.

PyTorch-NLP is a Python library for NLP. It is good for fast prototyping and is updated with current research. It comes with pre-trained embeddings, text encoders, dataset loaders, metrics, samplers, and neural network modules. It is open source software released under the BSD3 license. It is used in prototyping and preliminary construction work using the available innovative algorithms.

SpaCy is an open source software library for advanced NLP in the Python and Cython languages. It is possibly the main competitor to NLTK, being faster. It signifies everything as objects, which streamlines the interface for creating applications and helps to integrate it with other data science frameworks and tools. It supports fewer languages than NLTK. It has a simple interface and basic adoptions and organized credentials and several neural models for numerous components of language processing and study.

Textacy is a Python library for executing a variety of NLP tasks with ease and speed. It is based on the high-performance SpaCy library, which gives it core NLP functionality in processing work. It is used for text pre-processing, identifying keywords in context, key term extraction, quotation attribution, providing text and readability statistics, information extraction, topic modeling, and emotional valence analysis.

Retext is part of the unified Node Tools collective. It provides an interface that allows several tools and plug-ins to integrate and work collectively and efficiently. It basically uses plug-ins to simplify tasks such as correcting typography, sentiment detection, and spell checking.

Natural is one of the most popular Node Tools, incorporating many NLP functions. It supports phonetics, frequency of documents, tokenizing, stemming, string similarity identification, classification, WordNet, and some inflections. It is very similar to NLTK, but seeks to include a vast library of functions in a single package that is still at the development stage.

Compromise is a lightweight and fast NLP library. It has a very innate self-learning API. It supports a wide variety of useful text parsing and management functionalities through a browser interface.

OpenNLP is an ML-based toolkit for NLP developed by the Apache Foundation. It is easy to integrate with other Apache projects, such as Apache Spark, NiFi, and Flink. It provides common NLP processing components, and it can be used as a library in another application or from its command line. It supports multiple languages and NLP tasks, such as language detection, named entity extraction, POS tagging, tokenization, sentence segmentation, chunking, and parsing.

StanfordNLP is a set of tools providing deep learning NLP, statistical NLP, and rule-based NLP functionality. It can be used outside Java as another very powerful programming language. It offers a special license for commercial purposes.

CogCompNLP, developed by the University of Illinois, offers a Python library with analogous functionality. It is used to process text locally as well as on remote systems. It can eliminate a great amount of load from local devices. It delivers many processing functionalities, such as chunking, semantic role labeling, lemmatization, tokenization, dependency and constituency parsing, POS tagging, etc.

11.1.3 Graph of Words and Graph -based Natural Language Generation

A graphical illustration of a text item like passages, documents, or sentences is referred to as a text graph. It is a pre-processing step to support NLP tasks such as relation extraction and textual entailment.

In numerous NLP problems, objects are linked by relationships. Graphs are the usual way to capture connections among objects. Algorithms based on graphs are used in NLP in many applications such as finding objects that satisfy some structural properties which are different from those of other entities and finding optimal solutions for given relations among entities.

Graphs are all-pervasive in NLP, and are very powerful illustration tools. In any of the sentence/paragraph, it is possibly the utmost seeming representation of words based on graph. A graph consists of nodes and edges. Edges between nodes represent relationships between them. Several graph procedures are NP-hard. They are not scaled to present data sizes. Scalability is an important feature for algorithms, because they often process large amounts of data. This problem is significant in computational NLP methods, e.g., streaming graphs which change over time, such as graphs constructed from social media inputs. For example, on Twitter, networks represent users and their tweets, and the relationships among them alter quickly.

11.4 GRAPH EMBEDDING IN NLP

Embedding is the most important research area in NLP. Initially, embedding techniques were applied to words, but later they were also used in graph structures. Types of embeddings include word, sentence, document, and graph embedding. Graph embedding is the main technique in NLP.

11.4.1 Node Embeddings

Graph embedding methods based on nodes are divided into three types: matrix factorization methods, graph neural networks, and random walk-based algorithms.

11.4.1.1 Matrix Factorization Methods

Node representation techniques rely on removing a set of pair wise same information for vertices using dimensionality reduction. Dimensionality reduction is used to compress word vectors into lesser dimensions. Analogous statistical measures are used for approximating vertex likeness in graphs. For example an edge between two vertices shows their similarity, so an adjacency matrix in a graph can be used to determine pairwise similarities between vertices. This technique is called matrix factorization (MF), as it signifies graph properties as a matrix and calculates embeddings for each vertex by factorizing the matrix. MF methods are encouraged by dimensionality reduction techniques like Laplacian eigenmaps (Belkin & Niyogi, 2003), locality preserving projections and principal component analysis.

11.4.1.2 Graph Neural Network Methods

Node embedding techniques based on neural networks are called graph neural networks (GNNs). This is a wide field that either directly uses deep learning models like auto encoders for vertex illustration, or concepts taken from deep learning such as convolution operations. GNN-based models are classified into two key classes: auto encoder-based techniques and graph convolution networks (GCNs).

11.4.1.2.1 Auto Encoder-based Models

Auto encoders are the primary option for neural network architectures for dimensionality reduction. A given representation is encoded into a dense embedding in an unsupervised manner. From this, the same input can be reconstructed. Due to this property, auto encoders are suitable candidates to replace matrix factorization techniques. Auto encoder-based node embedding has two phases. The first stage examines the network structure and extracts a context vector for each vertex to represent their local or higher-order neighborhood. The second stage uses an auto encoder to compress the context vector into a dense, low-dimensional embedding.

11.4.1.2.2 Convolution-based Models

Convolution methods resolve the scalability and generalizability problems of earlier practices by resorting to local neighborhoods. It combines embeddings of neighboring nodes to build a target embedding. It is similar to the convolutional method. For computing the target node embedding, neighboring node embeddings are used. The neighboring vertices are inline embedded using their neighbors. This procedure is completed in an iterative manner. The total number of iterations is called the depth.

Embeddings of neighboring nodes are combined in each iteration for a target node t. The aggregation is simply element-wise, as in GCNs. This is then combined with the prior approximation of its embedding in the previous iteration. GCNs use a weighted sum to draw the graph. Thus convolutional methods can address both generalizability and scalability issues. New node embedding is computed using learned aggregation and combination functions and by looking up the present embeddings for neighboring nodes.

11.4.1.3 Random Walk (RW) Methods

In the matrix factorization method, the measure of node resemblance used is deterministic as it depends on a set of fixed statistical features. For very large networks, vast matrices need to be built, so MF is usually not scalable. RW-based methods use a stochastic method for determining similarity. In this way, they are different from matrix factorization methods. A sequence of truncated random walks is performed on the graph. During each walk, sampling of vertices is carried out to change the structure of the graph into a group of paths. These paths are regarded as artificial sentences which supply data about similar (topologically related) nodes in the graph. It is similar to natural language, where semantically alike words tend to co-occur recurrently.

Earlier methods took the direct normalized visit probabilities as vectors. These RW-based node depictions outperform conventional deterministic graph analysis methods such as the normalized graph distance used for encoding semantic networks in lexical semantic applications (Pilehvar & Navigli, 2015). However, the main constraint on conservative RW-based procedures is their high dimensionality. For this reason, newer RW-based techniques employ neural networks to address the dimensionality problem. DeepWalk (Perozzi et al., 2014) and node-2vec (Grover & Leskovec, 2016) are the two main techniques. Word2vec algorithms are efficient for node illustration. Another technique, LINE (Tang et. al., 2015), is not strictly RW-based, but is very closely connected. LINE combines two dissimilar objectives to learn node embeddings: first- and second-order.

11.4.1.4 Applications of Node Embedding

Node embedding evaluation revolves around the idea of similarity between node embeddings. Here are some of the applications.

Node classification is one of the main applications. Labels are assigned to vertices depending on the instructions learned from the considered subset vertices. This process is called label propagation. It is the first choice for evaluating node embeddings due to its supervised nature and ease of evaluation. For example, in calculating embeddings for the vertices in a WordNet graph, the task is to label the unlabeled nodes.

Node clustering is the same as node classification, but the labels are not predefined. It includes calculating similarities among vertices and then combining them depending on these similarities. One application of this approach is to lessen the intellect granularity of WordNet by assembling together word senses that are the same.

Node ranking involves recommending the top K nodes in a given target node according to certain criteria – e.g., finding the most semantically similar synsets to a given synset in WordNet. Its applications include question answering, recommending friends on social networks, and personalizing advertisements, just to name a few.

Graph visualization involves visualizing a given graph in a low-dimensional space like 2D to provide a high-level outline of the elements of the graph. Various categories of vertices can be shown with different colors. Node embeddings are of high dimensions, hence they are not directly visualizable, so dimensionality reduction techniques are applied, such as t-distributed stochastic neighbor embedding (t-SNE) (Tang et. al., 2015) and principal component analysis (Van der Maaten & Hinton, 2008) on the vertex embeddings prior to visualization. Graph visualization provides a qualitative testbed for assessing vertex embeddings. Some other applications of it are in fields like biology, bioinformatics, social network analysis, and software engineering.

Network compression involves quantifying the capabilities of vertex embedding techniques to encode structural information of a graph using reconstruction error. This approach uses node embeddings calculated for a graph to attempt to rebuild it. The difference between the original and the reconstructed graphs is the reconstruction error. Many researchers (e.g., Wang et al., 2016; Ou et. al., 2016) have shown that typical graphs can be rebuilt with good precision from their vertex embeddings.

11.4.2 Relation Embedding

In relation embedding, graph edges represent the associations between nodes.

11.4.2.1 Knowledge-based Relation Embedding

This is a representation technique that targets concepts and named entities from knowledge bases. Knowledge graphs or semantic networks are used to make representations of entities and relations. These are precisely embattled to the knowledge base completion task. A technique for embedding both entities and relations is given in Bordes et al. (2013).

11.4.2.2 Unsupervised Relation Embedding

Relations are stored in knowledge resources, as described earlier, but the distinct nature of these relations has inspired a novel field that examines their depiction as parts of constant vector spaces. Many methods have attempted to add continuity to discrete knowledge sources, but it appears that the complex nature of relations in the real world requires using fully continuous models of relations instead of joining continuity onto fundamentally discrete models of relations. An alternative method to model these relationships among ideas is by using a text corpus, as in word embeddings. Two main standards are co-occurrence and predictive models to learn relation embeddings.

11.4.2.3 Applications of Relation Embedding

Link prediction is the main application of relation embedding. The productivity of relations in a fundamental semantic network has a direct effect on the performance of a model using that source (Agirre et al., 2009). By observing interactions between nodes, relations in networks are constructed. Missing edges in a graph are predicted using link prediction. Applications of link prediction include biological network analysis (Pilehvar et al., 2013) and friend suggestions on social network sites. The main application of unsupervised relation embeddings is to model relationships between pairs of words.

11.5 GRAPH TOPOLOGIES FOR NLP APPLICATIONS

Graph topologies are utilized in numerous applications of NLP, such as finding answers for the given relations between elements.

11.5.1 Critical Analysis of Graph Architectures for NLP Applications

Construction of graph topologies is a crucial aspect of NLP as the architecture must develop the data appropriately. Graph representation plays an important role in resolving issues of NLP in a better computational manner with reference to time and memory space. For these reasons, a critical analysis of graph topologies is required, addressing issues such as text structure, discourse, generation, normalization, summarization, syntactic parsing, tagging, and machine translation. This section will analyze some issues of graph topologies or architectures such as heterogeneous graphs, multi-layered graphs, hypergraphs, and more complicated issues with graph data or embedding to improve computational procedures.

11.5.1.1 Text Formation, Conversation, and Generation

Altered messages and expanding sums lead to the requirement for message standardization and grammatical mistake revision to supply clean information to NLP procedures down the handling chain. This part reviews two or three strategies that address the issues with chart based strategies. At the point when an ideal text is procured, a plausible ensuing stage is inciting its development, to distinguish semantically sensible parts (14 Nastase et al., 2015).

11.5.1.1.1 Data Normalization

The vocabulary of web-based media is extremely powerful and elective spellings for words subject to extemporaneous or changed shortenings, phonetic substitutions or work related conversation language are continually made.Text standardization can be utilized to assist with tasks such as machine translation, text-to-speech, and information extraction.

11.5.1.1.2 Text Formation

This methodology decides the positioning of key phrases that can be utilized to depict the document. The subsequent stage is to use this data to fabricate. The main activity is to bunch sentences. The weight of the links between sentences relies upon the quantity and weight of the key phrases they share. Recognizing that the order in which sentences appear is important, the weight of the edge has an additional factor which is added when two sentences 'are near-by' or not. (14 Nastase et al., 2015). To bunch the sentences, explicit grouping is applied to the occurrence framework of the sentence chart to deliver a progressive bunching of sentences. Contingent upon the degree of rundown, groups at various levels can be utilized and then agent sentences are chosen from each bunch.

11.5.1.1.3 Language Production

Mapping between the syntactic trees and dependency diagram is necessary for interpretation. Lattices of words can be used to identify shared traits of comparative sentences (Barzilay & Lee, 2003). They then recognize sets of grids from various corpora that are paraphrases of one another - the distinguishing proof interaction checks whether the cross sections take comparative contentions; given an input sentence to be summarized, they match it to a lattice and utilize an paraphrase from the matched lattice's mate to produce a result sentence.The syntax or grammar of the resultant sentence words are encoded and determined as a hypergraph with their weights.

11.5.1.1.4 Communication

Another issue of communication is deciding which discussion string of every expression belongs to a similar discussion. The first step of artificial intelligence is to anticipate probabilities for sets of sentences as having a place with a similar discussion string rather than lexical, timing and communication. A graph is built with a vertex for each sentence and edges between sentences.

11.5.1.2 Language Rules and Classification

Labeling is used to label words or sentences in a collection of data. Graph approaches are very useful to provide a correlated view of data in the entire dataset. Consistent labeling is introduced to label the initial set of nodes by using supervised or unsupervised learning (14 Nastase et al., 2015).

11.5.1.2.1 Syntactic Parsing

Dependent relations in a statement produce an acyclic graph. This perspective can be utilized to project the dependency issues in a maximum spanning tree (MST). The MST is used to observe the most noteworthy scoring subgraph of a graph that fulfills the tree limitations over the arrangement of vertices. Diagram writing gives different algorithms for deciding the MST of a linked graph. Picking an algorithm relies upon qualities of the dependent diagram (Eisner, 1997).

11.5.1.2.2 Classification

Utilizing graph strategies for labeling relies on the principle that comparable elements should have similar tags. The nodes in the graph are used to address words or expressions and the weights are assigned to edges according to the similarity adjacent matric. A graph structure covers connected anchor texts of hyperlinks in organized partitions in Wikipedia editorials specifically records and tables. A CRF variety is utilized to classify vertices in the diagram as one of the twelve Named Entity types (Watanabe et al., 2007). Three sorts of connections are characterized between attach texts, in view of their connections in the organized parts of the text kin, cousins, and family members.

11.5.1.3 Context

In the area of lexical and message semantics, the most well-known portrayal is a graph having words as nodes. The manner in which boundaries are drawn and weighted differs a lot depending upon the assignment. It can depict directed/undirected relations, and might be obtained from different networks (e.g., as comparability/gap from WordNet) (Nastase et al., 2015).

11.5.1.3.1 Dictionary and Communication Models

One of the major graph architectures was developed by Widdows and Dorow (2002) to assist in NLP tasks. Their purpose is to assemble semantic classes by separating from crude corpora each of the components having a place with a specific semantic classification. The strategy first builds a huge graph comprising the multitude of elements in an enormous corpus, connected by the combination AND OR.

11.5.1.3.2 Similarity Measures

A huge class of techniques for syntactic likeness comprises measurements determined on existing semantic networks like WordNet and Roget, by applying the dijkstra algorithm (shortest path algorithm) that recognizes the nearest semantic connection between two information ideas. A Page Rank algorithm is used to ascertain the fixed appropriation of the vertices in the WordNet chart (Watanabe et al., 2007). When evaluated on standard word relatedness data sets, the method was found to improve significantly over previously proposed algorithms for semantic relatedness.

11.5.1.3.3 Word Significance Orientation

An outline of graph based techniques effectively used to handle the assignments by demonstrating the associations between expression of the words. A graph comprising the multitude of labeled and unlabeled models can be accommodated in a questionable word. A min-cut algorithm can be applied on a graph constructed over the sentences in a text, which is used to separate subjective from objective sentences. (Nastase et al., 2015).

11.5.1.3.4 Opinion Analysis and Social Networks

Opinion and subjectivity analysis is a region identified with both semantics and pragmatics. A methodology dependent on a min-cut graph algorithm can be viably applied to construct abstract concentrates of film reviews. A graph is developed by adding every person's sentences in a review as nodes, and by sketching boundaries dependent on sentence closeness. A minimum-cut algorithm is used to remove the irrelevant sentences from the goal ones. The graph that wraps the networks of tweeters and tweets connected on content similitude, incorporates extra edges that relocates and re-tweet data (Yan et al., 2012).

11.5.1.4 Machine Translation

The objective of the machine translation algorithm is to process delicate names for unlabeled vertices from the labeled vertices. The edge weight encodes (naturally) the level of conviction about the similitude of the delicate naming for the associated vertices. In this configuration, the procedure can be applied to machine interpretation, especially to energize smooth interpretation probabilities for comparable data sources. To assemble a graph consisting of training and testing information (word strings) associated through edges that encode pair-wise likenesses between tests (Nastase et al., 2015).

11.5.1.5 Knowledge Mining and Demonstration

Data extraction and portrayal is a complex issue, and this is reflected in the range of graph-based methodologies proposed. One characteristic of knowledge mining that makes it especially suitable for a graph approach is the fact that similar sorts of data can appear in various settings or structures (Coursey & Mihalcea, 2009). A well known way to deal with data mining is bootstrapping initiated with a couple of seed connection models or designs, and iteratively grow the set of relations and patterns based on occurrence in a large corpus. This perspective on bootstrapping as a shared reliance among examples and connection cases can be displayed through a bipartite chart.

11.6 CONCLUSION AND FUTURE WORK

NLP is a growing technology that enables systems to examine, recognize, and extract meaning from individual languages in a clever and effective way. This chapter has offered a detailed review of NLP tools, libraries, and graph- and node-based embeddings for natural language generation. Node embeddings were classified into three types and discussed in detail, along with applications of node embedding and relation embedding.

Character embeddings are deficient in semantic information, and word embeddings are deficient in morphological information. The grouping of characters and word entrenching can establish better vector depictions. Sentence embeddings are absolutely a step forward in allowing transfer learning for various NLP tasks. Word expression and graph implanting techniques can be used to tie together conditions and relations in the Unified Modeling Language to calculate semantic linking between concepts.

REFERENCES

Agirre, E., Alfonseca, E., Hall, K., Kravalova, J., Pasca, M., & Soroa, A. (2009). A study on similarity and relatedness using distributional and wordnet-based approaches.

Barzilay, R., & Lee, L. (2003). Learning to paraphrase: An unsupervised approach using multiple-sequence alignment. *arXiv preprint cs/0304006*.

Belkin, M., & Niyogi, P. (2003). Laplacian eigenmaps for dimensionality reduction and data representation. *Neural Computation*, *15*(6), 1373–1396.

Bordes, A., Usunier, N., Garcia-Duran, A., Weston, J., & Yakhnenko, O. (2013). Translating embeddings for modeling multi-relational data. *Advances in Neural Information Processing Systems*, *26*.

Coursey, K., & Mihalcea, R. (2009, June). Topic identification using wikipedia graph centrality. In Proceedings of Human Language Technologies: The 2009 Annual Conference of the North American Chapter of the Association for Computational Linguistics,Boulder, Colorado, Companion Volume: Short Papers (pp. 117–120).

Eisner, J. (1997). Three new probabilistic models for dependency parsing: An exploration. *arXiv preprint cmp-lg/9706003*.

Grover, A., & Leskovec, J. (2016). Node2vec: scalable feature learning for networks. *KDD*, *2016*, 855–864.

Nastase, V., Mihalcea, R., & Radev, D. R. (2015). A survey of graphs in natural language processing. *Natural Language Engineering*, *21*(5), 665–698.

Ou, M., Cui, P., Pei, J., Zhang, Z., & Zhu, W. (2016, August). Asymmetric transitivity preserving graph embedding. In Proceedings of the 22nd ACM SIGKDD International Conference on Knowledge Discovery and Data Mining (pp. 1105–1114).

Perozzi, B., Al-Rfou, R., & Skiena, S. (2014, August). Deepwalk: Online learning of social representations. In Proceedings of the 20th ACM SIGKDD International Conference on Knowledge Discovery and Data Mining (pp. 701–710).

Pilehvar, M. T., & Navigli, R. (2015). From senses to texts: An all-in-one graph-based approach for measuring semantic similarity. *Artificial Intelligence*, *228*, 95–128.

Pilehvar, M. T., Jurgens, D., & Navigli, R. (2013, August). Align, disambiguate and walk: A unified approach for measuring semantic similarity. In Proceedings of the 51st Annual Meeting of the Association for Computational Linguistics (Volume 1: Long Papers) (pp. 1341–1351).

Tang, J., Qu, M., Wang, M., Zhang, M., Yan, J., & Mei, Q. (2015, May). Line: Large-scale information network embedding. In Proceedings of the 24th International Conference on the World Wide Web (pp. 1067–1077).

Van der Maaten, L., & Hinton, G. (2008). Visualizing data using t-SNE. *Journal of Machine Learning Research*, *9*(11).(pp. 2579–2605).

Wang, D., Cui, P., & Zhu, W. (2016, August). Structural deep network embedding. In Proceedings of the 22nd ACM SIGKDD International Conference on Knowledge Discovery and Data Mining (pp. 1225–1234).

Watanabe, Y., Asahara, M., & Matsumoto, Y. (2007, June). A graph-based approach to named entity categorization in Wikipedia using conditional random fields. In Proceedings of the 2007 Joint Conference on Empirical Methods in Natural Language Processing and Computational Natural Language Learning (EMNLP-CoNLL) (pp. 649–657).

Widdows, D., & Dorow, B. (2002). A graph model for unsupervised lexical acquisition. In COLING 2002: The 19th International Conference on Computational Linguistics.

Yan, R., Lapata, M., & Li, X. (2012, July). Tweet recommendation with graph co-ranking. In Proceedings of the 50th Annual Meeting of the Association for Computational Linguistics (Volume 1: Long Papers) (pp. 516–525).

12 Graph-based Text Document Extractive Summarization

Sheetal Sonawane

CONTENTS

12.1 INTRODUCTION

On a daily basis, millions of web pages are being created, so there is a huge demand for condensing text documents. Text document summarization [1] is an important application in document classification, question answering systems, etc.

In the past two decades, much more attention has been paid to the problem of summarization, for example of web pages, research paper abstracts, and item/product review summaries are examples of document summaries. The text document is defined as below

Let D be the document corpus:

$$D = \{d_1, d_2, \ldots d_N\} \quad \text{(Equation 12.1)}$$

DOI: 10.1201/9781003272649-12

where N is the total number of documents and d_1, d_2 are documents. Document d is defined as a collection of paragraphs. A paragraph is a collection of sentences, and a sentence is defined as a set of terms in a document:

$$d_i = \sum_{k=i}^{\text{number of paragraphs in a document}} p_k \quad \text{(Equation 12.2)}$$

$$p_i = \sum_{k=i}^{\text{number of sentences in a paragraph}} s_k \quad \text{(Equation 12.3)}$$

$$s_i = \sum_{k=i}^{\text{number of terms in a sentence}} t_k \quad \text{(Equation 12.4)}$$

A text document summary is generated by selecting prominent sentences from a document in single-document summarization and from many documents in multi-document summarization.

The following are the key aspects of document summary [2]:

1. The theme of the document or documents should be preserved in a summary.
2. Summaries can be produced from a single document or multiple documents.
3. A brief and concise summary should be produced.

Based on need and use, summarization algorithms are divided into the following types:

1. *Based on generation of summary: extractive and abstractive summarization* – Extractive summarization is the extraction of high-quality sentences, paragraphs, etc. from the source document(s). The sentence quality is decided based on linguistic and statistical features of the sentences. Abstractive summarization extracts useful concepts from the document and constructs sentences using natural language processing (NLP).

   The following are the important factors that need to be considered for extractive summarization:
   (a) Important sentences are spread across the entire document
   (b) Size of the summary document
   (c) Order of the sentences
   (d) Lack of coreference resolution
   (e) Preserving the style of the writer
   (f) Possibility of inconsistency and redundancy in the text

   The following are the important factors that need to be considered for abstractive summarization:
   (a) Representing concepts from document
   (b) Generating sentences using NLP
   (c) The summary is dense and is presented in a conventional style

2. *Based on the dimension: single-document or multi-document summarization* – A summary generated from a single document is known as a single-document summarization, for example a webpage summary or research paper summary. In multi-document summarization, the summary is generated from multiple documents, for example news headlines from multiple related news feeds.
3. *Based on the context: query-specific or independent* – The extraction of a brief summary based on a query provides sentences/terms that are most similar to the query terms. An independent summary is generated based on the document sentences and their correlations with other sentences.
4. *Based on the application: critical or information* – The critical points from a document/documents are generated based on their importance and correlation with other elements, for example in the medical domain, a critical summary is used.

The summary generation workflow is described in Figure 12.1. The first step is identifying the type of summary based on the requirements and expected outcome. The contents are identified depending on the summary type. For example, if the summary type is query-based, the input query is taken from the user and the most similar sentences to the query are identified in the second step. The content ordering and relationships are calculated in the third step. According to the length of the summary expected, the top sentences are generated in the final step.

Deep learning approaches to summary generation have recently shown improvements over traditional approaches. Bidirectional encoder representation [3] is used for summarization, using a stack of transformer encoders pre-trained to understand text data.

This chapter will describe an unsupervised approach using graph-based methods for extractive summarization.

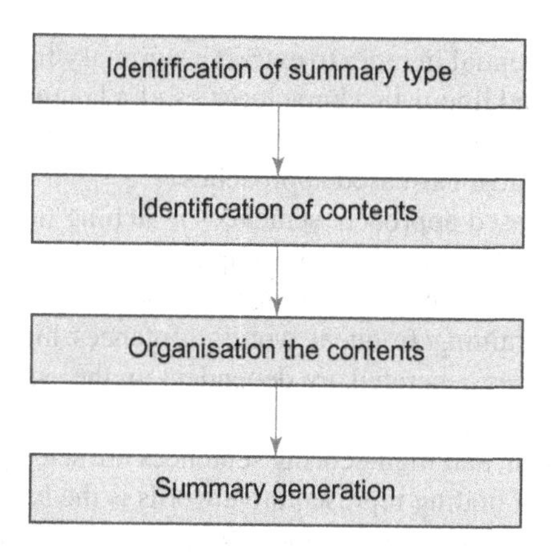

FIGURE 12.1 The workflow of summary generation

12.2 EXTRACTIVE SUMMARIZATION

The important consideration behind using extraction-based summary is the extraction of a set of sentences that present all the key ideas, or at least the majority of them, in the text. Hence, the main objective is to identify the parameters which reflect the importance of a sentence. The next step is to extract important sentences based on syntactic and semantic analysis of the text. The features used for extractive summarization will be explained in Section 12.2.1, and the summary length calculation methods will be explained in Section 12.2.2.

12.2.1 Commonly used Features in Extractive Summarization Method

Several features are commonly used in the extractive summarization process [4], some of which include:

- *Title sentence* – These are included in the summary.
- *Position of the sentence* – Sentences are extracted based on their position in the document.
- *Sentence length* – Lengthy and short sentences are generally avoided in the summary.
- *Proper noun feature* – Sentences that contain proper nouns are more likely to be included in the summary.
- *Cue phrase feature* – Sentences containing cue phrases (e.g., "in conclusion") are most likely to be included in the summary.
- *Font* – Changes in font in sentences can be important, hence sentences featuring this are included in the summary.
- *Frequent words* – The frequency of words in the document is considered to compute the sentence score.
- *Discourse relation* – The sentence relation should be considered and included in the summary.

These features are essential in order to extract a summary from a document. They cover the statistical and linguistic characteristics of a language.

Generally, methods for automatic extractive summarization can be classified into rule-based and statistical-based approaches.

In a typical rule-based approach, sentences matching the rules are extracted. The rules are constructed based on the importance of sentences, for example: sentence as headings, sentences containing title words, sentences containing noun terms, sentences containing frequent words, sentences highly similar to other sentences, etc. The rules generated are dependent on the system domain.

In statistical-based approaches, the ratio of important words/sentences in a document is calculated, and high-scoring sentences are selected for the summary. The traditional way of finding representative words is the bag of words approach. The term frequency and inverse document frequency (TF-IDF) scores are calculated, and sentences with high TF-IDF scores [5] are chosen.

The summarization problem is essentially a classification problem. Sentences are labelled as summary- or non-summary-based on their features.

The latent semantic analysis method [5] is used to find key terms and related sentences in documents. This method is useful to determine the context-based similarity of sentences.

The context of sentences is also identified by using the knowledge-based system of fuzzy logic. Knowledge sources like web data, Wikipedia, and WordNet are used to arrive at a contextual summary of the document.

12.2.2 Summary Length

The summary length depends on the application. For example, in a news summary, the summary length is generally 25% of the full item. In existing approaches, the summary length is specified by the user or decided implicitly by the algorithm. The summary size generally depends on the size of the document(s) and can be decided at runtime. This dynamic approach is very challenging, and is still an unexplored area.

The following methods are used for determining the length of a summary:

1. *Threshold* – The length of the summary is decided by user input.
2. *Oracle* – The number of sentences in the summary is considered to be the same as the total number of sentences in the system summary.
3. *Fixed number of sentences* – The static length is considered for all the documents in the collection.
4. *Summary function* – The summary length is proportional to the length of the input document(s).
5. *Size of summary* – Sentences of less than five words may not be considered in the summary. Similarly, longer ones may not be included.

12.3 GRAPH-BASED METHODS FOR EXTRACTIVE SUMMARIZATION

A graph can be described in the form $G = (V, E)$, where V represents the vertex or node and E is the edge between vertices.

Features [6] like terms/concept/context/sentences are considered as vertices, and the associations between them are described as edges. The associations between the features can be based on lexical, semantic, or contextual similarity.

For extractive document summarization, a vertex is a sentence, and an edge is a similarity between sentences. An example of a graph is given in Figure 12.2. V is a set of three sentences, and association is a similarity between sentences.

Graph G is defined as,

$$G = (V, E) \quad \text{(Equation 12.5)}$$

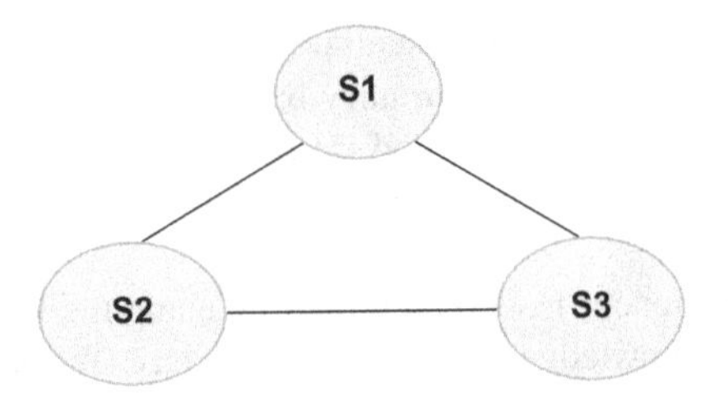

FIGURE 12.2 Graph example

$$V = \{s_1, s_2, s_3, \ldots s_n\} \quad \text{(Equation 12.6)}$$

$$E = \{e_1, e_2, e_3, \ldots e_{n*n}\} \quad \text{(Equation 12.7)}$$

In extractive document summarization, sentences are extracted based on their importance in the document. The following steps are carried out:

1. Identify features from the document, and represent them using vertices.
2. Use edges to define the relationships between features.
3. Assign a score to each vertex by applying a ranking algorithm iteratively.
4. High-scoring vertices denote the important sentences. Extract these vertices.

12.3.1 Graph-based Ranking Algorithm

The centroid-based summarization method [7] is used where terms are extracted which have a TF-IDF score above a threshold value. The sentences containing these terms are extracted in a summary. The LexRank [7] method applies social network measures such as eigenvector centrality and degree centrality to select sentences.

An example input document is given in Figure 12.2. The graph generated is shown in Figure 12.3. The associations between sentences are computed using cosine similarity, as shown in Table 12.1.

The TextRank algorithm [8, 9] is a graph-based approach for extractive document summarization. The iterative PageRank algorithm is used to compute the weights of the vertices. The high-weight vertices are selected as summary sentences.

12.3.2 Weighted/unweighted Simple Graph

A basic way of describing the relationships between sentences is to use a simple graph [10]. Edge scores are computed by applying a similarity measure, and vertices are ranked based on their associations with other vertices. The highest-ranking vertices are then extracted. An example of such a graph is given in Figures 12.3 and 12.4.

1. Information retrieval (IR) in computing and information science is the process of obtaining information system resources that are relevant to an information need from a collection of those resources.
2. Searches can be based on full-text or other content-based indexing. Information retrieval is the science of searching for information in a document, searching for documents themselves, and also searching for the metadata that describes data, and for databases of texts, images or sounds.
3. Automated information retrieval systems are used to reduce what has been called information overload.
4. An IR system is a software system that provides access to books, journals and other documents; stores and manages those documents. Web search engines are the most visible IR applications.

FIGURE 12.3 Sample document

TABLE 12.1
Edge Scores of the Sample Document in Figure 12.3

Sentences	1	2	3	4
1	—	0.47	0.46	0.40
2	0.47	—	0.39	0.42
3	0.46	0.39	—	0.39
4	0.40	0.42	0.39	—

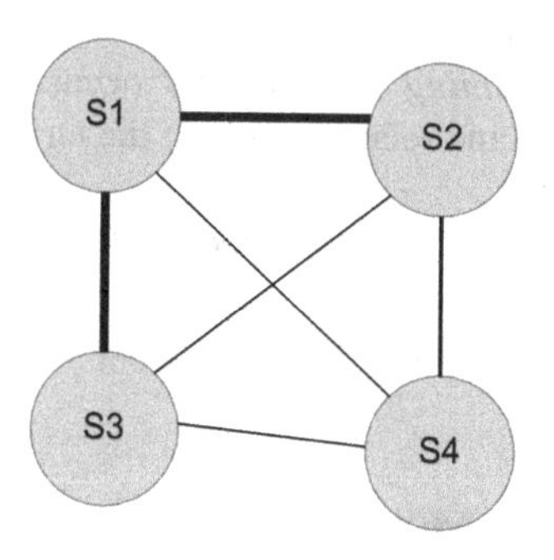

FIGURE 12.4 Graph representation of the sample document in Figure 12.3

12.3.3 Heterogeneous Graph Model

The heterogeneous graph model [4] shows the relationships between elements of text documents such as sentences, words, and topics. The document is modelled as heterogenous graph. The sentence score is calculated by using cosine similarity with other sentences, topics, and words.

Figure 12.5 shows the similarity between topic, sentence, and word.

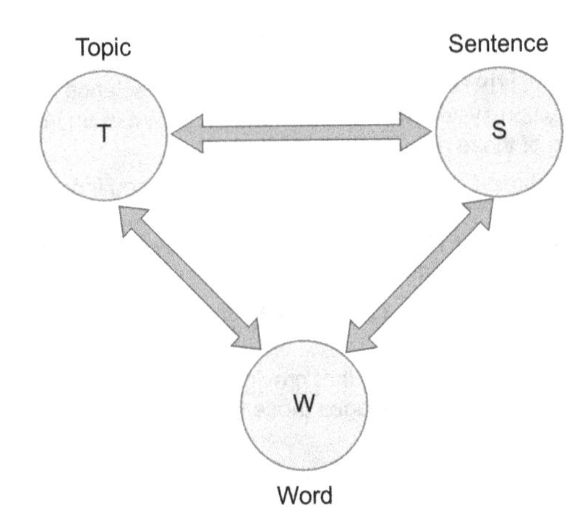

FIGURE 12.5 Heterogenous relationship graph

12.3.4 Correlation Graph Model

Correlation Graph Model is an interesting association-based approach [2] that is used to compute edge scores. The popular method of association rule mining is used to find correlations between sentences. The PageRank algorithm is used to compute the ranks of vertices. The semantic and syntactic relationships among the sentences are utilized to select the ranked sentences.

Figure 12.6 shows the four steps of graph-based summarization:

1. *Text processing* – Pre-processing steps such as tokenization, sentence splitting, and lemmatization are applied.
2. *Correlation graph mining* – Frequently occurring item sets in documents are identified, and relations among the terms are combined with a graph-based model.
3. *Graph indexing* – The PageRank algorithm is applied to nodes, and their relevance is calculated.
4. *Sentence selection* – A subset of sentences that providess an indexed graph is constructed.

12.3.5 Semantic Graph Model

In this approach, semantic and statistical relationships [11] between sentences are used to summarize text. The semantic relationships can be computed using WordNet or Wikipedia.

This approach helps to compute meaningful similarities, hence problems of ambiguity and redundancy can be avoided. The vertex scores are computed by applying the PageRank algorithm.

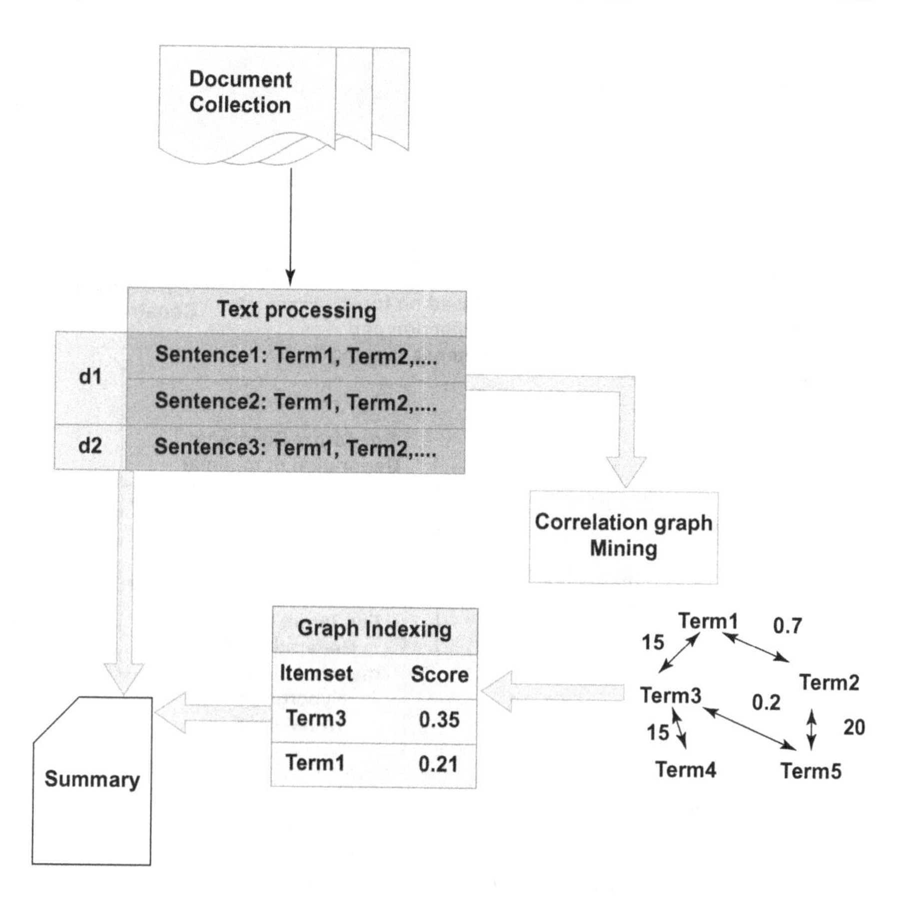

FIGURE 12.6 The GraphSum summarizer

Query-based summarization [12] is where the query terms are expanded and integrated into an existing summarization framework.

12.3.6 Hypergraph Model

An advanced type of graph, the hypergraph [13, 14], is widely used nowadays in solving NLP problems. The additional and advanced methods it offers help to make document processing effective and efficient. A set of documents with the user-defined query q are taken as the input.

Figure 12.7 shows the detailed steps. Pre-processing is carried out in step 1, then the topic detection algorithm is applied and the theme is generated. Each sentence is tagged with multiple topics.

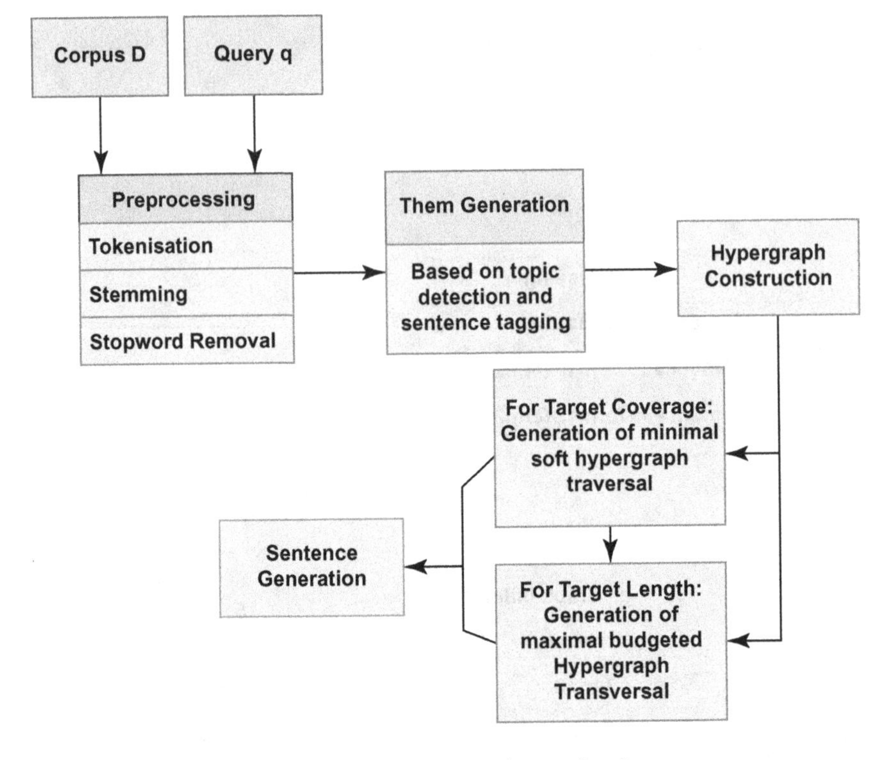

FIGURE 12.7 Summarization using a hypergraph stepwise chart

A hypergraph is built based on the theme where hyperedge weight is calculated based on its importance in the corpus and its similarity to the query.

Maximum budgeted hypergraph transversal is used to obtain a summary complying with the target summary length. Minimal soft hypergraph transversal is used to obtain a summary complying with the target coverage.

12.3.6.1 Hypergraph Construction

A hypergraph is defined as (V, E, φ, w), where V is a set of nodes, $E \subseteq 2^V$ is a set of hyperedges, φ is positive node weight, and w is positive hyperedge weight.

In a sentence-based hypergraph, nodes represent sentences and hyperedges define connecte or associated sentences. The φ of node weight is the length of a sentence.

$$V = \{1,2,\ldots,N\} \text{ and } \varphi_i = Li$$
$$E = \{e_1,e_2,e_3,\ldots,e_k\} \subseteq 2^V$$
$$e_l = T_l$$

The hyperedge weight is calculated as:

$$w_l = (1-\lambda)sim(T_l, D) + (\lambda)sim(T_l, q) \qquad \text{(Equation 12.8)}$$

where λ = [0,1] is a parameter, D is the corpus, and q is the query, $sim(T_l, D)$ is sentence similarity in theme T_l with the entire corpus, and $Sim(T_l, q)$ refers to the similarity of the theme with the user-defined query q.

12.3.7 Semigraph Model

Semigraph [15] is another advanced graph type that is used to produce document summaries. Feature-wise similarity can be handled easily using this approach, which computes features' associations with other features of other sentences.

A semigraph is defined as an ordered pair of two sets V and X. V is a set of vertices, and X is an edge connecting more than two vertices where two edges have at most one vertex in common.

Figure 12.8 shows the workflow. Pre-processing is applied in the first step. Then the features are calculated based on the proper noun (NP), thematic words, title words, and term frequency (TF) scores. These features representing each sentence are connected to other sentences using semi-edges. The association scores are calculated based on the weights of each feature.

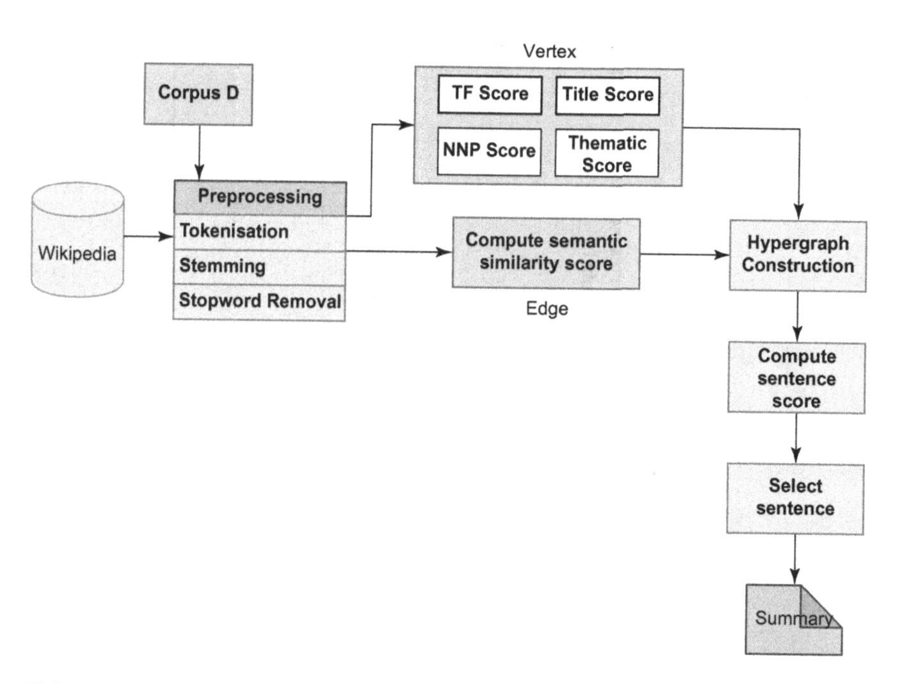

FIGURE 12.8 Summarization using a semigraph stepwise chart

TABLE 12.2
Graph Types Used in Different NLP Applications

Graph Node type	Graph Edge	Vertex weight/label	Edge label/weight	Application	Graph type
Sentence	Similarity between sentences	—	Similarity score	Simple graph	Extractive summarization
Term/token	Lexical/semantic similarity	—	Lexical/semantic similarity score	Multigraph	Coreference resolution
Term/token	Lexical/semantic similarity	Term weight	Lexical/semantic similarity score	Simple graph	Coreference resolution
Sentence terms	Term position in a sentence	Sentence and term position	Distance between terms	Simple graph	Abstractive summarization
Represents entities in one group as sentence	Entities mentioned in a document	—	—	Bipartite graph	Multi-document extractive summarization
Entities	Semantic relation	—	—	Knowledge graph	Summarization, question answering systems

12.4 CONCLUSION

The graph-based method [16] for summarization is very popular, and is widely used by researchers. The advantages of graph-based summarization include the following:

1. Graph-based methods are easily portable to other domains, genres, or languages.
2. The graph model does not make use of language-dependent corpora for training.
3. Deep linguistic knowledge is not necessary to model using graph methods
4. Advanced operations can easily be carried out by applying different methods.

In recent years, various summarization applications have been developed for news, email thread, medical information, research articles, voice conversations, broadcast news, and video and meeting recordings. A few Android applications such as Squash and SumIt have even been developed to summarize text. The extractive summarization of text document is carried out on the basis of entity or event describing sentences. Therefore, summarization can give concise information about what happened with/about/around an entity within a particular time frame. A graph is a mathematical structure that defines associations between entities using vertices and edges. Extractive summarization is an important NLP task where important sentences are extracted. The sentences are selected based on their context/content/theme scores, which are easy and efficient to calculate using graphs. Advanced data graph types like semigraph and hypergraph have recently been used to solve the problem of extractive summarization. Dynamic generation of Summary length can be explored more in the future. Various graph types and their applications are listed in Table 12.2.

REFERENCES

1. Kumar, Y. J., & Salim, N. (2012). Automatic multi document summarization approaches. *Journal of Computer Science*, 133–140.
2. Joshi, S. G., & Sonawane, S. S. (2015). A survey of extractive summarization approaches using graph model. *International Journal of Computer Engineering and Applications*, *9*(4), 145–156.
3. Abdel-Salam, S., & Rafea, A. (2022). Performance study on extractive text summarization using BERT models. *Information*, *13*(2), 67.
4. Ferreira, R., de Souza Cabral, L., Lins, R. D., e Silva, G. P., Freitas, F., Cavalcanti, G. D., ... & Favaro, L. (2013). Assessing sentence scoring techniques for extractive text summarization. *Expert Systems with Applications*, *40*(14), 5755–5764.
5. Das, D., & Martins, A. F. (2007). *A Survey on Automatic Text Summarization.* Language Technologies Institute.

6. Sonawane, S. S., & Kulkarni, P. A. (2014). Graph based representation and analysis of text document: A survey of techniques. *International Journal of Computer Applications*, *96*(19), 1–8.
7. Erkan, G., & Radev, D. R. (2004). Lexrank: Graph-based lexical centrality as salience in text summarization. *Journal of Artificial Intelligence Research*, *22*, 457–479.
8. Sarwadnya, V. V., & Sonawane, S. S. (2018, August). Marathi extractive text summarizer using graph based model. In 2018 Fourth International Conference on Computing Communication Control and Automation (ICCUBEA), Pune (pp. 1–6). IEEE.
9. Mihalcea, R., & Tarau, P. (2004, July). Textrank: Bringing order into text. In Proceedings of the 2004 Conference on Empirical Methods in Natural Language Processing, Spain (pp. 404–411).
10. Ge, S. S., Zhang, Z., & He, H. (2011, August). Weighted graph model based sentence clustering and ranking for document summarization. In The 4th International Conference on Interaction Sciences, Korea (South) (pp. 90–95). IEEE.
11. Ramesh, A., Srinivasa, K. G., & Pramod, N. (2014, February). Sentence rank: A graph based approach to summarize text. In The Fifth International Conference on the Applications of Digital Information and Web Technologies (ICADIWT 2014), Banglore, India (pp. 177–182). IEEE.
12. Wei, F., He, Y., Li, W., & Lu, Q. (2008, May). A query-sensitive graph-based sentence ranking algorithm for query-oriented multi-document summarization. In 2008 International Symposiums on Information Processing, Russia (pp. 9–13). IEEE.
13. Xiong, S., & Ji, D. (2016). Query-focused multi-document summarization using hypergraph-based ranking. *Information Processing & Management*, *52*(4), 670–681.
14. Van Lierde, H., & Chow, T. W. (2019). Query-oriented text summarization based on hypergraph transversals. *Information Processing & Management*, *56*(4), 1317–1338.
15. Sonawane, S., Kulkarni, P., Deshpande, C., & Athawale, B. (2019). Extractive summarization using semigraph (ESSg). *Evolving Systems*, *10*(3), 409–424.
16. Parveen, D., & Strube, M. (2014, October). Multi-document summarization using bipartite graphs. In Proceedings of TextGraphs-9: the workshop on Graph-based Methods for Natural Language Processing (pp. 15–24).

13 Applications of Graphical Natural Language Processing

S. V. Gayetri Devi, T. Nalini, and K. G. S. Venkatesan

CONTENTS

13.1 GRAPH THEORY IN NATURAL LANGUAGE PROCESSING

Graph theory is a mainstream discipline, just like the areas of natural language processing (NLP) and information retrieval. Conventionally, these fields have been seen as distinct, with diverse algorithms, a wide range of applications, and numerous types of end-users. But in fact these disciplines are closely connected, in that applications for NLP and information retrieval relevant use graph-theoretic frameworks to arrive at solutions. In an organized text, language units such as words, phrases, or even entire sentences are linked through several relationships, providing contributions to the total meaning and thereby sustaining the consistent structure and the related discourse unity of the input text. From the initial development phases of artificial intelligence, semantic or associative networks have been anticipated as representations that enable such language components and their interrelationships to be identified and stored, which enable diverse inference as well as reasoning methods to simulate functionalities pertaining to the human mind. The wide range of symbolic structures that arise from such representations

DOI: 10.1201/9781003272649-13

naturally conform with graphs, wherein text units are characterized as vertices and their interrelationships are represented by edges. Several text processing applications have the potential to be modeled with the help of graphs. Such data structures are capable of inherently encoding the structure and significance of a specific cohesive text and following up the Semantic or Associative Memory representations closely [4, 5].

This chapter intends to give an insight into lexical semantics, text mining, text summarization, classification of input text, construction of ontology, and subsequently information retrieval that are interlinked by the generic fundamental concept of employing graph-theoretic techniques for text and information processing tasks. The use of graph-centered algorithms and representations in NLP and information retrieval has seen enormous growth. The applications of graph theory to NLP encompass graph -based text summarization, topic identification, keyword extraction employing random walk language models, graph partitioning using normalized cut criteria for text segmentation, encoding discourse relationships with graph structures, use of word graphs to decode machine translations as well as in speech processing tasks, selection of translations, multilingual information retrieval using random walk methods, graph-oriented patterns and representations for extraction of information, and user question answering. Text graphs are used to represent texts on the basis of semantic relatedness or co-occurrences of words [14, 15]. The TextRank technique for the extraction of key phrases as well as summarization is possibly the most significant graph-oriented NLP method, and the algorithm is a chief component of NLP packages. Its basic idea is very simple. A text graph is built, then a centrality measure such as PageRank is used to determine the most significant words, phrases, or sentences. With current enhancements in the algorithm, text graphs are built from sentence or word embeddings. This method is one of the best unsupervised keyword extraction and extractive summarization tools currently available.

13.2 TEXT SUMMARIZATION

The graph-centered method for text summarization offers an unsupervised approach where sentences or words are ranked on the basis of a graph. The main objective of the graphical approach is to extract more significant sentences from a document. Essentially, we use it to find the rank of a vertex in a graph. Undirected and weighted graphs are used for text-oriented ranking. Sentences or documents are signified by nodes, and edges link any two nodes with shared common information. Sentence scoring is carried out by the attribution of weights to the graph nodes. The computed weights of a specific node word are oriented on the word-frequency, apart from the incidence of the word within keywords, title, proper nouns and domain-specific or predisposed lists. PageRank, LexRank, and TextRank are some of the important graph-based methods adopted for text summarization. Text graph creation methods parse the input text to build a model of the text graph. For every sentence, nouns are represented by graph nodes, an edge exists between every two resultant nodes, the edges are labeled using non-noun words among these nodes, and (c) starting and ending nodes exist for all the sentences signified by the text graph [5, 8].

The method thus comprises three major phases: document depiction, clustering of concepts, and selection of sentences. In order to construct a concept graph signifying the document, a fundamental task is to divide the text into multiple sentences and eliminate generic as well as highly frequent terms. After the sentences are isolated, the terms in every sentence are translated into suitable concepts based on various measures of relatedness as well as semantic similarity with disambiguation of word sense. This is carried out by assessing the semantic similarities among a word and its respective neighbors. The resultant concepts extracted from the common nouns are further extended using their superordinates, constructing a hierarchical form for every sentence in the input document, wherein edges signify the semantic relations that are unlabeled temporally, and a single node is created for every distinct concept within the text. This means that if two unidentical terms in a sentence represent the same concept, only one node is added to the graph to represent both the terms. Adverbs, verbs, adjectives, and proper nouns are not considered in this step. Then the sentence-related graphs are combined into an individual graph representing the entire document. This graph can be further extended using various more particular semantic relations among the vertices. Concept sets that are relevant to meaning are then constructed [9, 12]. It is assumed that every set signifies a sub-theme within the document and the most dominant concepts within a cluster provide the essential information connected to its sub-theme. After the concept clusters are formed, every sentence is allotted to a cluster. Hence, it is necessary to describe similarity measures among sentence graphs as well as clusters. Since the two illustrations are very dissimilar in size, conventional metrics of graph similarity are not suitable and hence, a vote mechanism is adopted. The final step is selection of the most important sentences for summary on the basis of the similarities among sentences as well as clusters. The similarity between two sentences, Sentence_1 and Sentence_2, is measured using the following mathematical model

$$\text{Similarity}_{\text{Sentence1},\text{Sentence2}} = 1 - \frac{2\sum_i^l (w_{jk} - w_{jk}.w_{ik}) \, . \sum_i^l (w_{ik} - w_{ik}.w_{jk})}{\sum_i^l w_{ik} \sum_i^l (w_{jk} - w_{jk}.w_{ik}) + \sum_i^l w_{jk} \sum_i^l (w_{ik} - w_{ik}.w_{jk})}$$

(Equation 13.1)

where each sentence is represented with l number of terms in a -dimensional space, and w_{ik} and w_{jk} are the components reflecting the weights of a corresponding term within a sentence.

The main objective is the extraction of the most significant sentences from the primary input document by first creating a semantic graph representing the document, then utilizing the document as well as graph structures to derive the document summary. It is necessary to pre-process the entire dataset prior to using it for text summarization. Verbs and nouns in the document are denoted by nodes and edges in the graph. Hence, the semantic representation developed in the graph is initially oriented toward the subject-verb-object triplet. Nodes are connected on the basis of associations among words. This is followed by the removal from the graph of nodes referring to the same entities. This step is also called the processing stage. Words are allocated to nodes according to their grammatical and semantic and significance. Subsequently to further simplify the graph, an established set of heuristic rules is applied using mapping and normalization.

Thus, the pre-processing stage uses a variety of NLP methods, such as sentence segmentation, part of speech (POS) tagging, word tokenization, lemmatization, and stemming. Scored are allocated to the sentences to allow them to be ranked. The heuristic reduction approach identifies nodes – subject–noun (SN), object–noun (ON), and main verb (MV). All the inappropriate words are removed. The processing stage therefore consists of sub-stages such as the creation of text representations to simplify ranking as well as analysis of the text, sentence ranking to reflect their significance, followed by the ordering of sentences from the highest to the lowest ranking, and extraction of high-scoring sentences from the document for the output summary to comply with the user's length requirements specified as a compression ratio, number of words, number of sentences, etc. The stabilization of candidate summary generation takes place as soon as the derived summary length cannot be further reduced with the subsequent iterations.

The final stage produces a logical graph with the help of the identified triplets wherein the associated nodes comprise subjects as well as objects. Sentences that have the highest scores are chosen for the eventual reduced graph. In the case of a significant semantic graph, the nodes have the text semantics stored dissimilar to the conventional semantic graphs that are unable to comprehend the sense of the sentences. The post-processing phase involves application of refinement methods to the summary sentences, followed by their concatenation to generate the final summary. Thus, within an input text the sentences are linked to one other. This feature of interconnection can be comprehended as lexical overlapping. In specific lexical connectivity notion, two sentences with shared lexis are linked to one other. This idea is utilized in computation of sentence significance within an input text. For the sole reason that a sentence significance within the input text is related with other different sentences within the same input text. Hence, graphs offer an appropriate method to represent the relationships as well as to compute the comparative significance of sentences through the analysis of the graph's structure. In order to implement this, the text must be represented as a completely connected graph with a set of a nodes and edges. The sentences form the graph nodes, while the graph edges signify the lexical similarities among the pairs of input sentences. After the completely connected graph is built, edge reduction methods can be used to minimize the graph so it is comprised of only significant edges. The most significant edge reduction method is the threshold method, which removes an edge when its weight goes beyond certain thresholds.

The algorithm for graph-based text summarization is illustrated by the flowchart in Figure 13.1. The process derives the eventual summary from the input document in several iterations, and involves the steps of text graph generation,

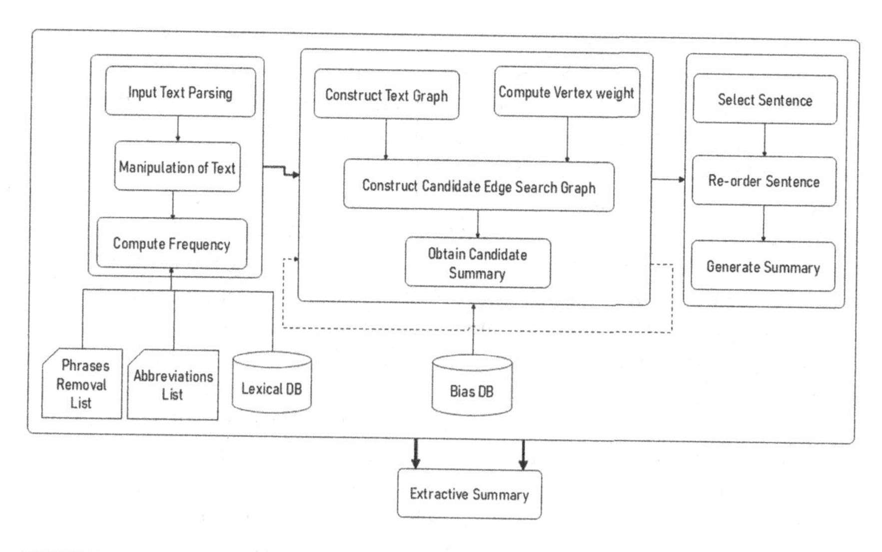

FIGURE 13.1 Graph-based text summarization framework

search graph generation, and obtaining the candidate summary. The iterations accomplish the summary length requested by the user in terms of maximum word count.

Extractive text summarization is a technique to identify crucial sentences in the text and then add those sentences to the summary. The summary generated consists of unaltered sentences present in the original text. *Abstractive text summarization* is an advanced technique to determine significant sections in the text, followed by interpretation of the context, then reproducing the text in a different way. This ensures that the main information is conveyed using the possible shortest text. The sentences in the summary are created by the model, and not just taken from the original data [16, 17]. The *random walk summarization* technique can be used to summarize single documents as well as multiple ones, since a graph can be constructed based on the information obtained from the input document(s).

13.3 KEYWORD EXTRACTION

An important feature of text summarization is keyword extraction, which determines what information within a text is crucial. Instead of using whole sentences, as in automatic summarization, keyword extraction chooses phrases or words that better reflect the details of a document. The keywords may establish valuable entries to build an automatic index for a specific document set, and can be utilized for classifying a text, or can act as a brief summary for a document. For example, keywords in research-oriented papers are often listed by their authors in order to assist in searching or browsing. Likewise, books are frequently provided with citations of keywords as an index in their endmatter, and this can be utilized as an outline of the chief concepts detailed in the book. On the Internet, image or blog repositories also employ important phrases in order to tag as well as identify the content. Keywords can also be utilized for terminology extraction, and for constructing domain-relevant dictionaries. For these purposes, random walk methods provide better performance than supervised techniques [2, 3].

Keyword extraction hence signifies the identification of the most pertinent terms and expressions in a provided text in an appropriate manner. During this period of information explosion, keyword extraction has received increased attention. The significance of keyword extraction across text summarization, comparisons, as well as documents categorization stressed on the importance of graph-oriented keyword extraction methods since they have the potential to infer better structural related information in comparison with other traditional methods for text analysis. The fundamental principle in graph-oriented keyword extraction is the estimation and identification the most significant nodes (words) on the basis of the information obtained from the structures of the text graphs. Such nodes can be identified using vertex centrality measures, such as degree, closeness centrality, PageRank as well as k-degeneracy measures. But keyword extraction methods differ in accordance with text graph creation methods, that influence the ranking of the potential candidate key phrases. Most of the prevailing graph-oriented keyword extraction methods rely on word co-occurrences, hence they do not essentially produce a collection of keywords that encompass the major topics covered in the text. Furthermore, most prevailing graph-oriented keyword extraction techniques need user parameters.

Graph-oriented approaches create a graph of relevant terms from the input document(s). A graph, for instance, interlinks terms which co-occur in the input text. These methods employ graph ranking techniques that consider the graph structure in order to score the vertex significance. TextRank is one method for the extraction of identifying keywords or relevant sentences.

Figure 13.2, illustrates the TextRank process. The first step is text tokenization and annotation with relevant POS tags. This is followed by construction of a word co-occurrence graph where the vertices represent words with the chosen POS tags. Two vertices are interlinked with an edge if they are present within the

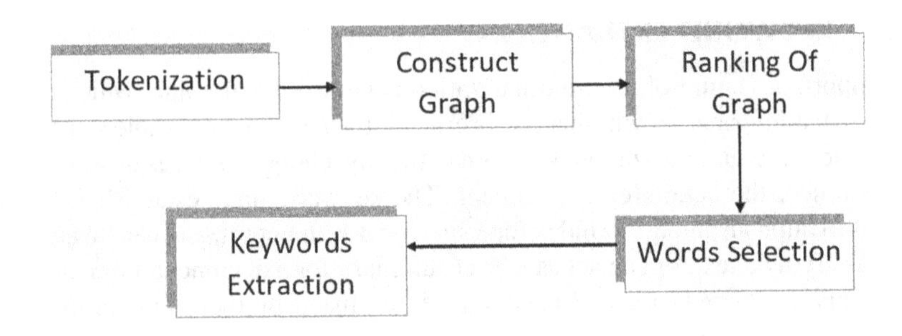

FIGURE 13.2 Graph-based TextRank keyword extraction

space of *N* words within the text. The graph formed is unweighted and undirected. The score of every vertex is then fixed to 1, and the ranking algorithm is deployed on the graph. The weight *S*(*Vi*) of a particular vertex *Vi* is assessed by taking into consideration the weights of vertices interlinked to *Vi*. *Inb*(*Vi*) signifies the inbound links to the vertex, while *Outb*(*Vj*) represents the outbound links from the vertex. Since this is an undirected graph, the inbound links and outbound links of the vertex are identical. The algorithm is executed on every node in multiple iterations until the weights of the vertices converge.

The vertices which denote words are ranked from the highest- to the lowest-scoring. The algorithm then chooses the first one-third of the words. In this step, words chosen in the previous stage are combined into multi-word keywords if they occur in the text together. For instance, consider the sentence "It is a beautiful world." If both "beautiful" and "world" are chosen as keywords, the algorithm outputs "beautiful world" as a keyword. The score of the newly built keywords represents the sum of the scores of the words. The algorithm is executed on each document separately, and does not require a body of documents to accomplish keyword extraction. The TextRank method is said to be language-independent.

Rapid automatic keyword extraction relies on the observation that keywords are regularly composed of several words and typically do not include punctuation or stopwords.

Figure 13.3 shows the keyword extraction process. The first step is candidate keyword extraction, wherein the text is fragmented into keyword candidates on the basis of the stopwords and phrase delimiters. A keyword candidate is a phrase which occurs between two phrase delimiters, such as punctuation characters or stopwords. This is followed by the graph construction comprised of the keywords. Here, the graph vertices are denoted by the words. They are interlinked if they are present together within candidate keywords. Also, the graph is weighted such that the weight signifies the number of instances where linked words are present together. The graph also comprises the connections to the node itself – every word appears within a candidate keyword along with itself.

The step that follows is word scoring – every word present in the graph is scored as follows: (1) word degree – degree(*w*) – represents the number of words

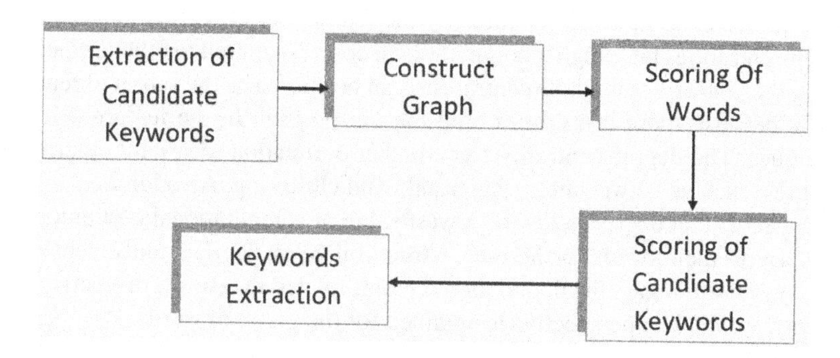

FIGURE 13.3 Graph-based automatic keyword extraction

that word w co-exists with (the sum of edge weights inclusive of an edge pointing to the vertex itself). The degree is inclined towards the words that appear frequently as well as lengthier keywords. (2) Word frequency – frequency(w) – represents the number of instances where a word is present in any candidate keyword. The frequency is inclined towards the words that are present more frequently. (3) The ratio of degree to frequency – degree(w)/frequency(w) – represents the metric that is towards the words that chiefly occur in the lengthier candidate keywords. It is recommended to use either the ratio of degree to frequency or the word degree. In this way, shorter keywords are favored.

The next step is the scoring of candidate keywords, wherein the score of every candidate keyword is represented by the sum of the scores of its member words. The connecting keywords are then established, where the candidate keywords are not comprised of stopwords. Since stopwords are sometimes part of a keyword, they are included in this specific step. The algorithm establishes pairs of keywords interconnected with a stopword within a text and includes them in the collection of prevailing stopwords. They must be present at least twice within the text to be included. The sum of the member keywords represents the score of the new keyword. Finally, one-third of the best-scoring keywords are identified through keyword extraction.

To give an example, keyword extraction is accomplished during web search performance optimization by attributing weights to every element of documents that are hyperlinked, thereby identifying the importance of every page. Two scores for the outgoing and incoming hyperlinks are determined for every node of the graph pertaining to the semantic or lexical graphs derived from the input text documents:

$$\text{Score}_{\text{Outgoing}}(N_i) = \sum_{Nj \in Out(Ni)} \text{Score}_{\text{incoming}}(N_j) \quad \text{(Equation 13.2)}$$

$$\text{Score}_{\text{incoming}}(N_i) = \sum_{Nj \in In(Ni)} \text{Score}_{\text{outgoing}}(N_j) \quad \text{(Equation 13.3)}$$

Eigenvectors as well as structural holes serve as the prevalent centralities determined in the most pertinent features by the feature selection methods. Because certain centralities have higher computational costs compared to others, eigenvector, degree, and structural hole centralities can be chosen as the subset of features. This is because these centralities hold the top position in the feature selection techniques. The degree centrality has a higher correlation to several determined measures, such as betweenness, PageRank, and clustering. An additional significant aspect is that degree holds the lowest value of computational cost among all the measures mentioned. Furthermore, structural holes, degrees, and eigenvectors represent intermediate, local, and global graph-related measures, respectively. In this way, a complete perspective is obtained for the graph of words.

After the best set of features is identified, it is utilized as the input for the feature selection approach, merging the connection assortment of keywords from every pairwise centralities, namely eigenvector, degree, as well as structural holes, as a solitary set. The performance of every centrality measure is then evaluated using recall, precision, and the F1-score for every input document and mean is obtained at the dataset extent. Higher values of precision signify that the method has returned more related results than irrelevant ones; on the other hand, higher values of recall imply that the method has returned the maximum of relevant outcomes. Candidate as well as reference keywords are then stemmed in order to reduce the number of mismatches. In certain datasets, keywords have been independently selected by individual coders using abstractive means, and some of them in reality are not available within the original input text. This renders it incredible to achieve a higher recall using extractive approaches. Taking into account, the same count of keywords humans being able to determine using the centrality measures about half of the coder-described keywords.

We can perform a statistical analysis of the keyword extraction results to gain a better understanding of the ranking and possible significant differences. To do this, we execute Nemenyi post-hoc grouping by datasets. On the top of the diagrams is the critical difference (*CD*), and on the axis are plotted the average ranks of the methods, where the lowest (best) positions are on the left side. When sets of methods have no significant differences, they are connected by a black line in the diagram. In order to understand the structure of our underlying data and to examine whether the centrality measures are good separators for clustering, we present the mean values found for each attribute – i.e., the centrality measures of the words in the full dataset and in the clustering algorithms, respectively, in Table 8. When used with text data, clustering can provide an alternative way to organize the thousands of words in a document.

Deep learning-based methods chiefly identify a list of potential candidate keywords. They subsequently have the document as well as candidate keywords embedded within the same space, and features such as cosine similarity are measured between the embeddings of the document as well as the keywords. Keywords that are most identical to the document text are selected based on the similarity measure.

13.4 GRAPH -ORIENTED TOPIC ANALYSIS

Graph-based techniques for topic identification enable automatic extraction of meanings from input text by identifying recurrent topics or themes. The approach of topic identification extends beyond keyword extraction because related topics are not required to be specified within the document, but rather have to be attained from certain sources of external knowledge. The task also differs from text classification because the topics are unknown in advance or are furnished as a controlled variant of vocabulary with multitude of entries, hence no classification is performed. In its place, with topic identification we aim to identify categories or topics pertaining to the available document to enhance its content with related external sources of knowledge [1, 4].

For dynamic ranking of topics relevance, external knowledge from an encyclopedia can be utilized to determine the related topics for a provided document. The approach comprises two major steps [7, 14]. In initial step, a knowledge graph containing encyclopedic perceptions on the basis of Wikipedia is constructed, wherein the vertices in the graph are signified by the categories and entities defined within the encyclopedia. The edges among the nodes are denoted by their relation of closeness within the specific Wikipedia articles. The graph is constructed once, and subsequently it is saved offline in such a way that it can be used to identify topics within new documents.

In the next step, for every input document the major encyclopedic concepts within the text are identified, and links are created between the external encyclopedic graph and the content of the document. A biased graph-based centrality algorithm is then applied to the complete graph such that all the vertices within the repository of external knowledge are ranked on the basis of their significance to the input document. Graph-oriented ranking techniques such as PageRank are fundamentally a method of determining the position of a node within a graph on the basis of repeatedly drawn global information from the complete graph. One construction is represented by the lines of a random walk over a directed graph. This involves visiting the vertices of the graph, and has a certain probability of hopping to a certain other vertex of the graph at random. The rank of a specific node is a sign of the likelihood that one would place the random walker at that particular node at a specific time.

Two major parameters need to be set for topic identification. First, the set of preliminary nodes utilized as bias within the ranking comprise (1) the preliminary collection of articles interconnected by original primary document, (2) the topics that are specified in the articles interlinked by the primary document, and (3) both the preliminary articles and the topics listed by the primary document. The dynamic ranking technique can be executed via dissemination on an encyclopedic graph that consists of entire articles from external knowledge source, all the topics from an external repository, or all the categories and articles from an external source.

Thus, a weighted graph is built to signify the relations between words. The relations chiefly consist of two characteristics: entity–centroid relation and dependency relation. Topic identification is considered as a graph partitioning problem addressed by the spectral clustering method. Hence, a graph-oriented model is first constructed, followed by the specification of an algorithm to model the documents in the form of a weighted graph.

13.5 TOPIC SEGMENTATION

Expertise in automatic summarization of documents is growing, and has the potential to offer solutions to the problems arising from information overload. These days, document summarization has a crucial role in aspects of information retrieval. With larger extent of documents, that present a summary of every document the user, importantly enables the work of identifying the required documents. Document summarization serves as a method of constructing automatically a condensed version of a document that offers beneficial information to end users, and multiple-document summarization aims to create a summary furnishing most of the information content in a collection of documents concerning an implicit or explicit main topic. Topic segmentation can be accomplished by various means, depending on the aim, such as (1) to derive linear topic segmentation (i.e., detection of the sequence of various segments within a text), or (2) to derive hierarchical topic segmentation (i.e., definition of a structure of sub-topics among the segments detected).

After the related topics are determined within a text, the next step is to divide the text into segments Topic segmentation aims to divide the text into coherent chunks on the basis of the topics it addresses. For example, for an article that encompasses three news stories, the aim would be to automatically determine the stories and outline their boundaries. The partitioning of a text as topics can be achieved at various degrees of granularity, ranging from dividing a book into chapters to identifying subtopics within a single-page article. Several applications can benefit from topic segmentation, including text summarization, keyword extraction, question answering, and information retrieval.

The volume of data is a crucial factor in selecting supervised versus unsupervised modeling frameworks. Supervised models usually address shortcomings of unsupervised models – primarily by employing binary classification to merge all the significant aspects and similarity functions as well as decisions made using other models requiring a very restricted volume of labeled information, and then creating a complete graph to take into account all pairs inter-sentence relations.

A meaningful graph for text segmentation can be built by adding all the sentences within a text as vertices in the graph and creating weighted edges reflecting pairwise similarity for sentences. Sentence similarity can be computed using metrics such as cosine similarity or to measure text-to-text similarity. A graph method that can be utilized to divide a text into segments is the normalized cut criteria approach, which can assess both the dissimilarities between various segments and the similarities within them. In this way, unlike earlier segmentation methods that relied fundamentally on local consistency within a segment, similarity relationships among several segments in the input text can be identified and then minimized. Thus, a graph-oriented method aims to apprehend semantic similarities among segments, rather than approximating using topical similarities. Every node of the resulting graph represents a sentence, and the edges are formed of pairs pertaining to semantically relevant sentences. Comprehensible segments are then established by identifying maximal groups in the relevancy graph.

First, the text is pre-processed and stopwords are eliminated. Then the stems of the words are determined and the relevant parts of speech are identified using tagging. Only verbs and nouns are utilized within the text. The method commences from the start of the key text, and words are taken from the knowledge repository to provide a two-tier tree where the root of a specific word is a similar word, and the children of the tree are words that are relevant to the specific target word. The children of the target word within the input text are then examined to construct a graph utilizing the target word as well as the words that represent both children in the earlier step tree and the input text. Thus, text segmentation consists of two stages. First, a two-tier tree is created from the connections of the abstract of the word, followed by creation of a graph from this earlier phase, then the selection of crucial segments that were identified using the graph created earlier.

The integration of external knowledge repositories dependably includes beneficial information as compared to the baselines which exclusively depend on the available text. The graph-oriented centrality method provides a way to produce topics ranked dynamically across a framework and offer the potential to use heuristics or knowledge from other resources such as encyclopedias which are then converted into a graph representation.

To summarize, all the sentences within a text are represented by the vertices of the relatedness graph. Semantic similarities are computed among all the pairs of sentences within the input document. For every pair of sentences whose semantic relatedness is higher than a certain threshold value, an edge is added among the equivalent nodes of the graph. The set of all potential maximal cliques in the graph is then computed. A preliminary set of segments is obtained by merging the adjacent sentences identified in minimum of single maximal clique for the graph. In the next step, the adjacent segments that have one clique at the minimum holding single sentence at bare minimum from each adjacent segment. For the specified minimal segment size, the adjacent segments are merged with sentences having a segment size less than the maximum value along with those which are more highly semantically related among the two adjoining segments. The relatedness between the two adjoining segments is calculated as the mean relatedness in their corresponding sentence.

13.6 DISCOURSE RELATIONSHIPS

Text segments, whether or not they belong to different topics, are normally linked using discourse relationships. Identifying them in a text is vital for various text processing applications, such as question answering, text summarization, and topic segmentation. Discourse relationships are usually characterized using conjunctions or various content-oriented words that contribute toward the consistency of the text. For example, words like "before" and "after" designate a temporal sequence involving two specific statements, as in the sentence, "Before he wrote the article, John visited the library." Similarly, "because" specifies a cause-and-effect relationship, as in the sentence, "Travel was delayed because of technical reasons." "Furthermore" or "also" precede an elaboration, as in the sentences, "Additional edges are included in the graph. A weight is also computed and later assigned to every edge." On the other hand, "however" or "but" designate a contrasting statement, as in "Mary liked the latest novel, but Tom had no interest in it."

To obtain discourse-oriented information in order to answer logical questions, first the elementary discourse units are encoded, followed by a module for reasoning of graphs, then a model to predict the answers. For a specific say

j^{th} option in the choices of answer for a question, a graph $Gi = (Vi, Ei)$ is constructed with $v_j \in V$, where the node v_j relates to the corresponding discourse unit e_j. After propagation of messages with relevant weights, the representations in a specific vertex v_i are updated with vertex embeddings and message representations using:

$$v_j^{\text{updated}} = ReLU\left(v_{\text{message}} + bias^u + weight^u\right) \quad \text{(Equation 13.4)}$$

The updated vertex representation is utilized to improve the token embeddings contextually through summation of relevant vertex positions, with $bias^u$ and $weight^u$ representing the bias and weight. The probabilities of answer options are then derived by feeding discourse-improved token embeddings to the answer prediction component. The model is entirely trained with cross entropy relevant loss. The high- and low-level discourse token characteristics are merged, resulting in singular individual feature vectors. The features can be concatenated and input as a new vector to obtain the output features for further classification.

The data structures that are normally utilized to detail discourse relationships are tree structures, which are easier to derive and formalize and can encode the text segments within a relationship along with their respective discourse connectors. However, recent research has shown that graphs are more appropriate than other methods for discourse representation since they show cross-dependencies between statements. Graph structures are useful representations for such discourse relationships, and offer the capability to encode richer collections of dependencies to compared to alternative forms of tree structures. Discourse relation graphs are built on the basis of dependency-oriented discourse relations among utterances that are intertwined. Modeling the relations among such utterances in conversations explicitly can enable models to recognize major key contents for concise and useful summarization.

13.7 MACHINE TRANSLATION

Machine translation is a vital emerging field in NLP, aiming to automatically translate texts from one natural language to another. Earlier methods of machine translation mainly comprised rule-oriented systems that despite being precise in their abilities to create translations held very low level of coverage and were not transportable across the domains. Such disadvantages have been addressed by current statistical approaches that depend on larger parallel input texts in order to automatically learn the translation models, which then can be applied to the translation of new texts. Generally, statistical-led machine translation creates the best translation for an input text, but there are some applications where it is necessary to have access to a greater number of potential alternate translations, ranging from several hundreds to several thousands, thus leading to storage and processing challenges. A potential solution for the sophisticated representation of a collection of candidate translations is the utilization of word graphs, which avoid the redundancies most frequently identified among the candidate translations. For example, candidates may exist that vary by just a single word.

A word graph is comprised of an acyclic graph that is directed and has one selected root vertex. The edges are labeled with the words, and a path across a translation graph represents a candidate translation. As an option, the graph can also be comprised of scores associated to the words on the graph edges, which can be utilized to compute the score for a specific translation path. The main differences between word- and phrase-level translations involve three further steps. The first step is to include phrases in the graph by introducing new edges among words. Such edges can be considered as shortcuts which link all the words pertaining to a phrase. The second step is to translate phrases within the graph by introducing an additional edge for every potential phrase translation. The third step adapts the phrase-to-word edge labels by replacing the phrase edges with a sequence of one-word edges.

13.8 MULTILINGUAL RETRIEVAL OF INFORMATION BASED ON GRAPHS

The two main techniques conventionally used for multi-language information retrieval are: (1) automatic translation of input documents into the language in which the query was posed query, and (2) automatic translation of the query into the language of the input documents. Of these two methods, translation of the input query is used most frequently since it takes less time and does not require the re-indexing of the input document collection. In order to create a translation of a specific query, the commonest method is the use of a bilingual dictionary. Although machine translation and translation based on parallel texts are also potential methods, they normally need the availability of greater parallel systems, and these exist only for a few languages [13]. On the other hand, bilingual dictionaries are available for a number of languages, and can be used to translate input query words into the language of the objective documents. Graph-oriented representation can be used effectively to determine the correct translations by utilizing random walks across a co-occurrence graph. To build the co-occurrence graph, potential candidate translations are included as vertices connected by weighted edges taking into account the link strength identified by a larger system in the target language.

13.9 INFORMATION RETRIEVAL USING GRAPHS

Information retrieval applications' results normally return complete documents that are related to the query posed. When the information required is more specific, it is usually more useful to use an information extraction system. Information extraction is used to identify knowledge in unstructured, raw forms of text. An efficient scheme to handle this is mutual reinforcement, which is based on the concept that ideal patterns produce good instances, and good instances are followed by good patterns. Such reinforcement may be naturally modeled using bipartite graphs that are coupled by a centrality algorithm. In such a representation, patterns and instances are signified as nodes in the graph, while the edges reflect creation links among instances and patterns. Once the graph is built, a centrality measure is deployed iteratively to identify a score for every node. This score serves as a confidence level for both patterns and seeds that may be utilized as a filter to avoid introducing errors within the bootstrapping procedure. Hence, the choice of patterns and instances at every bootstrapping step is determined on the basis of global information repeatedly inferred from the whole graph of patterns as well as seeds, instead of local information determining the quality of the immediate seeds they produce.

13.10 GRAPH -BASED QUESTION ANSWERING

Overlapping with both information retrieval and information extraction, graph-based question answering is the task of automatically answering a question posed in natural language [6, 7]. In graph matching, question–answer graphs that are learned from training data are utilized to construct graph rules that may find answers to new questions. In this technique, a set of questions and answers is annotated manually, then rules are automatically learned by matching their respective graphs. The graphs are built using the output of a specific dependency parser, capturing the syntactic relationships among the words as well as their associated roles [10, 11]. Despite not having overall performance in question-answering approach oriented on graphs, with no competency in comparison with the prevailing methods, the approach is worthy of attention since it is easily portable to newer domains does not require a different question classification phase, and does not use entity recognizers that may not be readily available for languages other than English.

REFERENCES

1. Yang, S. & Tang, Y. (2022). News topic detection based on capsule semantic graph. *Big Data Mining and Analytics*. 5(2). 98–109. 10.26599/BDMA.2021.9020023.
2. Xiong, Ao, Liu, Derong, Tian, Hongkang, Liu, Zhengyuan, Peng, Yu, Kadoch, Michel. (2021). News keyword extraction algorithm based on semantic clustering and word graph model. *Tsinghua Science and Technology*. 26. 886–893. 10.26599/TST.2020.9010051.
3. Chen, Chaoxian & Yang, Bo & Zhao, Changjian. (2020). *Keywords Extraction Based on Word Relevance Degrees*. 60–65. 10.1145/3395260.3395262.
4. Wang, Dongyang & Su, Junli & Yu, Hongbin. (2020). Feature extraction and analysis of natural language processing for deep learning english language. *IEEE Access*. 1–1. 10.1109/ACCESS.2020.2974101.
5. Lakshika, M. & Caldera, H. & Welgama, W. (2020). *Abstractive Web News Summarization Using Knowledge Graphs*. 300–301. 10.1109/ICTer51097.2020.9325453.
6. Zhang, Jie & Pei, Zhongmin & Xiong, Wei & Luo, Zhangkai. (2020). Answer extraction with graph attention network for knowledge graph question answering. 1645–1650. 10.1109/ICCC51575.2020.9345000.

7. Feng, Yanlin, Chen, Xinyue, Lin, Bill, Wang, Peifeng, Yan, Jun & Ren, Xiang. (2020). *Scalable Multi-Hop Relational Reasoning for Knowledge-Aware Question Answering.*
8. Hark, Cengiz, Uçkan, Taner, Seyyarer, Ebubekir & Karci, Ali. (2018). *Graph-Based Suggestion For Text Summarization.* 1–6. 10.1109/IDAP.2018.8620738.
9. Yongkiatpanich, Chuleepohn & Wichadakul, Duangdao. (2019). *Extractive Text Summarization Using Ontology and Graph-Based Method.* 105–110. 10.1109/CCOMS.2019.8821755.
10. Mital, Piyush, Agarwal, Saurabh, Neti, Bhargavi, Haribhakta, Yashodhara, Kamble, Vibhavari, Bhattacharjee, Krishnanjan, Das, Debashri, Mehta, Swati & Kumar, Ajai. (2018). *Graph based Question Answering System.*
11. Hu, Sen, Zou, Lei, Yu, Jeffrey, Wang, Haixun & Zhao, Dongyan. (2017). Answering natural language questions by subgraph matching over knowledge graphs. *IEEE Transactions on Knowledge and Data Engineering.* 1–1. 10.1109/TKDE.2017.2766634.
12. Gambhir, Mahak & Gupta, Vishal. (2017). Recent automatic text summarization techniques: a survey. *Artificial Intelligence Review.* 47. 10.1007/s10462-016-9475-9.
13. Bastings, Jasmijn, Titov, Ivan, Aziz, Wilker, Marcheggiani, Diego & Sima'an, Khalil. (2017). *Graph Convolutional Encoders for Syntax-aware Neural Machine Translation.*
14. Kipf, Thomas & Welling, Max. (2016). *Semi-Supervised Classification with Graph Convolutional Networks.*
15. Agirre, Eneko & Soroa, Aitor. (2009). Personalizing page rank for word sense disambiguation. Proceedings of the 12th Conference of the European Chapter of the Association for Computational Linguistics. 33–41. 10.3115/1609067.1609070.
16. Samerhassan, Radamihalcea & Carmenbanea. (2012). Random walk term weighting for improved text classification. *International Journal of Semantic Computing.* 01. 10.1142/S1793351X07000263.
17. Mihalcea, Rada & Tarau, Paul. (2004). *Text Rank: Bringing Order into Text.*

14 Analysis of Medical Images Using Machine Learning Techniques

Nikita Jain, Mahesh Kumar Joshi, Vishal Jain, and Manish Dubey

CONTENTS

DOI: 10.1201/9781003272649-14

14.1 INTRODUCTION

In recent years, a major focus in the areas of medical science and imaging has been tumor identification. Tumor detection is still considered to be a hugely challenging area of research in medical science. The primary motive of medical imaging analysis is to detect brain tumors accurately so that proper and timely treatment can be provided for those suffering from them. In identifying tumors, magnetic resonance imaging (MRI) is used to provide an input image source. Any unusual growth in brain cells and tissues is called a brain tumor. Brain tumors can occur in any age.

Brain tumors' symptoms depend on their size, type, and location. The symptoms may include vomiting, headaches, vision problems, mental changes, difficulty in walking, changes in speaking, and hearing and memory changes. In 2016, the American Brain Tumor Association found that nearly 80,000 men, women, and children in the USA had been diagnosed with brain tumors.

The research described in this chapter used wavelet transformation to process the MRI images, then reduction of the dimensions of the features detected was carried out by principal component analysis (PCA). Binary classification of the medical images was carried out using the support vector machine (SVM) method. A kernel support vector machine (KSVM) with four kernels was used for accurate measurement using radial basis functions, linear functions, polygonal functions, and quadratic functions. Many techniques were applied, such as standard deviation, energy, mean, variance, entropy, root mean square (RMS), inverse difference moment (IDM), kurtosis, contrast, smoothness, correlation, and skewness.

14.1.1 OVERVIEW

The brain is an essential organ in the body's nervous system which receives input from sensory organs and sends output to muscles. The human brain is divided into two hemispheres, the left brain and the right brain, which are connected together. Brain tumors can cause critical or severe disease due to unrestrained growth of unusual tissues.

Brain tumors, can be divided in benign and malignant tumors. Benign tumors are not cancerous, do not spread, and remains in their current form, while malignant tumors are cancerous, and spread and grow. Generally, benign tumors are not dangerous for human health, but malignant tumors are very dangerous and can lead to death because they can grow and spread rapidly into surrounding tissues. Malignant tumors have the ability to increase the amount of abnormal brain tissue uncontrollably.

Many imaging techniques are used to diagnose brain tumor, but MRI is very popular because it provides high-definition images showing the internal structure of the brain and provides a variety of useful information that can be used in medical diagnosis and biomedical research.

When searching and browsing image data, image features (essential data patterns) such as color, texture, and shape enable the recognition of an image complying with a user query. In the method proposed in this chapter, medical images were targeted for search in a database. Because most of the images have similar colors and textures [1], edge detection can be helpful in finding appropriate images in the database, so this study explores a variety of edge detection techniques in order to design a new and enhanced methodology.

14.1.2 Motivation

Research has found that many people have died due to inaccurate detection of brain tumors. The work in this chapter was motivated by an article by Selvakumar et al. [2] which described how the k-means algorithm was applied to noise-free MRI images to extract the tumor data more accurately then apply the fuzzy C-means algorithm to identify the features that needed to be extracted.

Tumors vary greatly, and every type of tumor has a different treatment. Many scanning techniques are available to identify tumors, such as computer tomography (CT), positron emission tomography (PET), and MRI, but MRI scanning is the most accurate. It can be very difficult to identify relevant features among those isolated and decide which technique is best suited for brain tumor imaging, and we found that PCA was a frequently chosen technique for finding patterns in high dimensions and was very widely used in analyzing the data [3].

14.1.3 Objective

The primary aim of this study is to detect brain tumors using appropriate segmentation techniques to identify various features, and then apply a classification process using support vector machines with different kernel functions.

14.1.3.1 Study of Different Segmentation Techniques

In this section of study, we will study various image processing and viewing them on computers. In this the elementary step is to identifying an object, understanding the image, image processing. Some researchers start with the image segmentation like threshold strategies, Otsu's technique, primarily graph-based strategies, contour technique, primarily region-based strategies, edge detection strategies, clustering strategies, and various hybrid techniques. Histogram or bar graph methods don't work well for images whose histograms are nearly unimodal. For multifaceted and noise-based data, primarily edge-based techniques are not appropriate they concentrate on detecting pixel on the edges of objects. In region growing techniques, over-segmentation and under-segmentation are important problems. Graph-based strategies are highly complex processes [4]. Because of its simplicity, Otsu's technique is used.

14.1.3.2 Selection for Appropriate Features

To select the appropriate features to identify, wavelet transformation was applied to compute a coefficient matrix with the help of discrete wavelet transformation (DWT). DWT can be used to selected the features. This method degrades the input image into a chain of sub-band images. These are then passed through PCA to reduce the features, then go through gray level co-occurrence matrix (GLCM) processing to calculate features such as energy, contrast, correlation, and homogeneity.

14.1.3.3 Performance and Classification of the Proposed Model

After implementation of the chosen classification technique, using SVM and various kernel functions, the system is evaluated and the results are summarized.

14.1.4 Expected Outcomes

After successful implementation, the following results were obtained from the study:

- *A rich collection of literature on image segmentation techniques* – Literature on various image segmentation techniques was studied, and Otsu's technique was selected based on the expected outcomes.
- *A feature detection technique* – The final implementation produced an efficient feature identification technique which can help to calculate various texture-based and statistical-based features.
- *Analysis of the performance of the technique* – The performance of the algorithm designed was evaluated using SVM techniques with numerous kernel functions, which are suitable for binary classification tasks.

14.2 LITERATURE SURVEY

Aslam, Daxiang, and Cui suggested that the system is going to be used for the intensity of brightness from its gray scale image. Thresholding can be used to detect diseased tissues. A series of filters such as mathematician, linear and average, were used to get rid of noise [5].

Zhang and Wu suggested the technique in which they have discussed about the tool which will distinguish the normal and abnormal brain and identify the Gaussian Radial Basis (GRB) kernel. This brain imaging classification system supported by PCA and KSVM could probably be a valuable tool to be employed in computer-aided clinical identification [6].

Panigrahi et al. concluded that tumor detection benefited from the assistance of fuzzy C-means clustering applied repeatedly to genetic formula parameters. This method is divided into pre-processing and post-processing stages. The proposed system of the author is applied to various sizes and intensities of primary and secondary varieties of abnormal images [7].

Kohir and Karaddi proposed a new approach to brain cancer classification for astrocytoma kind brain recognition that may be a part of image process exploitation GLCM. Astrocytoma is the kind of brain tumor which begins from the brain or the spinal cord [8].

Tirpude and Welekar suggested that the gray level distribution of the image pixels was not sufficiently distinct, so the employment of a distinct, comprehensive threshold value was not a good choice to segment the entire image, including the tumor itself, and concluded that global thresholding techniques provide poor results when attempting to section MRI images of tumor-bearing brains [9].

Malik and Baharudin concluded that the experimental comparative analysis of the applied math quantized bar chart texture characteristics for the effective image retrieval in terms of exactness and recall within the discrete cosine transform (DCT) domain supported the median and Laplacian filters. Then the applied mathematical texture options like kurtosis, smoothness, energy, skewness, mean, standard deviation, and entropy were calculated by intensity levels in the bar chart bins of all blocks. The results of the quantized bar chart texture options supported Laplacian filters, median with edge extraction and median that provide the simplest performance in terms of image retrieval in a vary DCT domain [10].

Hassan and Aboshgifa suggested that programs with graphical user interfaces (GUIs) give far superior results than the traditional techniques for tumor detection as they permit users to change parameters easily [11].

Thiagarajan and Bremananth proposed a unique algorithm rule supported the mixture of conditional random filed and changed artificial bee colony improvement with changed fuzzy chance c means is employed, conditional random field may be a widely used technique for image segmentation. The mixture of changed Artifical Bee Colony (ABC) optimization algorithm rule with Fuzzy Possibility C-Means (FPCM) is employed to search out the best label that minimizes the posterior energy operate to segment the image. This provides important results for the applied mathematics parameters taken for thought and it outperforms the prevailing approaches like the exiting approach and Markov Random Fields Artificial Bee Colony (MRFABC) [12].

Reddy et al. proposed a perspective for distinguishing the growth of tumor size and bone cancer stage victimization region growing algorithmic rule. This technique segmented the region of interest by victimization region growing algorithmic rule. Tumor size is mathematically calculated consistent with the amount of pixels within the selected tumor part. Rely on the entire pixel worth cancer stage is discovered. Choice of seed point depends on the image and it is troublesome to pick out accurately [13].

Asuntha et al. proposed a system for detecting bone cancer from MRI scan images. Features extracted from images enable details to be understood. The main motive for extracting these characteristics is to make the process simpler and more accurate [14].

Jeevitha and Narendran proposed a segmentation approach that enables users to quickly and efficiently segment tumors in MRI images of the brain. Their approach uses the Otsu thresholding technique to improve efficiency [15].

Borole et al. concluded that digital image processing techniques are necessary for tumor detection in MRI images. The pre-processing techniques "embody completely different ways like Filtering, Contrast enhancement, Edge detection is employed for image smoothing" [16].

Reddy et al. concluded that the classification techniques are measure rising because the key factors for the diagnosis of carcinoma sickness Breast cancer disease. SVM model using radial basis function (RBF) and polynomial kernel functions with variable arguments such as RBF sigma, BoxConstraint, and poly-order. SVM kernel functions like RBF and polynomial (non-linear) are measure applied to come up with the hyper plane. The SVM model is used to test the data and classify tumors as benign or malignant [17].

Yogamangalam and Karthikeyan advised that segmentation is completed to estimate the surfaces. Segmentation may be used to any form of image. Examination to different techniques thresholding is the simplest and computationally quick. Depending on the application technique varies [18].

14.3 THE PROBLEM DOMAIN AND PROPOSED SOLUTION

This section will give a detailed description of the problem domain and propose our functional model as a solution.

14.3.1 Domain Description

Image processing uses mathematical models to improve image quality. Nowadays, these techniques are highly involved in real-world applications for object recognition, information extraction, and search engines. There are various image retrieval and extraction models available that promise to be efficient and effective. These models frequently employ methods for feature extraction and calculation to retrieve more accurate results. Basically, during a search, an image is compared to another image. If both images are similar then the image is returned as a search result. Searching for similar images is a complex process, therefore content-based image extraction is used [19].

In the last 20 years, a variety of useful algorithms have been developed for the segmentation of medical images, each with its own set of characteristics. Daily growth of medical knowledge volume guided in uplift human mistakes in their manual analysis and increases the requests to explore mechanically. The study and analysis of the brain could be a major interest because of its capability for learning early development patterns and morphologic changes within the tumor method. Segmentation of structural regions of the brain is that the basic downside in medical image analysis [20].

A mass of tissue originating from development of abnormal cells is termed a tumor. Ordinarily, in our body the cells age and die, then new cells develop to replace them. However, in the case of and cancers, this death–rebirth cycle is disrupted, often resulting in tumor formation [21].

Tumor cells grow unceasingly, and don't expire. The tumors keep on adding more and more tissue to the mass, which grows into a cyst. Tumors are classified into primary and secondary tumors [22]. Once the tumors going outside from the tissues of the brain itself area unit state to be primary tumors. Secondary brain tumors are caused by cancer that spreads from a different part of the body. In this context, shape, texture, and color analysis help to identify the relevant images in huge databases. Therefore, this study aims to find an optimum method for feature calculation for medical databases. In the medical domain, most of the tumor image data available has similar color and texture features, so shape features are helpful for distinguishing the images more effectively [23].

Li (2012) suggested that texture can be defined as a recurrent pattern of arrangement of structures with constant intervals. In general, texture refers to surface characteristics associate degree look of an object given by the form, concentration, size, arrangement and proportion of its straightforward components. A fundamental step in gathering such characteristics is texture feature extraction, which is helpful in numerous image processing applications, such as medical imaging, remote sensing, and content-based image retrieval [24].

14.3.2 Problem domain

The medical domain and image search approaches are faced by some fundamental issues that our proposed model seeks to address. The following issues need to be resolved:

- *Images are defined using color, shape, and texture* – For this reason, these features need to be focused on when searching medical databases to find accurate image matches.
- *Choice of image segmentation method* – This is a fundamental step in object identification, image reclamation, and image understanding [25].
- *Selection of appropriate features* – Feature extraction is one of the main processes in a texture classification system. The main purpose of this process is to extract useful information to explain or represent a texture in the input image. Feature extraction is also required as a prior step for the classification process. Texture images which belong to the same group should provide similar texture features.

- *Selection of an appropriate feature reduction tool* – Many mathematical tools are working successfully in the field of image processing. The main problem with graphical authentication mechanisms is that the images tend to be large, therefore processing is slow. In image compression and recognition PCA method is effectively applied [26]. Principal component analysis is useful to improve security and compress huge amounts of data. The motive for using PCA is to decrease the number of observed variables i.e., dimensionality of the data to independent variables i.e., smaller spontaneous dimensionality of characteristic, which are necessary to explain the data cost effectively. The deed that PCA might do is redundancy confiscation, data compression, prediction, feature extraction, etc. [27].
- *Gauging performance and classification of the proposed model* – After implementation of the chosen technique, the performance of the system needs to be evaluated and the results summarized [28].

A brain tumor dataset was provided by the Institute of Oncology, University Medical Centre Ljubljana, Yugoslavia. This dataset specifies two categories of tumors – benign and malignant. Otsu's technique was employed in MRI data for segmentation the divided knowledge used SVM as learning algorithms with four kernel functions [29].

14.3.3 Solution Domain

The structure of tumor recognition systems usually consists of the following features:

- *Image acquisition* – This is the initial stage of image processing. In this area of medical science, brain MRI images can be acquired from databases.
- *Image pre-processing* – This step involves segmenting the required image into its constituent regions. The foremost objective of this step is improve the quality of the image data and decrease the effects of noise.
- *Feature reduction* – Processing and storing large amounts of feature data increases calculation time and memory requirements, so principal component analysis is used to reduce the number of features.
- *Classification* – This process assigns class levels to the data and examines whether any fresh data fits into these levels.
- *Accuracy assessment* – The accuracy of the system can be gauged by applying a wide variety of techniques and algorithms.

14.3.4 Algorithms Used in the Study

This section describes the algorithms utilized in implementation of our model.

14.3.4.1 Otsu's Method

In image processing, Otsu's technique, named after Nobuyuki Otsu, is used to mechanically implement the thresholding of clustering based image, the dearth of a gray level image into a binary image. This system be of the opinion that the image put up with two categories of pixels following bimodal bar chart foreground and background pixels their combined intra class variance is stripped down, or equivalently (because the total of pair wise square distances is constant), in order that their inter class variance is peak. For this reason, Otsu's technique is mostly a one dimensional, separate analog of Fisher's discriminant analysis.

14.3.4.2 Wavelet Transformation

14.3.4.2.1 Wavelet Transform

Wavelet transform has the power to analyze an image by factoring it into a series of sub-band images. These sub-band images can be thought about as one form of wavelet coefficients where texture features are calculated [30]. Any function can be considered a wavelet function $\Psi(t)$ if it satisfies the following conditions:

- *The wavelet function's square integral is finite* – The wavelet must have (a small amount of) finite energy:

$$\int_{-\infty}^{+\infty} |\Psi(t)|\hat{}\ 2dt < \infty \qquad \text{(Equation 14.1)}$$

- *The integral of wavelet function $\Psi(t) = 0$* – The function must be oscillatory (a wave):

$$\int_{-\infty}^{+\infty} \Psi(t)dt = 0 \qquad \text{(Equation 14.2)}$$

14.3.4.2.2 Continuous Wavelet Transform (CWT)

CWT computes wavelet coefficients at each achievable range and location, has made plenty of computing influence and moment in time. To create wavelet transform to become additional economical efficient and sensible in real world applications.

14.3.4.2.3 Discrete Wavelet Transform

DWT is accomplished by iteratively filter an indication or likeness from beginning to end the high pass and low pass filters, and later down sampling the filtered information by two. This procedure can decompose the input image into a series of sub-band images. Figure 14.1 illustrates associate example of DWT, whereas the image with a down arrow within a circle represents the downsampling operation.

In Figure 14.1, an image S at resolution level it was decomposed into four sub-band images after going through one stage of decomposition process. The approximation image is concretely the low frequency module of the original

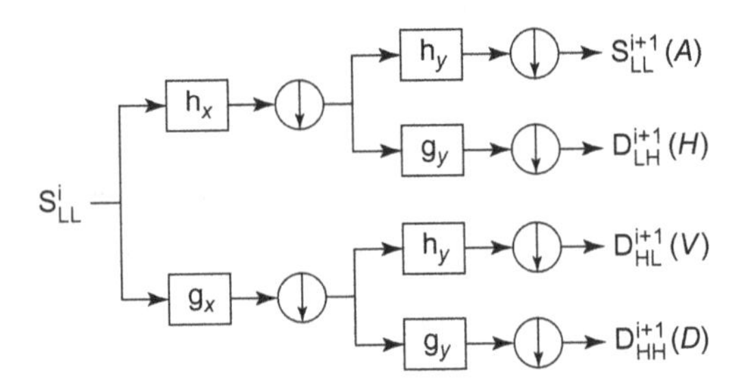

FIGURE 14.1 Example of DWT

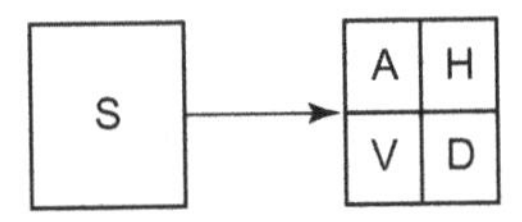

FIGURE 14.2 Output of a decomposed image using wavelet transform

image *S*. The output of a decomposed image using wavelet transform is shown in Figure 14.2.

Every detail image comprises the information of specific orientation and scale. This implement that the spatial information is also hold on within the sub-band images.

The sub-band images acquired through the low-pass and high-pass filters can be calculated by using the following equations:

$$\begin{aligned} A &= \left[h_x * \left(h_y * S \right)_{\downarrow 2,1} \right]_{\downarrow 1,2} \\ H &= \left[h_x * \left(g_y * S \right)_{\downarrow 2,1} \right]_{\downarrow 1,2} \\ V &= \left[g_x * \left(h_y * S \right)_{\downarrow 2,1} \right]_{\downarrow 1,2} \\ D &= \left[g_x * \left(g_y * S \right)_{\downarrow 2,1} \right]_{\downarrow 1,2} \end{aligned} \quad \text{(Equation 14.3)}$$

where *S* represents the original input image, and ↓ represents the downsampling operator.

Therefore, downsampling is a procedure to remove redundant filtered samples from the sub-band images in the decomposition process.

14.3.4.2.4 Discrete Wavelet Frame Transform (DWFT)

Some investigators have suggested the DWFT method of texture classification. DWFT is similar to the traditional DWT method. The only difference between them is that DWFT does not implement downsampling operations, and hence create a translation invariant property for the decomposition results, as shown in Figure 14.3.

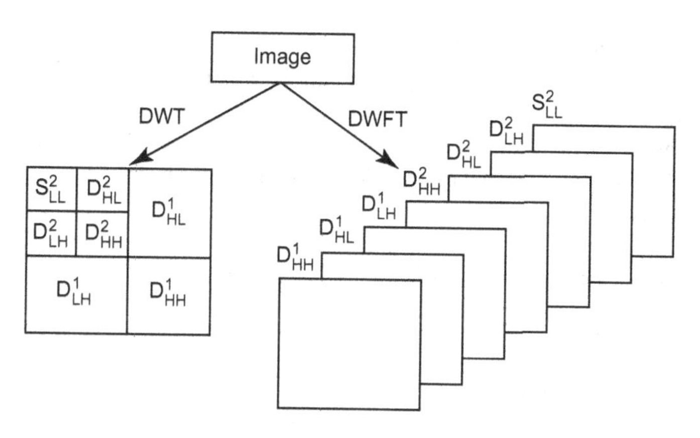

FIGURE 14.3 A translation-invariant property for the decomposition results

14.3.4.3 Principal Component Analysis

PCA is a mathematical system that uses an orthogonal variation to convert a set of observations of possibly connected variables into a set of values of linearly unrelated variables known as principal components. PCA was originated in 1901 by Karl Pearson. PCA is principally used as a data analysis tool and for creating prognostic models. The number of principal components is a smaller amount or adequate smaller of the quantity of original variables or the quantity of considerations.

The results of PCA are typically in the form of component scores, known as factor scores, and PCA is that the simplest of the true eigenvector-based variable analyses. Frequently, its operation will be thought of as manifest the inner structure of the information in an exceeding approach that best illuminate the variance within the data. If a variable dataset is envisioned as a collection of coordinates in an exceedingly high dimensional data, PCA is closely associated with correlation analysis. Correlation analysis generally covers additional space specific assumptions concerning the underlying structure and solves eigenvectors of a rather completely different matrix.

14.3.4.4 Gray Level Co-occurrence Matrix

The GLCM serves as a robust foundation for texture classification. Many textural parameters matrix facilitates comprehend the small print concerning the image content. Texture includes vital data concerning the structural preparation of surfaces. The textural characteristics supported gray tone abstraction dependencies have a general relevancy in image classification. The three essential framework components utilized in human importance of pictures are contextual, textural and spectral characteristics. Textural property contains data concerning the abstraction distribution of tonal variations inside a band. Feature Extraction could be a technique of capturing visual content of pictures for categorization & retrieval. Primitive or low level image option will be either general options, like taking out options of form, texture and color or space specific.

14.3.4.5 Support Vector Machine

SVM is a useful method for data classification, which usually involves separating data into training and testing sets. The goal of the SVM method is to create a model supporting the training data that predicts the target values of the test data attributes. SVM demands that every information instance is delineated as a vector of real numbers.

14.3.5 Our Proposed Algorithm

The steps involved in this process are shown below:

1. Read the input image.
2. Convert the image to black and white using Otsu binarization.
3. Apply discrete wavelet transform. This allows analyzing of images at various levels of resolution.
4. Extract the useful features using principal component analysis.
5. Apply the GLCM to determine the homogeneity, mean standard deviation, variance, smoothness energy, entropy, RMS, contrast, correlation, kurtosis, skewness, IDM, mean square error, etc. utilized for the performance evaluation.

These algorithm steps are shown in Figure 14.4.

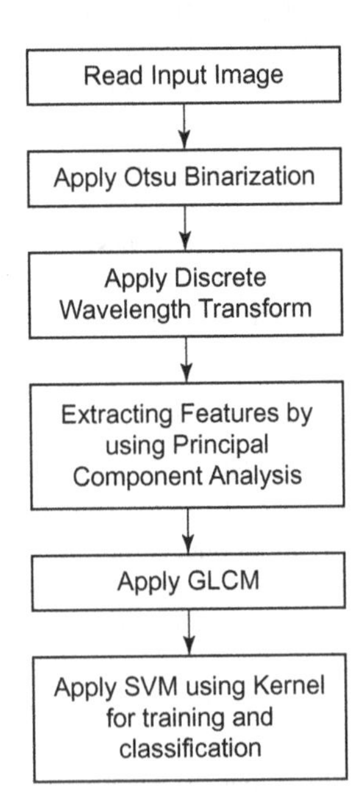

FIGURE 14.4 Block diagram of the proposed algorithm

The algorithm determines which pixels go below foreground and which pixels go below background levels. An image with abundant gray levels is regenerated into fewer gray level pictures and comparison is completed on each pixel intensity with a reference value of T (threshold). If the input picture is $f(x, y)$ and the binary version is $g(x, y)$, then $g(x, y) = 1$ if $f(x, y) >= T$, otherwise it is 0. PCA is used to reduce the number of surplus characteristic sets in the dataset.

14.4 IMPLEMENTATION

This section describes the hardware and software requirements of the proposed system, in addition to the different functions and methods involved.

14.4.1 Tools and Techniques

The development of the desired techniques was carried out using the following system configuration:

1. Development environment: MATLAB® 8.1 (R2013a)
2. SVM classifier with kernel functions for training the data
3. DWT, GLCM, and PCA for feature extraction
4. Operating system: Windows 7
5. RAM: 2 GB and above
6. Disk space: 9,216 MB
7. Processor: Intel Core i5

14.4.2 MATLAB

MATLAB is a high-performance language used for technical computation that connects visualization, programming, and computation in a user-friendly environment. MATLAB stands for MATrix LABoratory. MATLAB features an application-specific family of add-on solutions called toolboxes.

Specialized technology is used by toolboxes that allows us to apply and find out the MATLAB, MATLAB functions which provides the collections of Toolboxes such as signal processing, neural networks, control systems, fuzzy logic, simulation, and wavelets.

14.4.3 Methodology

This research project used MRI brain images as inputs for the algorithms. Instead of different scan of the brain MRI picture provides the comprehensive information of the brain tissues. Initially, the brain reflection is checked whether it is pretentious by the tumor or not. So, if the tumor constituency is extracted from the brain picture then the quantity of pixel for the tumor section is computed.

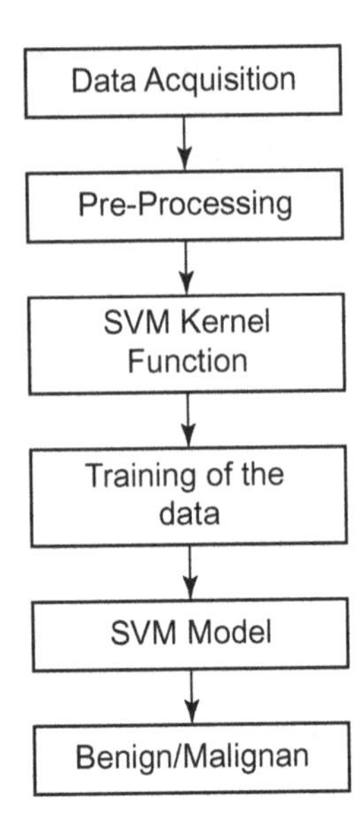

FIGURE 14.5 Training and testing the data using the SVM classifier

If the amount of pixel is zero the classification displays the brain image without tumor region. Otherwise, the brain image with tumor region is displayed by the image. If the brain image has tumor province, this image is required to try to do the subsequent more stepladder. Figure 14.5 shows that however we training and testing the data through SVM Classifier.

In the next step, filtering is employed to get rid of noise from the brain image. Heaps of noise is not adulterate by MRI. Thus to eliminate the noise from the brain image during this system average filter is employed. The regularize image is obtained once pre processing, and it is able to use within the next step. To handle quickly in the next step the regularize image is used.

Input data from the feature set is passed to the SVM classifier to divide it into two categories. High dimensional feature the nonlinear SVM works in a very great way. Kernel functions are used to enhance the margin of the classification. It is simple to use in sensible image processing and also provides the clear understanding of the classification. The proposed model used strategies such as RBF, linear, and polygonal functions to produce the segmented image. The classification method measured many characteristics of the dataset, such as energy, homogeneity, correlation, mean, entropy, standard deviation, RMS, variance, smoothness, skewness, kurtosis, IDM, contrast, etc.

14.5 RESULT ANALYSIS

This section evaluates the results and performance of the model.

14.5.1 Means

Means functions are simple methods commonly utilized in pure mathematics, analysis, and computation. A large range of types of means have been developed for these functions. In contest of image processing filtering through mean is assessed as abstraction filtering and used for noise reduction:

$$\bar{\mathbf{X}} = \frac{\sum_{i=0}^{n} X_i}{n} \qquad \text{(Equation 14.4)}$$

14.5.2 Standard Deviation

SD is a most extensively used to assess variability in statistics. In terms of image processing, it is used to show the proportion of variation or dispersion from a common value. A low SD is a sign that the data points tend to be very close to the mean, whereas a high SD indicates that the data points are spread out over a large range of values:

$$s = \sqrt{\frac{\sum_{i=1}^{n} (X_i - X)^2}{(n-1)}} \qquad \text{(Equation 14.5}$$

14.5.3 Entropy

Entropy is massive once the image is not texturally uniform and plenty of GLCM components have terribly little values. Complicated textures tend to process high entropy. Entropy is physically powerful, however contrariwise related to energy:

$$Ent = -\sum_{X_{i-1}} p(i,j) \log_2[\mathbf{p}(i,j)] \qquad \text{(Equation 14.6)}$$

14.5.4 RMS

RMS is the measure of the root mean square value of an image:

$$\bar{\mathbf{X}}_{rms} = \sqrt{\frac{\sum_{i=0}^{n} X_i^2}{n}} \qquad \text{(Equation 14.7)}$$

14.5.5 Variance

The variance could be a computation of however so much a group of numbers is detached. It is a variety of descriptors of a likelihood distribution, recitation how distant the figures lie from the mean:

$$s^2 = \left(\sqrt{\frac{\sum_{i=1}^{n} \left(X_i - X^2\right.}{(n-1)}} \right)^2 \qquad \text{(Equation 14.8)}$$

14.5.6 Smoothness

It is a measure which is a relative of region intensity.

$$SM = \mathbf{1} - \frac{1}{1+s^2} P(i,j) \qquad \text{(Equation 14.9)}$$

14.5.7 Kurtosis

In statistics, kurtosis is an approximate of the form of the probability distribution of a real valued random variant. It is closely associated with the fourth moment of a distribution. A low kurtosis distribution has shorter, thinner tails, and sometimes an additional rounded peak.

$$\text{Kurt} = \frac{1}{s^4} \sum_{X_{i=1}}^{n} \left(\mathbf{X}_i - \bar{X}\right)^4 P(i,j) \qquad \text{(Equation 14.10)}$$

14.5.8 Skewness

Skewness is a statistical measure of the dearth of equality of the distribution of a random variant having real value. The skewness worth may be positive or negative, or may be non specific. A negative skew shows that the tail on the left facet of the density operates is greater than the correct facet. Also the values (possibly as well as the median) which are in bulk missing from the correct of the mean. A positive skew indicates that the tail on the right facet is longer than the left facet and also the bulk of the values lie to the left of the mean.

$$\text{Skew} = \frac{1}{s^3} \sum_{X_{i=1}}^{n} \left(X_i - \bar{X}\right)^3 P(i,j) \qquad \text{(Equation 14.11)}$$

14.5.9 IDM

IDM is determining of image texture as known as homogeneity that computes homogeneity of a picture. Inverse Difference Moment characteristics obtain the analysis of the distribution closeness of the GLCM components to the GLCM diagonal. IDM includes a scope of values thus on decide either the image is rough or non textured.

$$IDM = \sum_{i=1}^{n} \frac{1}{1+(i-j)^2} P(i,j) \qquad \text{(Equation 14.12)}$$

14.5.10 Contrast

The contrast is an evaluation of intensity of a pixel and its neighbor over the image. In the visual cognition of the real world, contrast is determined by the difference in the color and brightness of the object and other objects within the equivalent ground of observation. It is the difference between the very best and the lowest values of a contiguous group of pixels. It calculates the quantity of native variations present in the picture.

$$Con = \sum_{i,j} |i - j|^2 \, p(i, j) \qquad \text{(Equation 14.13)}$$

14.5.11 Correlation

Correlation evaluates the dependency of gray levels should be linear of neighboring pixels. An optical method that makes use of tracking and image registration methods for 2D and 3D accurate measurements of changes in digital images is known as digital image correlation.

$$\text{Cor} = \sum_{i,j} \frac{(i - \mu i)(j - \mu j)p(i, j)}{\sigma_i \sigma_j} \qquad \text{(Equation 14.14)}$$

14.5.12 Energy

The energy characteristics compute the uniformity of the magnitude level distribution. If the worth is high, then the distribution is to a little variety of intensity levels. It measures the textural uniformity that is pixel pair repetitions. It discovers disorders in textures.

$$\text{Energy} = \sum_{i,j} \mathbf{p}(i, j)^2 \qquad \text{(Equation 14.15)}$$

14.5.13 Homogeneity

Homogeneity is that the distribution closeness of components within the GLCM. It is energetic animate of close to diagonal components in the GLCM. It has highest worth once all components within the identical image.

$$\text{Hom} = \sum_{i,j} \frac{p(i, j)}{1 + |i - j|} \qquad \text{(Equation 14.16)}$$

Several characteristics of the dataset were measured, such as kurtosis, skewness, entropy, RMS, mean, homogeneity, deviation, variance, smoothness, IDM, contrast, correlation, energy, etc. for the classification methods (Table 14.1).

These are shown in Table 14.1, in which the benign dataset is employed and the parameters are calculated.

In Table 14.2, the malignant dataset is used and the calculations are performed on it for the different features.

TABLE 14.1
Accuracy Observed Using Different Features for Benign Dataset

Benign Tumor Data\ Image	1	2	3	4	5	6	7	8	9	10
Mean	0.0031107	0.00235179	0.0032427	0.00250954	0.0020681	0.0019318	0.00352304	0.000686592	0.00193931	0.00341193
Standard Deviation	0.0897608	0.0897839	0.0897562	0.0897796	0.0897909	0.0897939	0.0897456	0.0898121	0.0897938	0.0897499
Entropy	3.17346	3.26983	3.57973	3.31556	3.51816	2.66316	3.15619	2.74648	3.65493	2.9949
RMS	0.0898027	0.0898027	0.0898027	0.0898027	0.0898027	0.0898027	0.0898027	0.0898027	0.0898027	0.0898027
Variance	0.00804787	0.00805116	0.00801859	0.0080626	0.00803049	0.00805185	0.0080274	0.00806289	0.00798716	0.00805202
Smoothness	0.920457	0.897422	0.923447	0.903246	0.884969	0.877845	0.929107	0.718636	0.87826	0.926967
Kurtosis	7.32819	7.95668	6.27346	6.23204	6.7672	7.27071	7.48478	10.9703	5.81169	7.68008
Skewness	0.469022	0.886238	0.633152	0.312064	0.441261	0.611709	0.52124	0.73646	0.340779	0.631759
IDM	0.057689	0.492585	0.52567	0.563091	0.546199	-0.0366395	-1.03921	0.119006	1.00105	0.38163
Contrast	0.208843	0.271691	0.24416	0.216073	0.224972	0.233315	0.234149	0.26891	0.203281	0.23654
Correlation	0.199005	0.0930892	0.100677	0.138167	0.0991065	0.128439	0.132059	0.0976505	0.112589	0.129391
Energy	0.7621	0.76857	0.740911	0.754802	0.769087	0.749118	0.752994	0.786145	0.755387	0.760611
Homogeneity	0.935159	0.933815	0.926261	0.93249	0.936531	0.930775	0.931526	0.940953	0.933106	0.934441

TABLE 14.2
Accuracy Observed Using Different Features for Malignant Dataset

Malignant Tumor Data	1	2	3	4	5	6	7	8	9	10
Mean	0.00630907	0.00425992	0.00458293	0.00423595	0.00571502	0.00282896	0.00528247	0.00365066	0.00458293	0.00423595
Standard Deviation	0.0895928	0.0897136	0.0896977	0.0897148	0.0896327	0.0897701	0.0896592	0.0897405	0.0896977	0.0897148
Entropy	3.20515	3.6046	3.54839	3.55162	2.66218	3.62834	3.19429	3.37095	3.54839	3.55162
RMS	0.0898027	0.0898027	0.0898027	0.0898027	0.0898027	0.0898027	0.0898027	0.0898027	0.0898027	0.0898027
Variance	0.00801767	0.00804977	0.00806942	0.00803605	0.00804695	0.00803589	0.00805359	0.00805956	0.00806942	0.00803605
Smoothness	0.959133	0.940642	0.944594	0.940326	0.955076	0.913222	0.951576	0.931415	0.944594	0.940326
Kurtosis	12.2408	5.99721	6.5235	6.06145	13.0402	5.32384	9.73182	7.35059	6.5235	6.06145
Skewness	1.10481	0.521797	0.620389	0.510428	1.31237	0.322997	0.991423	0.635044	0.620389	0.510428
IDM	1.2156	0.36996	0.503033	0.313019	1.27783	1.04188	1.85456	-0.137806	0.503033	0.313019
Contrast	0.305895	0.227197	0.243882	0.231368	0.292547	0.215517	0.278643	0.243326	0.243882	0.231368
Correlation	0.142097	0.13258	0.107227	0.107236	0.158376	0.0950755	0.142678	0.0932787	0.107227	0.107236
Energy	0.786231	0.743862	0.731029	0.741808	0.758837	0.737835	0.76042	0.761293	0.731029	0.741808
Homogeneity	0.937931	0.929018	0.924625	0.92976	0.932983	0.927359	0.932114	0.932884	0.924625	0.92976

14.5.14 Kernel Functions

To select a correct classification algorithm for image is de facto a tedious assignment. Therefore the nonlinear SVM works in a very great way on high dimensional characteristics sets.

In this research, some of kernel functions methods like RBF, linear, and polygonal are used to locate the segmented image. Table 14.3 shows the accuracy of the results for different kernel functions for the benign dataset, which proves that the linear accuracy method gives good results. Table 14.4 shows the accuracy of the

TABLE 14.3
Accuracy Observed Using Different Kernel Functions for Benign Dataset

Benign Tumor Data with Images	RBF Accuracy (%)	Linear Accuracy (%)	Polynomial Accuracy (%)	Quadratic Accuracy (%)
1	90	90	80	90
2	80	90	80	80
3	70	90	70	70
4	70	90	80	80
5	80	80	80	70
6	80	80	80	80
7	70	90	70	80
8	70	80	80	70
9	70	90	70	80
10	90	90	80	70

TABLE 14.4
Accuracy Observed Using Different Kernel Functions for Malignant Dataset

Malignant Tumor Data/ Image	RBF Accuracy (%)	Linear Accuracy (%)	Polynomial Accuracy (%)	Quadratic Accuracy (%)
1	90	90	80	90
2	80	90	80	80
3	70	90	70	70
4	70	90	80	80
5	80	80	80	70
6	80	80	80	80
7	80	80	80	80
8	70	90	70	70
9	90	90	90	80
10	70	80	70	80

results for different kernel functions for the malignant dataset, which proves that the linear accuracy method gives good results.

14.6 CONCLUSION AND FUTURE WORK

This chapter has presented the research work carried out for segmentation of different MRI brain images and their classification using machine learning techniques and the SVM method.

14.6.1 Conclusion

Nowadays, information extraction from the web and large databases is common. The users frequently place their queries for obtaining the results according to the queried data. In this presented study, the image extraction techniques and the features extraction techniques are learned.

The study addressed issues related to image searches in the medical domain and the features used to accurately distinguish images in a database. In this research it is observed during content based image retrieval process three main features are computed but two of them are not much effective due to similar color and texture of images in medical database.

Therefore, MRI segmentation cannot be resolved employing simple, traditional image processing methods. Due to the options of MRIs, evolution of machine driven algorithms is difficult. There is kind as a result of fragmentary volume impact, implicit noise and big selection of imaging parameters that have a control on the tissue intensities.

The brain tumor identification could be a facilitate for the physicians and a privilege for the medical imaging and industries engaged on the assembly of CT scan and MRI imaging. MATLAB simulation was carried on totally different brain images, and tumors were detected using Otsu's methodology for image segmentation and optimum global thresholding.

The nonlinear SVM works on elevated dimensional characteristic sets. To extend the periphery of the classification, kernel functions are used. There are various kernels utilized in SVM like linear, polynomial radial basis function etc. Kernel SVM provides the clear understanding of the classification and really simple to use in sensible image processing. During this approach some of its methods like RBF, linear, and polygonal are used to find the segmented image.

14.6.2 Future Work

Otsu's segmentation works very well for brain MRI dataset to segment and PCA performed higher results for feature reduction. Specifically, we have analyzed and compared four of the kernel functions of SVM with a paradigm brain MRI data. In future we are able to use others feature reduction technique and can compare and realize the accuracy. The scientist also can use numerous hybridized learning algorithms with the of dataset.

REFERENCES

1. B. B. Ghotekar and K. J. Mahajan, "MRI Brain image Segmentation and Classification: A Review", *International Research Journal of Engineering and Technology (IRJET)*, vol. 3, pp. 1170–1176, 2016.
2. J. Selvakumar, A. Lakshmi and T. Arivoli, "Brain Tumour Segmentation and Its Area Calculation in Brain MR Images using K-Mean Clustering and Fuzzy C-Mean Algorithm", IEEE-International Conference On Advances In Engineering, Science And Management (ICAESM -2012), March 2012.
3. M. Arif and G. Wang, "Fast Curvelet Transform Through Genetic Algorithm for Multimodal Medical Image Fusion," *Soft Computing*, vol. 24, pp. 1815–1836, 2020.
4. D. Kaur and Y. Kaur, "Various Image Segmentation Techniques: A Review", *International Journal of Computer Science and Mobile Computing, IJCSMC*, Vol. 3, Issue. 5:809–814, May 2014. ISSN 2320–088X.
5. D. C. Aslam, "Brain Tumour Detection from Medical Images: A Survey", *Nano Biomedical Engineering*, vol. 9, no. 1, pp. 72–81, 2017.
6. Zhang and Wu, "An MR Brain Images Classifier via Principal Component Analysis and Kernel Support Vector Machine", *Progress in Electromagnetics Research*, vol. 130, pp. 369–388, 2012.
7. G. Panigrahi and Mallick, "Detection of Brain Abnormalities from MRI Images Using MATLAB", *International Journal of Advanced Research in Electrical, Electronics and Instrumentation Engineering*, vol. 5, no. 10, pp. 7887–7892, 2016. ISSN (Print): 2320 – 3765 ISSN (Online): 2278 – 8875.
8. K. Kohir, "Detection of Brain Tumour using Back-Propagation and Probabilistic Neural Network", *Proceedings of 19th IRF International Conference*, 25th January 2015, Chennai, India, pp. 74–80, 2015. ISBN: 978-93-84209-84-1.
9. N. N. Tirpude and R. R. Welekar, "Effect of Global Thresholding on Tumour-Bearing Brain MRI Images", *IJECS*, vol. 2, no. 3, pp. 728–773, 2013.
10. Malik and Baharudin, "The Statistical Quantized Histogram Texture Features Analysis for Image Retrieval Based on Median and Laplacian Filters in the DCT Domain", *The International Arab Journal of Information Technology*, vol. 10, no. 6, 157–163, 2013.
11. Hassan and Aboshgifa, "Detecting Brain Tumour From MRI Images Using MATLAB GUI Programme", *International Journal of Computer Science & Engineering Survey (IJCSES)*, vol. 6, no. 6, pp. 47–60, 2015.
12. B. Thiagarajan, "Brain Image Segmentation Using Conditional Random Field Based On Modified Artificial Bee Colony Optimization Algorithm", *International Scholarly and Scientific Research & Innovation*, vol. 8, no. 9, pp. 674–684, 2014.
13. Reddy et al., "A Novel Approach for Detecting the Tumour Size and Bone Cancer Stage Using Region Growing Algorithm", International Conference on Computational Intelligence and Communication Networks, 2015.
14. A. Asuntha et al., "Feature Extraction to Detect Bone Cancer Using Image Processing", *Research Journal of Pharmaceutical, Biological and Chemical Sciences*, vol. 8, no. 3, pp. 434–442, 2017. ISSN: 0975-8585.
15. Jeevitha and Narendran, "Brain Tumour Segmentation Based on Otsu Thresholding", *Paripex – Indian Journal of Research*, vol. 2, no. 2, pp. 53–55, 2013. ISSN - 2250-1991.
16. N. Borole and Kawthekar, "Image Processing Techniques for Brain Tumour Detection: A Review", vol. 4, no. 5(2), pp. 28–32, 2015. ISSN 2278-6856.

17. Reddy et al., "An SVM Based Approach to Breast Cancer Classification using RBF and Polynomial Kernel Functions with Varying Arguments", *International Journal of Computer Science and Information Technologies*, vol. 5, no. 4, pp. 5901–5904, 2014. ISSN: 0975-9646.
18. K. Yogamangalam, "Segmentation Techniques Comparison in Image Processing", vol. 5, no. 1, pp. 307–313, 2013. ISSN: 0975-4024.
19. R. K. Vijila and S. Joseph Jawhar, "Novel Technology for Lung Tumour Detection Using Nano Image," *IETE Journal of Research*, vol. 67, no. 5, pp. 1–15, 2021.
20. S. M. Kurian, S. J. Devaraj and V. P. Vijayan, "Brain Tumour Detection by Gamma DeNoised Wavelet Segmented Entropy Classifier," *CMC-Computers, Materials & Continua*, vol. 69, no. 2, pp. 2093–2109, 2021.
21. G. Sheejakumari, "Brain Tumour Detection from MRI Images Using Histon Based Segmentation and Modified Neural Network", *Biomed Res- India*, Vol. 2016, Special Issue ISSN 0970-938X: S1-S9, 2016.
22. R. Bahadure and Thethi, "Image Analysis for MRI Based Brain Tumour Detection and Feature Extraction Using Biologically Inspired BWT and SVM", *International Journal of Biomedical Imaging*, Article ID 9749108, pp. 1–12, 2017.
23. S. Albahli, H. T. Rauf, M. Arif, M. T. Nafis and A. Algosaibi, "Identification of Thoracic Diseases by Exploiting Deep Neural Networks," *Computers, Materials & Continua*, vol. 66, no. 3, pp. 3139–3149, 2021.
24. A. Miglani, H. Madan, S. Kumar and S. Kumar, "A Literature Review on Brain Tumour Detection and Segmentation," 2021 5th International Conference on Intelligent Computing and Control Systems (ICICCS), 2021, pp. 1513–1519, doi: 10.1109/ICICCS51141.2021.9432342.
25. Das et al., "Detection and Area Calculation of Brain Tumour from MRI Images Using MATLAB", *International Journal of Computer Engineering in Research Trends*, vol. 4, no. 1, pp. 37–40, 2017. ISSN (O): 2349-7084.
26. A. Sakshi, B. K. Panigrahi and T. Gandhi, "Transfer Learning Based Brain Tumour Detection and Segmentation using Superpixel Technique", International Conference on Contemporary Computing and Applications, 2020.
27. H. Cherguif, J. Riffi, M. A. Mahrez, A. Yahaouy and H. Tairi, "Brain Tumour Segmentation Based on Deep Learning", International Conference on Intelligent Systems and Advanced Computing Sciences (ISACS), 2019.
28. Isin et al., "Review of MRI-based Brain Tumour Image Segmentation Using Deep Learning Methods", ICAFS, Vienna, Austria, *Procedia Computer Science*, vol. 102, pp. 317 –324, 2016.
29. C. L. Choudhary, C. Mahanty, R. Kumar and B. K. Mishra, "Brain Tumour Detection and Classification using Convolutional Neural Network and Deep Neural Network", International Conference on Computer Science Engineering and Applications (ICCSEA), 2020.
30. G. Minajagi, "Segmentation of Brain MRI Images using Fuzzy C-Means and DWT", *International Journal of Science Technology & Engineering*, vol. 2, no. 12, pp. 370–378, 2016. ISSN (online): 2349–784X.

Index

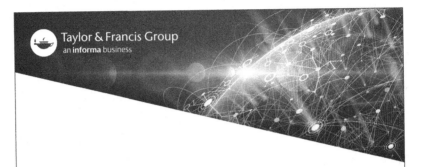